Another Humanity

Contemporary Continental Ethics
Series editors: Bryan Lueck, Southern Illinois University Edwardsville and Lucian Stone, University of North Dakota

Normative Ethics from a Continental Perspective

The books in this series address pressing and difficult ethical questions from the perspective of Continental philosophy. They offer new ways of thinking about moral phenomena and raise challenging questions that have not been considered before. The series includes work in the field of normative ethics, both theoretical and applied. Space is also given to treatments of social, political and aesthetic questions that intersect with ethical considerations.

Editorial Advisory Board
Andrew Benjamin, Alphonso Lingis, Ladelle McWhorter, Eduardo Mendieta, Ann V. Murphy, Kelly Oliver, Danielle Petherbridge, Anthony Steinbock

Books available
Obligation and the Fact of Sense
Bryan Lueck
The Responsibility to Understand: Hermeneutical Contours of Ethical Life
Theodore George
The Fragility of Concern for Others: Adorno and the Ethics of Care
Estelle Ferrarese, translated by Steven Corcoran
Choose Your Bearing: Édouard Glissant, Human Rights and Decolonial Ethics
Benjamin P. Davis
Another Humanity: Decolonial Ethics from Du Bois to Arendt
Benjamin P. Davis

Visit our website at: edinburghuniversitypress.com/series/epcce

Another Humanity

Decolonial Ethics from Du Bois to Arendt

Benjamin P. Davis

EDINBURGH
University Press

Edinburgh University Press is one of the leading university presses in the UK. We publish academic books and journals in our selected subject areas across the humanities and social sciences, combining cutting-edge scholarship with high editorial and production values to produce academic works of lasting importance. For more information visit our website: edinburghuniversitypress.com

Edinburgh University Press Ltd
13 Infirmary Street
Edinburgh EH1 1LT

First published in hardback by Edinburgh University Press 2025

A CIP record for this book is available from the British Library

ISBN 978 1 3995 4858 8 (hardback)
ISBN 978 1 3995 4861 8 (paperback)
ISBN 978 1 3995 4859 5 (webready PDF)
ISBN 978 1 3995 4860 1 (epub)

EU Authorised Representative:
Easy Access System Europe
Mustamäe tee 50, 10621 Tallinn, Estonia
gpsr.requests@easproject.com

For Frieda, Shahrzad, Derefe and Gerard – with love and thanks

And to the Columbia University student journalists of WKCR who, on the night of 30 April 2024, scraped together a radio broadcast of the police raid on their campus and, when they returned to music on the afternoon of 1 May, uplifted us with Donald Joyce's organ, playing Philip Glass

Contents

Acknowledgements

In this very serious book, I remain unable to write with *any* sense of humour, which is a shame, because philosophy is fun, and writing this book involved much shared laughter among many people, whom I would like to acknowledge here.

Thanks to Derefe Chevannes for so many phone calls, and for emphasising that when we say 'God help us', it is *not* a turn of phrase, as we are truly hoping for divine intervention in our lives. Apologies to Ms D and the Black Studies Department at Saint Louis University for never ironing my shirts (and thanks for so many debates and discussions – I have never laughed so much in a Department). Apologies to Steve Tamari for supporting England's football team (I might already lose you here, reader – what else would we expect from a defender of 'the human', you say! – but if it's any defence, it's because I love David Beckham). A special thanks to Gerard Aching for making me feel like a Madrileño for *una noche inolvidable*, for reading my work, and for courageously bringing up whether it could be morally OK to support Real Madrid – gracias por todo y un abrazo fuerte, Gerard.

Thanks to my dad for working so hard and never complaining, and to my mom for sending me your granola, which I have literally lived on for years. Thanks to my brother for being so playful despite being an elite surgeon, and so for making my days lighter. And to Thomas Mathews for always being thoughtful and for making our family closer. I hope we have been as welcoming to you as you have been to us. Lindsay Poplinski, for making so much time for me every damn day – despite being a very productive doctor. You are all my family.

Thanks to Shahrzad Sabet and Ben Schewel for building the Center on Modernity in Transition, which remains a home for me.

Thanks to Lili Nkunzimana for walking with me as I submitted this book.

Jane Gordon, for making me a better thinker with each conversation. Lewis Gordon, for your example of humanism. Paget Henry, for your writing, which has opened many paths.

A heartfelt thanks to Frieda Ekotto for encouraging me to write, and for helping me see South Africa. Chanel, Rozena and Crain, for conversation in SA. Lebo and Wonga for hospitality and humour (and Chenin blanc) during my time there. I miss you both!

Thanks to Lucian Stone and Penny Mitchell, as well as Sandra and Steve Tamari (again), for encouraging me to visit Palestine – and to Ahmad, Josh, Ben, Amani and A. for conversation there. Dirk Moses, for courageous writing, and Sam Moyn, for ongoing support.

Thanks to Bernard Harcourt, for reminding me to do more than speak to an esoteric academic debate, for inviting me to Columbia, and for your warmth as a mentor. I so value your presence and work.

Wael Hallaq and Bachir Diagne, for conversation during those days in New York. reakash walters, for a wonderful time, a joyful time, in New York, Madrid and Avilés as I finished this book.

Nikolas Kompridis, for showing me how to keep the faith in humanism, and for introducing Bina Gogineni to our Stuart Hall reading group. And Bina for conversation in Montreal!!

Helen Kinsella, of course – thanks for everything. You mean the world to me.

Janine Jones, I wish I had met you sooner! Thank you for conversation as I edited this book.

And Derik Smith, for your example of thinking, and for hours of conversation after Mukasa's wedding.

I would like to acknowledge my friends who might disagree with the ideas here but who have always believed in my work: Eric Aldieri, Jeta Mulaj, Miguel Gualdrón Ramírez, Jon Catlin, Sid Issar, Robert Beshara, Osman Nemli, Lizzy Wong, Megan Campbell, Callum Shepard, Lucy Benjamin, Matt Elia, Ashleigh Elser, Mukasa Mubirumusoke, Raisa Elhadi, Adam Lugsch-Tehle, Annabelle and Teddy Fleming, Scott Ritner and Chelsea Jack.

I would also like to thank my colleagues for their ongoing support: Kris Sealey, Cindy Willett, Adrien Wing, John Lysaker, George Yancy, Chris Tinson, Bukky Gbadegesin, Jonathan Fenderson, Ayça Çubukçu, Vincent Lloyd, Mohammad Salama, Lori Gruen, Chris Harris, Jill Stauffer, Max Tomba, Jess Whyte, Manisha Desai, Elaine Webster, Miguel Vatter, Zinhle ka'Nobuhlaluse, Valérie Loichot and Banu Bargu. Special thanks to Banu, the title whisperer, for directly vetoing a previous version of this book's title as we ate Max's risotto in Santa Cruz.

It has been a great pleasure to begin working with my new colleagues at Texas A&M. Alberto Moreiras and Adam Rosenthal are two scholars critical of 'the human' from whom I have learned so much, and with whom I enjoy every discussion and debate. It has been my absolute pleasure to contribute to the work in Africana Studies alongside Alain Lawo-Sukam and Rebecca Hankins; no work is more important, perhaps especially in Texas, and I remain so grateful for your warm welcome and your intellectual spirit. Don Deere, Selin Islekel and Constantine Karathanasis remain both colleagues and friends. Omar Rivera and Ted George have been mentors who make my life a lot easier and have made me feel fully supported. I would also like to thank Teresa Vilarós-Soler, Donnalee Dox and Rick Curry for ongoing support, Claire Katz for sharp discussion on Levinas, and Stefanie Harris and Christoph Konrad for welcoming me into the robust, multifaceted and successful Department they have been running.

A number of universities invited me for lectures where I got to test out the arguments I made in this book: Nelson Mandela University; the European University Institute; the University of California, Irvine; the University of California, Santa Cruz; Columbia University; Wesleyan University; the University of Connecticut; George Mason University; the City University of New York; and Grinnell College. Thank you for these opportunities.

I thank Christine Barton for thoroughness and attention in copyediting this book.

In Chapter 4, all my archival materials come from the Edward W. Said Papers (1940s–2006), MS 1524, Rare Book and Manuscript Library, Columbia University Library. I thank Tara Craig and the staff there for facilitating my visits to what is truly a wonderful library. Excerpts from archival material by Edward Said. Copyright © by Edward Said, used by permission of The Wylie Agency LLC.

For legal reasons, I need to say that the epigraph is a quote from Freud and the Non-European by Edward Said. Copyright © 2003 by Edward W. Said, used by permission of The Wylie Agency LLC.

Finally, I would like to thank my editor, Carol Macdonald, for her ongoing support of my work.

Preface

In his appraisal of Picasso's 1937 painting *Guernica*, named after the small Basque town on which German planes dropped bombs in the Spanish Civil War, the Trinidadian historian and activist C. L. R. James noted that the painting was 'produced at the time of universal crisis'.[1] Paying particular attention to the woman with the lamp, James read her suffering as itself 'open opposition to the total chaos' as well as a form of 'intellectual resistance'.[2] Thinking across species, James saw in the bull not just the invincibility of the Spanish people, but 'a solid, material living figure which stands for the eternal human value of survival'.[3]

When I look at the painting today, I see an almost photographic report in the greys, blacks and whites. I see unnamed creatures trying to hold on.

It strikes me that our time is not the time of the Spanish Civil War. I don't know anyone who has given up their position to fight against fascism. No, our time is a much more professionalised time, a time when solidarity is more likely to be proclaimed loudly than lived out humbly and through sacrifice. But ours is still very much a time of war.

I finished writing this book as Israel's planes dropped US-made bombs on Palestinian people during an ongoing war on Palestine. Al Jazeera played in the background of my days, sleep felt like the impossible goal of my nights, and my phone continually dinged as friends let me know they are 'OK' (whatever that means) or that they can't say much via text because, for instance, in Jerusalem random body searches have increased and they could be arrested for what they send to me. My phone rang and rang as colleagues who started to write, speak or post about Palestine for the first time began to face repercussions and wondered if their sudden feeling of paranoia made any sense. (It does.)

From October to now, as I write this Preface in December, I have watched the survival of ordinary families in Gaza. I have wondered whether my friends in the West Bank are still alive amidst increasing settler/military aggression there. I have seen in the ordinary resistance of Palestinians, in their courage and witness, a compelling spirit of human survival. And I have returned yet again to the philosophers who, for a number of years, have been those to whom I turn in times of 'total chaos', my lights making visible how people over time have stood together for 'human value': W. E. B. Du Bois, Édouard Glissant, Sylvia Wynter, Edward Said and Hannah Arendt.

This book is about these philosophers' inviting and imaginative visions of what it means to be human. It is about how we might together re-construct, perform and defend a truly universal sense of humanity, another humanity, one that responds to, and might lead us beyond, our time of universal crisis.

Benjamin P. Davis

Madrid

20 December 2023

Notes

1. C. L. R. James, 'The Olympia Statues, Picasso's *Guernica* and the Frescoes of Michelangelo in the Capella Paolina', in *The Future in the Present* (Westport, CT: Lawrence Hill and Company, 1977), p. 229.
2. Ibid. pp. 230, 232.
3. Ibid. p. 232.

Freud's uneasy relationship with the orthodoxy of his own community is very much a part of the complex of ideas so well described by Deutscher, who forgets to mention what I think is an essential component of it: its irremediably diasporic, unhoused character . . . But I would want to qualify Deutscher by saying that this needn't be seen only as a Jewish characteristic; in our age of vast population transfers, of refugees, exiles, expatriates and immigrants, it can also be identified in the diasporic, wandering, unresolved, cosmopolitan consciousness of someone who is both inside and outside his or her community. This is now a relatively widespread phenomenon, even though an understanding of what that condition means is far from common.

—Edward W. Said, 'Freud and the Non-European'

Introduction: Thinking Race and Humanity Together (An Attempt)

When I read academic books, my biggest wish is usually that the authors would tell me how they arrived at their questions – not just what their questions are, but how they got there.

I wrote this book as a settler in the United States who has come to see the present as a time of war – a global war about land against Indigenous peoples, a war that is deeply tied to the forced labour of Black people, a war densely bound up with racism and with race.[1] I have seen this ongoing war, with its tremendous dispossession of land and labour, play out not just in the United States, but also in Brazil, Palestine and South Africa. From that position and those travels, I wrote as a way of testing out ideas for living otherwise.

When I tell you about a place before I offer an argument, it is because I am sympathetic to the writer Binyavanga Wainaina's suggestion that 'maybe all that is required of us is to document, to simply document our times if we are writers, document in the flawed way that seems true to us'.[2] When I move to my reading of a philosopher and make an argument based on that reading, I try to do so in what Frantz Fanon called a 'concrete language', which he contrasted to a 'technical language' that, by obscuring ideas and making people feel they cannot understand the world around them, is itself another form of dispossession.[3]

By writing personally and concretely, I am trying to respond to social problems. When I cite a theorist, it is because they helped me to think about the series of ethical questions that motivates this book: What does it mean to be part of war and dispossession? How to own up to that violence? How to account for that suffering? How to challenge the structures and forces and companies and people that create that displacement, and how to see what new relations (and possibilities) emerge as a result? What are my responsibilities, and what is my place (in every sense), amidst a dispossessive form of life that predominates today? How to criticise every element of that coercion without losing sight of what we can construct?

'Wrong life cannot be lived rightly', Theodor Adorno asserted, and that insight seems correct in this context.[4] So too does Sylvia Wynter's observation that empire's educational apparatus 'instructs us' – all of us – 'to want to be of a specific ethnoclass of humanity'.[5] This means that even if most of us, in practice, side against Adorno and try to live our wrong lives a little more rightly, we are still susceptible (even likely) to follow social incentives that implicate us in dispossession – that normalise owning property, accumulating investment assets and dressing like the member of a rowing club (in our blazers, loafers and neutral sweaters, all made far away by people we don't know and don't really think about). What can ethical theory do, given all that? What can any of us do, given all that?

The authors I read in this book don't necessarily answer these questions, but they have sustained my belief in the importance of raising them. By staying with the questions and theories that have emerged from dispossession (and, relatedly, from racialisation), and by thinking with five diasporic philosophers as the book proceeds, I am ultimately asking: What would the theory and practice of humanity look like if it started from and referred back to the dispossessed?[6] If at times I take too moralising of a tone in these pages, it is because I also want to stress the corollary question: Are we who are *not* part of what Fanon called *les damnés de la terre* willing to redistribute or repatriate – to give up with a view towards repair – the wealth and the land (and the psychological status they provide) that we have gained from this dispossession?[7]

When Said says in the epigraph that an understanding of where humanity is today is 'far from common', I include myself in the group that lacks understanding. I read the work of the aforementioned authors in order to dwell with this lack, to sit with the many forms of displacement that mark our time, and even, in an intellectual sense, to pursue exile (as Said encourages) – to consider 'what that condition means' for how we have come to understand ourselves, one another, and the political forms that we inherited but did not choose, that we uphold in accepting and performing their reality, and that we can make anew and make differently. By testing out my guiding authors' concepts in documented situations and through the essays that make up this book, and by tracing the figures of 'the human' and 'humanity' in their work, I read Du Bois, Glissant, Wynter, Said and Arendt as instructing us towards different wants, towards different forms of life – ultimately, towards another way of practising 'the human', what Glissant describes in terms of *living* 'another . . . humanity'.[8] In this way, I follow the philosopher Zahi Zalloua in saying that 'it is not at all clear that decolonizing the mind is a metaphor'.[9]

* * *

This book is a sequel to my 2023 book *Choose Your Bearing: Édouard Glissant, Human Rights and Decolonial Ethics*. In that book, I re-constructed the concept of 'human rights' by focusing on the utility of rights claims for organising across communities and countries.[10] I still believe in the importance of connecting ethics and rights – beginning from, in Said's words, 'recognition of the fact that *citizens with rights* . . . are the moral norm'.[11] But rather than elaborate on that argument further, in this book I will enter a more esoteric debate: the contemporary debate in critical theory around the status of 'the human', a debate that perhaps initially seems further removed from ordinary life than the question of rights. It will be my task to bring this debate back to the ground in the pages that follow, to demonstrate how fundamental this question is, not least because the notion of 'the human' subtends any claim to human rights. Moreover, competing ideas around what it means to be human – and whether 'the human' is an ideal that is useful at all – continue to inform what the legal scholar Patricia Williams called 'the alchemy of race and rights' we all live amidst.[12]

Importantly, the authors who are the focus of this book are not just the authors to whom I have returned in searching for different forms of life; they are also – alongside Frantz Fanon, Joy James and a few others – the foundational sources to whom both promoters and critics of 'the human' and 'humanity' return in advancing two remarkably separate lines of critical theory today. By starting from Du Bois, Glissant and Wynter in this book, I am starting from three foundational authors in debates around the human, humanity and human rights today – debates that have also taken on Said and Arendt in varying ways, which I will elaborate upon in later chapters.

One response to the critics of 'the human' and 'humanity' would be to philosophically oppose their claims point for point. This role, the philosopher as the one who performs a scholastic refutation, can be important, and I will address some central criticisms below. But this mode of philosophising did not call to me following October 2023, as I existed in a state of what Said described as being 'emotionally reclaimed . . . by Palestine', as being at once 'shattered' and 'reinvigorated'.[13] No, what I was after then, as now, was a much more constructive approach – a way of reading and thinking that returns us to that ancient, anchoring question of philosophy as a way of life or as an art of living.[14] It is in that spirit, more ancient than medieval, more about practices of repair than about scholarly refutations, that I have written what follows in regard to the question of the human today.

In *Another Humanity*, I will argue that the concepts of 'the human' and 'humanity' are sufficient tools to motivate a transition towards a decolonised future. My claim is not that critical theories are wrong in pointing out the limitations of 'the human' with respect to its historical and ongoing operations of exclusion based on race, gender, species and other axes of power. Rather, I start from the premise that in our modern/colonial world, all concepts are contaminated by histories of asymmetrical power, indeed by histories of domination, such that the task becomes not to throw out problematic concepts (which would leave us with none) but instead to strategically leverage the concepts that could be the most politically useful. To put this another way: if we are indeed living in a time of 'the coloniality of being', then our search for an untainted 'exteriority' no longer makes sense.[15] The needed conceptual work becomes strategic; we need what the cultural theorist Stuart Hall called 'strategic points of departure'.[16] I contend that 'the human' is a strategic point of departure for necessary political work today: the work of building a world where human rights are truly universal and defended by our very forms of life. I will make this argument throughout the course of this book. But at the outset, I need to qualify my argument. To do so, I will just tell a story.

* * *

One of the most rewarding parts about having written a book is receiving invitations to speak about it and being received by others with their questions and critiques and confirmations. As someone who grew up in a small river town in Minnesota, I never take for granted the opportunity to learn how people in various places experience the world. This is also a research method I have actively pursued for some time, only realising it could be called a method when I first read Du Bois's Preface to *Color and Democracy*, where he justifies that book's thesis based on 'long study and wide travel'.[17] Speaking about *Choose Your Bearing* has only heightened my fascination with how theory travels, and it has made me want to study more in turn.

After I submitted this book, but before I revised it, I was invited to speak at Nelson Mandela University in Gqeberha, South Africa. There I learned for the first time about a position of 'non-racialism' advanced by a group of scholars who rely on the language of 'the human'. I was told that the anthropologist Zimitri Erasmus is part of this group – I had asked a colleague about her because I enjoyed and learned from her book *Race Otherwise*, especially how it called for a 'double politics', meaning 'to acknowledge the ways in which race continues to matter, while working towards its undoing'.[18] As I understand Erasmus in this claim, both steps are crucial, as is their order: settlers and white people often zoom to the second element without starting from, referring back to, and allowing the first acknowledgement to bear on our theory and praxis. We cannot start from the working beyond, the undoing, without first being conditioned by the initial acknowledgement of how 'race continues to matter'.

For Erasmus, 'double politics' also involves taking action 'against racism as a power structure, as well as against the meanings of race that underpin this structure'.[19] The promise of 'double politics' is to outline a practice that could lead to 'unity among the subjugated in defiance of colonial racial codification and its consequences'.[20] Such a 'double politics' still sounds good to me – and yet, as always, the way we get to this 'unity' matters very much, as does defining who counts as 'subjugated'. And even more so I wonder what this double politics would look like in everyday life: in our ordinary interactions on the bus, in the classroom, or as we make food with friends in our kitchens – other spaces we theorists rarely discuss.[21]

To be honest with you as we begin, reader, I do not know how to practise this double politics. I do not know what it means, precisely and concretely, both to acknowledge and to undo race in conversations with colleagues, friends and partners. I do not know how to minimise harm in even having these conversations, given where we are at, right now, as a species, and given how race is often experienced as simultaneously a form of alienation and a site of belonging. Perhaps it is out of this deeply personal uncertainty – and the missteps and connections that have come from it in community and friendship and loss – that I have written this book.[22] If that is true, then my guiding questions have emerged, as Du Bois said in reflecting on his work, 'not so much of my study, as of my human companionship'.[23]

In any case, one morning in Gqeberha, a few days after my conversation about Erasmus, I had breakfast right when the dining room opened (half past six) at the four-star hotel where the conference organisers had generously put us up. As I sat drinking English breakfast tea after eating a hot meal that was prepared for me by a short-order cook, a colleague who is part of this non-racialism group of scholars asked to join me. I said yes, and we began talking about our research. I told him about this book, and he explained that my archive here is more or less that of the non-racialists, especially insofar as I take inspiration from Paul Gilroy's work in and following his 2000 book *Against Race*. In response, I asked my colleague about his approach. Likely due to my time in a Black Studies Department – and specifically due to Chris Tinson's magnanimous and continual invitation for me to think more about *how* arguments about race are made – the more I heard about my colleague's specific version of the non-racialist position that morning, the less sense it made to me.

For to travel extensively in a short period of time is also to witness how densely the colour line still belts the world, meaning that we have not, in this century, yet surpassed the greatest problem of the past century, which Du Bois diagnosed in his famous words: 'The problem of the twentieth century is the problem of the color-line.'[24] From the Senegalese man who approached me at a Florence café and asked me to buy his self-published book on migration, to the Ethiopians who scrub the floor of Ben-Gurion Airport, to the Black woman who makes coffee at the LAX Hyatt before 5 a.m. for frequent flyers travelling early or for hotel guests (like me) who can't sleep, it is evident that race still conditions/determines mobility and labour, as well as exposure to pollution and accumulations of fatigue, across the planet today.

As the winter breeze came off the Indian Ocean that morning in South Africa, I made this observation about mobility and labour to my colleague, and I noted that some would say it makes good sense to think with race for descriptive sociological accuracy, or to organise politically on the lines already set by a structuring force, just as workers do. And I heard in reply – a collegial reply, as this was a genial and generative conversation – points that I myself have made before: that to think or to organise through race is *nationalist* or *reductive* or *too easy* or *a capitulation to colonial categories*.[25] But I have come to disagree with these characterisations of theory that starts from questions of race. More and more they strike me as trying to read the world as if reading Du Bois's *Color and*

Democracy and only wanting to talk about democracy; they avoid what is foregrounded, determining and demanding to be worked through.

Indeed, and perhaps to the surprise of some friends, I have become part of the 'we' that the philosopher Norman Ajari describes in writing, 'We have all grown weary of the endless reminders that there is no biological basis to race.'[26] Those reminders usually function to shut down conversations that would be more helpful – socially and personally – if they were only just beginning. But instead, in the contexts with which I am most familiar, and as the political theorist Utz McKnight has argued, although 'the US is still very much a racial polity', the fact is that '[t]he conversation about race is attenuated in public so as to guard against its leading to questions about the place of Whiteness in society today'.[27]

Stuart Hall said that race is 'the modality in which class is "lived"'.[28] That line applies to white people as much as to Black people, rich people as much as to poor people. It explains why middle-class people around the world have no problem – or perhaps remain deliberately ignorant about – investing their money in the companies that make the weapons that ultimately kill Palestinians. In practice (that is, in our financial and affective investments, because practices are always already value-laden; practices are lived judgements), the deaths of racialised people are seen as a small price to pay for climbing towards the status of a dominant ethno-class, or for maintaining one's position there. After all, isn't race one compelling explanation for how Christians in the US vocally and financially support the plight of white Ukrainian Christian refugees while staying much quieter about African Christians and Palestinian Christians who are Black or Arab refugees?[29] In the past few years, have you seen a US Christian church that flies the Nigerian and Palestinian flags alongside the Ukrainian flag? As a lawyer at the Palestinian human rights group al-Haq (declared a 'terrorist organisation' by the Israeli government) explained to me in Ramallah, the way Israeli chemical factories have moved their operations to Tulkarem in the West Bank always made a certain kind of sense to him, because he grew up in Louisiana's 'cancer alley', where pollution from chemical plants disproportionately affects Black communities. And as South African scholars who draw from Black consciousness (instead of non-racialist) approaches stressed to me, to talk about Gaza is to talk about race.[30] Racialisation serves nation-states' and companies' and middle-class investors' military and economic goals; it is not, Hall says, 'as if the politics of race fell out of the sky'.[31]

Might we do well, then, to dwell with the multiple histories and facets of 'the politics of race' before we jettison a potentially powerful analytical and political tool? Don't our social movements and relations often break down precisely when we start to avoid, instead of having open conversations about, how race has shaped all of us? Could our discomfort talking about race signal its necessity? Might race be most influential precisely in the moments when we think it is least obvious, when we think it no longer bears on us?[32] Wouldn't it be worthwhile to talk about (to perhaps *begin* to understand) how race and war – as well as structures of labour, mobility and fatigue – inform each other *before* we say that thinking through race is a capitulation? Couldn't these conversations be enlivening and enlightening, as theorising together so often is – not, as Hall cautions, out of some 'moral intellectual duty', but because such difficult conversations help us place ourselves, because 'the issue of race provides one of the most important ways of understanding how this society actually works and how it has arrived where it is'?[33] 'What better way of beginning to come to terms with each other', Said adds, 'than to open one community to the other's history, actuality, and aspirations?'[34] Perhaps in this one instance, *contra* Marx, we do need to interpret the world before we try to change it.

These were my thoughts as I sipped tea with my colleague as the hotel's Black staff waited on us.

* * *

One lesson from Négritude is that philosophy 'placed in the service of black peoples' is always already pro-human philosophy.[35] 'I am not burying myself in a narrow particularism', the poet and philosopher Aimé Césaire wrote in his 1956 letter resigning from the Communist Party.[36] 'My conception of the universal', he went on, 'is that of a universal enriched by all that is particular, a universal enriched by every particular: the deepening and coexistence of all particulars.'[37] More recently, the Black Studies scholar Rinaldo Walcott has echoed Césaire: 'Black freedom is not just freedom for Black subjects; it is a freedom that inaugurates an entirely new human experience for everyone.'[38] But the reverse does not hold. Claims to humanity and cosmopolitanism and global citizenship and love and universality do not necessarily suggest a position that is not anti-Black, which is also to say that they do not necessarily address historical and ongoing dispossession. As Césaire put it, '[I]t does not go without saying.'[39]

How can we with Northern passports speak of global citizenship without addressing our countries' policies that make it very difficult for African or Muslim scholars to travel to our countries? Might the nationalism or identity politics be found less in the racialised scholar who starts from race and more in our lack of interrogating and challenging the lack of reciprocity demonstrated by my own country's closed borders? As Said stressed over and over, dispossession remains the test case for claims to universality.[40] There can be (and often is) intellectual but not material reflexivity.[41]

One implication of my above analysis is that the onus should not be on the Black scholar to prove their ultimate humanism in making their 'nationalist' or 'biologically reductive' or 'un-deconstructed' argument that starts from Black strivings; the onus lies with theorists of humanity and cosmopolitanism and global citizenship and human rights (myself included) to first and sufficiently demonstrate our accountability to the dispossessed (those we are dispossessing). Then the conversation about humanity can proceed. To the extent that this book insufficiently owns up to this responsibility in painting its portrait of another humanity, it remains theoretically and practically limited.

Critiques of 'The Human'

Critiques of the concept of 'the human' remain important and necessary precisely because the history of pseudo-humanistic thought is ongoing. The *locus classicus* is the Dominican theologian Bartolomé de las Casas's advocacy for the humanity of Indigenous peoples in the sixteenth century while arguing for enslaved Africans to replace Indigenous people as labourers.[42] Las Casas would be included in Du Bois's observation that, in the modern historiography of white European Christians, Africa and its diasporas have been 'read almost out of the bounds of humanity'.[43] With past and present examples in mind, much contemporary critical theory has remained resolutely critical of using the concept of 'the human' for emancipatory political work. Indeed, my argument in this book runs against the contemporary grain in critical theory. A brief survey of recent literature shows an effort to jettison 'the human' across various disciplines and approaches.

Writing in 2009 from a position that has come to be known as decolonial theory, the decolonial thinker Walter Mignolo argues that:

[f]rom the sixteenth century to the Universal Declaration of Human Rights, He who speaks for the human is an actor embodying the Western ideal of being Christian, being man and being human. In other words, 'human' in human rights is an invention of Western imperial knowledge rather than the name of an existing entity to which everyone will have access.[44]

In his influential 2016 book that was translated and published as *Necropolitics* in 2019, the historian Achille Mbembe calls for going beyond the 'internal' critique of Western humanism (made by Césaire, Fanon, Glissant, Wynter, Gilroy – the archive of this book) and draws our attention to 'the external critique', describing Afropessimism as 'a war that would be waged against the very concept of humanity since this concept is indeed the Trojan horse that has trapped the Negro in a permanent state of death, social or otherwise'.[45] Intervening in questions of human rights and international law, in her 2017 article 'Thinking against Humanity', the anthropologist Ayça Çubukçu reads Malcolm X and Frantz Fanon to argue that 'violence is central, and hierarchy is intrinsic to the political and ethical operations of "humanity"'.[46] Bringing together Continental metaphysics and Afropessimism, the literary theorist Calvin Warren takes 'a world of antiblack brutality' as a point of departure in his 2018 book *Ontological Terror* and articulates the titular concept as 'the terror that ontological security is gone, the terror that ethical claims no longer have an anchor, and the terror of inhabiting existence outside the precincts of humanity and its humanism'.[47] In her category-challenging 2020 book *Becoming Human*, the literary scholar Zakiyyah Iman Jackson reads African, African American and Caribbean texts as working to 'critique and dispose prevailing conceptions of "the human" found in Western science and philosophy'.[48] Jackson finds in these texts resources 'to generate new possibilities for rethinking ontology: our being, fleshy materiality, and the nature of what exists and what we can claim to know about existence'.[49] Commenting on Afropessimism, the critical theorist Alberto Moreiras noted in 2022 that '[t]he space of humanism has defined the space of modern politics, and it still does', and he has gone as far as to argue against '[h]uman narrative' because '[n]arrative subjects, particularly those in a political narrative, are always parasitic on Black suffering'.[50] 'The human and its subcategory, the inhuman', the geographer Kathryn Yussof notes about geology and the racial erasures of the term 'Anthropocene', 'are historically relational to a discourse of settler-colonial rights and the material practices of extraction', such that one contribution of Black and Indigenous studies is to articulate and challenge 'intimate confinements and ongoing containments of humanist thought'.[51] As the theologian Norman Wirzba observes, 'The current question is whether the category of humanity itself should be retained.'[52] In sum, numerous prominent scholars from various disciplines engaged in critical theory – and often following one particularly theoretical line of Black Studies – currently maintain that the category of 'the human' is part of the white supremacist colonial problem, not a solution to it.[53] These modes of theory are part of what the philosopher Lewis Gordon, in *Existentia Africana*, had already diagnosed at the turn of the millennium as 'a pervasive ethos *against* humanistic solutions'.[54]

The aforementioned critics (and their work) have become influential enough to exemplify a wider trend in critical theory: to criticise and avoid appeals to 'the human' and 'humanity'. While I disagree with this theoretical strategy, it is nevertheless important here to give it more of its due. For this criticism, like all criticisms, emerges from a particular place and in response to specific needs. Indeed, it is worth noting, as Ajari does, that the success of Afropessimism in shaping discourse 'stems from its resonance with the lived experience of young Black people in the twenty-first century', and this lived experience always justifiably deserves theoretical attention.[55] Moreover, much of the aforementioned criticism of 'the human' is accurate in important ways.

As the literary theorist Rei Terada has recently commented, 'the humanism of liberals' has a way of 'tak[ing] the place of analysis' and allowing one 'to be confirmed in one's political reality'.[56] For many critics of humanism, appeals to humanity have become inseparably bound with the most minimal appeals to institutional reform, which lack imagination and courage. More personally, in practice we humanists too often work first to maintain or improve our own institutional and economic position, an effort that requires an abandonment of thinking, a replacement of analysis with respectability, complacency and selfishness. In regard to what will be the guiding example in this book, in no place has the liberal humanist's lack of analysis and courage been more striking than in regard to the question of Palestine. While many critics of 'the human', including Mignolo and Çubukçu, have long been vocal about Palestine and theorised Palestine together with other contexts of racialisation and colonialism, I am sure that every reader of this book could name a colleague who identifies themselves as a liberal and a humanist but who has remained resoundingly silent in their teaching, research, writing, editing and programming on campus long before and especially since 7 October 2023.[57] This silence has extended to even the most basic appeals to first-amendment free speech and academic freedom on campus as well as to even the most minimal, fact-based teaching of the history of Palestine and Israel.

All of this to say, my sense is that part of the frustration behind criticisms of 'the human' today, perhaps a significant part, is motivated through this experiential (instead of theoretical) site of disagreement. When humanists whose publications and conference presentations most loudly call for universalism and humanity in the abstract remain most silent when the question of the scope of human rights is actually on the table, appeals to universalism and humanity severely lose their credibility.[58] The legacy of Du Bois and Césaire we trade on becomes suspect, or at least hackneyed. Our peers and students see this very easily, and at some level surely we know it ourselves.

Although my above point remains anecdotal, it will soon be more publicly and widely proven. Even some scholars who remained silent in the wake of this most recent battle of the hundred years' war on Palestine will feel the need to comment and focus their respectable scholarly agendas on the campus protests, thus ironically becoming shapers of the discourse around a question they didn't have the courage to talk about or take action on when it mattered most.[59] This anecdotal point nevertheless remains important regarding my argument in this book: it suggests that contemporary debates around 'the human' arise not simply out of disagreements about how we read Césaire or Fanon but also through daily performances of protest or silence on our campuses. It remains true, as Said wrote in introducing *The Politics of Dispossession* in the early 1990s, that 'to defend Palestinian self-determination, and even to pronounce the word *Palestine* has been more difficult than any other political cause today'.[60]

Talking about Palestine wakes us from our respectable scholarly slumber in another way. As Said taught, and as I will argue throughout this book, to pronounce the word *Palestine* is also to invoke an idea, 'a vision of the future – the Palestinian idea – based not on exclusivism and rejection, but upon coexistence, mutuality, sharing'.[61] In that way, to say 'Palestine' is to talk about Indigenous land, reparations to communities of African descent, and where our endowment funds get invested. In other words, the idea of Palestine has become about much more than a particular place; it has also started conversations about human rights and repair. It is 'a long-standing corrective'.[62]

This is why Said says, 'It would be wrong to consider the struggle for Palestine only as a local struggle for land; it is that, of course, but equally, it is a far-reaching struggle for democratic rights and principles.'[63] Thought this way, supporting Palestine means that 'we must together formulate the modes of coexistence, of mutuality and sharing, those modes that can take us beyond fear and suffering into the future, and an extraordinarily interesting and impressive future at that'.[64] It means that the struggle for Palestine is 'the struggle for a new world order on the side plainly of freedom, knowledge, human rights – that is, on the side of everything that enhances life and humanly productive values'.[65] And here Said already begins a response to critics of 'the human'.

Indeed, the position the rest of this book develops will follow that of Said, who maintained a humanism until his passing, asserting in his late work, such as in the Introduction to *Reflections on Exile*, a clear path forward: 'If Western humanism was discredited by its practices and hypocrisy, these needed to be exposed, and a more universal humanism enacted and taught.'[66]

Defences of 'The Human'

Pace the above criticisms of 'the human', a few voices within critical theory nevertheless stand out for maintaining a commitment to a humanistic vocabulary. Lewis Gordon's work has been accurately characterised as offering a 'decolonial humanism'.[67] Gordon has gone as far as to define philosophy itself as 'humanity reaching beyond itself' coupled with a deep reflection on 'human responsibility not only to each other but also to other aspects of reality'.[68] Gordon's attention to human life as it is lived in food, music, dance, conversation and joy, as well as his emphasis on an ethics of responsibility, has deeply shaped this book.

Stuart Hall's student and cultural studies scholar Paul Gilroy has developed a concept of 'planetary humanism' that also works against the contemporary critical grain.[69] In his 2019 Holberg Lecture, 'Never Again: refusing race and salvaging the human', Gilroy says, 'I think we should be sceptical about the seductions of the ontological turn recently promoted in the study of race politics'.[70] While he does not identify the purveyors of this 'ontological turn' in that lecture, the anti-humanist work of the aforementioned critical theorists, especially those advancing what has come to be called Afropessimism, provides points of contrast with both Gilroy's humanism and what the performance studies scholar Tavia Nyong'o calls Gilroy's 'critical sympathy' for active pursuits of human rights and humanitarian politics.[71] Importantly, Gilroy's criticism of ontological approaches is not a critique of all methods that focus on or start from race. As I read it, his own work often starts from questions of race, and the Black Atlantic sources and archives he works within (and named) remain foundational for thinking race and humanism together.

Returning to Hall in 2021, Gilroy was clear in arguing that '[r]acism is not another layer of misery to be logged and added to the dismal effects of other social processes. It has a constitutive power. It shapes and determines economic and political relations.'[72] This line complicates readings of Gilroy that see him as dismissing race, a reading his work admittedly invited explicitly in and following his 2000 *Against Race: Imagining Political Culture beyond the Color Line*. In that book, he lamented that '[n]obody ever speaks of a human identity' and that instead many people rely on more particular identity claims (such as race, gender and generation) that function 'to delineate and subdivide humankind'.[73] But his early work and his recent return to Hall's work nevertheless allow us to read Gilroy's corpus as overall starting from that first aspect of

Erasmus's 'double politics', namely, the acknowledgement of 'the ways in which race continues to matter'.

Drawing out questions of history and politics instead of proceeding through ontological claims also allows Gilroy to highlight the relevance of past struggles, including coalitions across born-into lines. For instance, he uses photos of protest signs saying 'Jews and Arabs Unite! Against British Imperialism' to suggest that his planetary humanism involves recycling what was fruitful about previous anti-imperial projects – 'I thought recycling was good, obviously it's not to everyone's taste here', he said to an audience in 2008 with characteristic good humour regarding criticism of his work.[74] Overall, Gilroy draws on a Black Atlantic archive of abolition focused more on risk than respectability, writing in his 2004 *Postcolonial Melancholia* that the kind of anti-racism he has in mind 'came via a disreputable abolitionism and translocal, multicultural, and anti-imperial activism that was allied with the insurrectionary practice of those who, though legally held in bondage, were subject to the larger immoralities of a race-friendly system of domination'.[75] Criticising 'race-friendly' ways of thinking in his later work is part of his overall critique of ontologising approaches to race, which is a more specific critique than simply evading or neglecting what Hall called 'the politics of race'. Gilroy advocates instead for a specific practice, namely, 'the ability to imagine political, economic, and social systems in which "race" makes no sense', which he presents as 'an invaluable transitional exercise' to a more just world.[76] This practice, experiment or 'exercise' resonates with the second part of Erasmus's double politics regarding race ('working towards its undoing').

Thought in terms of Erasmus's double politics, Gilroy's planetary humanism starts from the historical struggles around who counts as 'human' and outlines a strategy for imagining the world anew. Such an exercise in no way refuses to recognise the economic and political realities that race continues to shape, structure and determine; it starts from that reality and attempts to think Relation otherwise, as Gilroy notes citing Glissant's concept. Glissant's 'creative use of [Relation]', Gilroy explains, 'brings a concern with what has been relayed together with a critical interest in relative and comparative approaches to history and culture and attention to what has been related in both senses of that word: kinship and narration'.[77] 'Approaching the issue of relation in this spirit', Gilroy goes on, 'requires a sharp departure from all currently fashionable obligations to celebrate incommensurability and cheerlead for absolute identity.'[78]

In this book, I follow Gilroy in attempting to think Relation otherwise. I would not position my argument polemically as against race. Just as I have learned from Black Studies scholars' call to recognise the tremendous enduring significance of the global colour line and caution about moving naively beyond race in theory before and without first shifting how race continues to shape practice ('continues to matter'), so too have I learned from Gilroy's insistence on avoiding ontology, incommensurability and absolutism in outlining a new form of Relation, what I am calling here 'another humanity'. I will try to hold those two lessons together, in a productive tension, in the rest of this book.

* * *

Beyond the work of Gordon and Gilroy, I have more specifically learned from how Joseph Drexler-Dries and Kristien Justaert thread a decolonial emphasis through the idea of the human in their collection *Beyond the Doctrine of Man: Decolonial Visions of the Human*. The essays that make up *Another Humanity* further resonate with the approach the anthropologist Gary Wilder offered in *Concrete Utopianism*. 'The task of critical analysis', Wilder begins there, 'is to delineate the challenges that must be

confronted and the possible pathways that could help emancipatory forces overcome the existing order so as to promote
human flourishing on a planetary scale.'[79] The pages of this
book move through a similar spirit of criticism, one with its eye
on paths that lead to planetary human flourishing. I am additionally sympathetic to the task Wilder outlines for critical theory when he writes, reading Marx, that our goal is 'to awaken
humanity to its obscured and forgotten dreams without which
it will continue to reconcile itself to the existing world'.[80] At
the same time, however, I disagree with Wilder's assertion that
'revolutionary change . . . cannot rely upon or unfold within
the parameters of existing concepts and consciousness'.[81] My
claim is not that we need new 'social realities' that 'exceed the
existing conceptual terms and frames', but rather that we need
to truly live out our concepts in order to bring about new social
realities.[82]

While the academic purpose of this book is to make an
intervention into this textual question of how we read some of
decolonial philosophy's foundational sources, I have suggested
above that another question, the more significant question,
has less to do, for instance, with how we read 'No Humans
Involved' and whether or not we can say, in turn, that Wynter is ultimately a humanist. No, the bigger question here has
to do with how each of us responds when the liberal goal of
extending human rights is actually on the table. Because we
still live in a world in which the post-war Bretton Woods and
Dumbarton Oaks institutions limit more expansive imaginaries, we cannot avoid negotiating with this liberal agenda,
including its concepts.[83]

From where I stand, we should remain critical of all nation
states, indeed of the nation state itself as a political form,
while strategically supporting decolonial/Indigenous claims
to sovereignty, self-determination and human rights. This is
a political exercise that has more to learn from the cautions

of deconstruction than decolonial methods often do. (I will return to this point below.) This is another form of 'double politics', acknowledging (and even leveraging) today's predominant political categories as we work towards their undoing, as we imagine and experiment with political forms in which the concepts of sovereignty and property no longer make any sense. This transitional exercise remains the most important political task of our time.

To make this point, let me again start with a story.

Conceptual Sufficiency and Stuart Hall's Politics without Guarantees

In the summer of 2022, I returned home to rural Minnesota to visit my parents. This was just after the US Supreme Court overturned *Roe v. Wade*, and I was thinking hard about the kind of political responsibility that Lewis Gordon says should be 'borne by every member of society, for the actions of their government'.[84] When I would 'head into town', as we country people say, I would come across an anti-choice billboard with a photo of a foetus alongside text in all caps: 'ALL HUMANS HAVE HUMAN RIGHTS'. This billboard indicates how both 'the human' and 'human rights' are being deployed against women's rights today. Our post-*Roe* moment also recalls Stuart Hall's conclusion to his 1979 essay 'The Great Moving Right Show', where he notes that conservative politicians have 'change[d] the nature of the terrain itself on which struggles of different kinds are taking place'.[85] 'That', he says, 'is exactly the terrain on which the forces of opposition must organize, if we are to transform it.'[86] If you want to move a concept, 'to rearticulate it another way', Hall goes on, 'you are going to come across all the grooves that have articulated it already'.[87]

In line with Hall's suggestion, during that summer I found that to think from rural Minnesota meant more than simply thinking alongside anti-choice billboards. It was also to think with Indigenous-led organisations, such as Honor the Earth, which led the charge in challenging the legality of the Line 3 pipeline in Minnesota. Honor the Earth's mission states:

> We believe a sustainable world is predicated on transforming economic, social, and political relationships that have been based on systems of conquest toward systems based on just relationships with each other and with the natural world . . . [W]e are committed to restoring a paradigm that recognizes our collective humanity and our joint dependence on the Earth.[88]

For Honor the Earth, 'humanity' is a term that can explain the violations of the Line 3 pipeline and invite actors to mobilise against the pipeline, as part of restoring a different paradigm of life on a shared planet. 'Humanity' is a term that, even after oil began flowing through the pipeline, has been used to make connections between Line 3 and other anti-pipeline struggles up and down the Mississippi River, from Minneapolis to St Louis to New Orleans. Moreover, it is not necessarily an anthropocentric concept, oriented towards a single species. For Honor the Earth, the concept of humanity is a political, legal and spiritual tool that reflects a larger practice of being human, itself situated within right relations to the Earth and thus receptive to it; and in this way, the concept also speaks to new (or old) ideas of rights, gender, maternity, species and time.

In suggesting that the human is a sufficient concept for decolonial work today, I follow the work of the legal scholar Patricia Monture-Angus, who has argued that the problem for decolonial politics is often not a conceptual one, but rather an ethical and political one about whether people are willing to live out what the concept demands. She makes this point clear regarding how citizens of so-called Canada often choose to address questions of Indigenous rights:

It boggles my mind to think that all of this constitutional debate, the number of conferences, the amount of federal money and federal energy spent trying to figure out what Aboriginal people want is merely the struggle to accept that we want to be responsible as Peoples. At the centre of our demands is one simple thing: I want and I need and I have the right to live as a responsible person in the way that the Creator made me, as a Mohawk woman. That is the only right I need. When I have the right to live in my territory as a Mohawk woman then I will have justice.[89]

As I read Monture, she is not saying that the problem preventing her from living on her land as a Mohawk woman is that the concepts of 'people', 'responsibility', 'territory' or 'justice' are inadequate and so need to be deconstructed. She treats those concepts as sufficient. Because those concepts are not inadequate (even if they are limited, as all concepts are), the solution to recognising Indigenous rights is not really one of debates, conferences or increased grant money for non-profit organisations. The actual social problem is that settlers want to hold on to their settler states; the actual social solution is 'the significant letting go of Canadian government power over the lives of Aboriginal citizens'.[90] If the problem is not necessarily with the concepts, then one pressing political task that remains is creatively using already existing concepts.

When I make this point, some people say that I am implying that we are no longer talking about theory or philosophy, which I have deemed unhelpful. But that is not my point at all. Further, this critique only makes sense in a context where we have ceded the ground of what is philosophical to a modern understanding, because in an older sense philosophy is not just the transmission of knowledge; it is also about the formation of habits. And those habits are formed via reading as well as in conversation and activism and silence and passivity. So when we talk about something as banal and ordinary as who has title to the land or how we invest our money, we are talking about how an idea or a thought comes to life and informs our practice and otherwise 'spaces itself out into the world', as Glissant says in opening *Poetics*.[91] What I am trying to do, then, is to shift the task of philosophy or critical theory away from totalising critique and towards the decidedly nuanced and difficult skills of recognising which concepts are sufficient in a given context and using those concepts productively in dialogue with a given (and always fractured, contradictory and changing) community or struggle. To say that such work is not philosophical relies on a recent and predominantly academic idea of philosophy as tied to logical proofs and argumentation, on the analytic side, or critique and rupture, on the Continental side. But the skill I am beginning to outline here, the skill of using concepts to shape our practice anew or to dwell with ideas and thus reorient our lives, recalls perhaps the most timeless meaning of philosophy as guided by truth and pursued in relation to others (through dialogue, politics and friendship). This is the mode of philosophy that still leverages our most ambitious ideals. This is the spirit of philosophy that follows Adorno when he writes, 'The need to allow suffering to speak is a condition of all truth' and Du Bois when he writes, 'Humanity is one and its vast variety is its glory and not its condemnation.'[92]

Before I further defend my reliance on 'humanity' in the next chapter, it would be helpful to zoom out and consider for what purposes we rely on concepts and what we expect them to do in the first place.

* * *

In February 2003, in one of his last major speeches, Edward Said reflected on his ethical obligations in a time of war: 'I feel it is my moral and intellectual duty to oppose the unjust use of [US] military, economic, and political power abroad for what is, it claims falsely, to be its national security interests.'[93] 'I have no power', he goes on, 'so I have to resort to the tools of education, to writing and speaking.'[94] Said's reflection, spoken painfully as he watched another imperial invasion and occupation advance across the Middle East, raises the question of what tools those of us who oppose war, colonialism and anti-democratic regimes have in order to work towards what he had previously called a 'noncoercive human community'.[95] As we resort to education, writing and speaking, which concepts can help us to make the political gains we so gravely need today?

What, to begin, can we expect concepts to do? After all, no one criticises a hammer as an insufficient tool for picking up green beans at the dinner table; we simply do not expect a hammer to do the work of a fork. Further, many schools of philosophy, from US Pragmatism to French deconstruction, have cautioned us against expecting that a concept, by its very being (or ontologically or per se), can bring about some predetermined outcome. Perhaps it was Arendt who made this point most poignantly in critiquing a natural-rights understanding of human rights in her book *Origins of Totalitarianism*, writing, '[T]he world found nothing sacred in the abstract nakedness of being human.'[96] Following these cautions, *Another Humanity* does not proceed as if a use of a concept can do something by itself. Rather, it offers an examination of what different uses of concepts do, including how they inspire various actions. 'The challenge', the anthropologist Ann Stoler writes, 'is both to discern the work we do with concepts and the work that concepts may explicitly or inadvertently exert on us.'[97]

Even given this specification, there are further difficulties. The way to examine what concepts inspire is to draw on anecdotal, textual and historical examples. But different experiences will show up in our anecdotes and result in different conclusions. For instance, whereas Afropessimists see the argument for the humanity of Black people, and the human rights thus entailed (or demanded), as a failed political strategy, humanists continue to deploy this argument.[98] In response, my aim is not to legislate which concepts work and which do not in some time-out-of-mind way, but rather to invite my readers to consider further how concepts function *in their own contexts* – to examine what works and what does not in the situations in which we find ourselves.[99] After all, the fact that our creative uses of concepts are limited in what they can do does not mean, as Hall jokes, that we are left with a single option – 'read the *Guardian* and pray!'[100]

My implicit focus throughout this book will be on how different uses of concepts function to *explain* material conditions, *invite* actors into political struggle or *organise* towards a new vision of community. Although a clear explanation of the world does not necessarily lead an actor to try to change it, although a creative use of a concept that openly draws out political implications is an invitation that is often declined, and although work to organise communities often faces entrenched barriers to change, it remains true that explanation, invitation and organisation are part of how concepts work as (political) tools. For instance, decolonial uses of self-determination explained why independence movements were necessary in Africa following World War II, and those uses were flexible enough to invite actors in many countries to leverage the concept.[101] The Standing Rock Sioux's use of the language of human rights both explained why moving the route of the Dakota Access Pipeline closer to their treaty-bound land violated their water rights and sovereignty and invited actors to participate in decolonial struggle.[102] And as the political theorist Christopher Paul Harris notes in his recent study of the Movement for Black Lives, in the wake of the murder of Trayvon Martin, the multiracial organisation Million Hoodies Movement organised their work through claims to human rights. 'That they foregrounded "human rights" is not accidental', Harris writes, 'nor is the fact that they specifically linked anti-Blackness with systemic violence', because their work was to advance 'a broader rhetorical shift . . . toward explicitly highlighting the different ways anti-Blackness reduces Black people to subhuman status as structural rather than incidental, much like the explicit assertion of Black humanity that would later anchor the phrase "Black Lives Matter".'[103] It is also noteworthy that in pursuing Black self-determination at the level of the city, the people of Jackson, Mississippi – through ideologically different organisations such as the Jackson Human Rights Institute, Cooperation Jackson, the Malcolm X Grassroots Movement, the Black Left Unity Network, and the Jackson branch of the NAACP – worked together to turn Jackson into a 'Human Rights City'.[104] Thus, social movements inspired by and following Standing Rock and Black Lives Matter – the movements of this century that have theorised race, class, gender and land together – have used the concepts of 'the human' and human rights to explain, invite and organise. While it is not my claim that the role of critical theory needs to be to bring about certain ends, theory nevertheless can thus inform and inspire and learn from practice, and practice can and does dialectically inform ethical and political theory. 'The big emancipatory dreams of progressive and anticolonial movements of the previous century seem to be in pieces', the writer Isabella Hammad has recently observed in connecting narrative and politics, yet 'some are trying to make something with these pieces, taking language from here and from there to keep our movements going.'[105]

My claim is also not that sufficient concepts are *external to* anti-egalitarian uses or inherently check against co-optation. No concept is *a priori* safe from state or elite capture.[106] Rather – and again, this is part of living under what Maldonado-Torres calls 'the coloniality of being'[107] – concepts are always already saturated with history and are always able to be co-opted. 'History will always find you', the poet Joy Harjo writes, 'and wrap you / In its thousand arms'.[108] That concepts are saturated with history, that history finds us, means that we would do well to acknowledge that 'the human', as many of us have come to know and practise it, is 'always already an effect of coloniality', as the theorist and artist Denise Ferreira da Silva puts it (reading Wynter).[109] But this colonial mediation is perhaps less of an obstacle to political struggles than it initially might seem, because its recognition allows us to quit searching for an unmediated or un-capturable concept. This is part of what Hall means when he teaches us that in politics there are no guarantees.

* * *

Like in *Choose Your Bearing*, in this book I take my methodological cue from Stuart Hall. I read Hall's claim '[t]here are no political guarantees' to mean that all concepts are saturated with history and that no use of a concept can prevent itself from being co-opted.[110] The contribution of this reading is that it asks critical theorists to turn down our emphasis on critiquing concepts and to turn up our emphasis on using concepts to build new coalitions, collectives and communities. If all concepts carry limitations and can be used to further domination, then we need not search for pure concepts, worry about how to prevent a concept from being captured, or spend too much time showing how concepts are contaminated or co-optable.[111] (This can become the fate of any concept.) [112] The practical question then becomes: Which concepts – no matter their history, even if that history (as it always does) shapes their limitations and possibilities – are most helpful to achieve those goals?[113]

In the final lecture of his 1983 series of lectures on cultural studies, 'Culture, Resistance, and Struggle', Hall said about 'the rule of law' – and he would later say about the term 'black' – 'People who were being excluded, whether the working classes, the poor, women, servants, et cetera, did not need another term; they needed *that* term, the term which the bourgeoisie already understood, in order to conduct the struggle.'[114] 'The fact that these struggles were stitched into a fabric of ideas which were bourgeois in origin', he went on, 'does not guarantee that they always remained inscribed in just this way.'[115] 'This is as true of the present as of the past', he concluded.[116]

Politics without guarantees, then, goes both ways: no concepts are per se or fundamentally this or that, because all concepts can be re-articulated differently. Just as no emancipatory use of a concept can prevent itself from being co-opted to serve structures of domination, as when alt-right actors begin to talk about their 'lived experience' being white men or when Hillary Clinton mentions 'intersectionality' on the campaign trail while maintaining her commitments to prisons and pipeline-funding banks, so too are no concepts that have advanced domination safe from re-inscription by emancipatory actors, as Hall's example of 'the rule of law' shows.[117] If this is true of the present as much as of the past, then a clear conclusion emerges: our task today is neither merely to de-stabilise or to play with problematic concepts we have inherited (often the post-modern approach), nor to search for some concept 'outside' of, or free from contamination by, unjust structures (often the decolonial approach), but instead to strategically *leverage* the always already limited concepts that will nevertheless allow us to win collectively on the terrains on which we are currently losing (we might call this 'the Du Boisian approach', upon which I will elaborate below and in Chapter 1).

In his 1997 lecture 'Race, The Floating Signifier', Hall elaborated upon his sense of politics without guarantees:

The one thing we are not is guaranteed in the truth of what we do. Indeed, I believe that without that kind of guarantee we would need to begin again, begin again in another space, begin again from a different set of presuppositions to try to ask ourselves what might it be in human identification, in human practice, in the building of human alliances, which without the guarantee, without the certainty of religion or science or anthropology or genetics or biology or the appearance of your eyes, without any guarantees at all, might enable us to conduct an ethically responsible human discourse and practice about race in our society.[118]

Here Hall develops what we might call a 'humanism without guarantees', that is, a humanism that refuses to be based on the old 'certainties' of Western (social) science.[119] He hints at what this new humanism requires in his emphasis on not narrow or national but 'human' identification, practice and building alliances. Resonating with Said's call for theorists to focus on beginnings more than origins, Hall notes that this new beginning for 'human identification' and 'human practice' might finally allow a more honest conversation about what race is and how it functions.[120] And he stresses the importance of new beginnings not just for discourse, but also for ethical practice, for how responsibility to one another ought to play out within a society – as well as, for Hall in other places, *across* different societies.[121]

Hall's idea of 'politics without guarantees' ultimately implies the need for some methods of contemporary critical theory – those that examine a concept only to deconstruct, destabilise or abandon it without a return to the question of what we can build together – to shift their approach.[122] Once we have studied and practised deconstruction or critique, we can always deconstruct or critique a concept.[123] With Hall, I am more interested here in considering the skill of recognising when an imaginative use of a concept can do the work we want it to do – that is, the skill of knowing when and how to wager that a term is what he calls '*that* term' needed to conduct the struggle or to build alliances. If some use of a concept (a) does extensive explanatory work and (b) does that work in a widely legible, accessible, and thereby invitational way, then, no matter the concept's history or how it has been captured, it remains a valuable political concept.[124] It is sufficient for the task at hand given what we can expect of a concept. It is from that point of recognising sufficiency that we 'begin again', and we do so strategically, with all our human-all-too-human emotions, prejudices, traditions, accomplishments, vulnerabilities and limitations.[125] In sum, while it is not at all clear to me that the concepts of 'the human' and 'humanity' (or for that matter a general sense of species-being) were Western inventions or find their origin in Europe, part of the point of recognising conceptual sufficiency is that a problematic provenance of a given concept does not disqualify it; we can re-articulate concepts no matter their origin. In the final instance, what matters is not origins but beginnings: how we begin, and begin again, with the conceptual terrain that confronts us.

* * *

What I have called 'conceptual sufficiency' – here the sufficiency of 'the human' and 'humanity' – is important not just for ethical theory but also for political theory.[126] To acknowledge the sufficiency of a certain concept entails changes to inquiry. It points critical theory in a direction different from spinning around in aporias as we begin our work. That new direction would include (1) clarifying and making more accessible what the concept implies as well as (2) inquiring into the barriers that prevent actors from carrying out what the concept implies.

In regard to (1) clarification, we can consider the claim – in the face of a differentially borne climate emergency and amidst an ongoing global pandemic – that the earth as one 'country' that humanity shares is a better understanding of the reality of our species than divisions of planet earth and humanity into nation states and races (and thereby into different civic and ascriptive statuses).[127] If we believe this humanist understanding is correct, then there remains work to be done in order to clarify its implications. For instance, if a country currently allows its citizens to come and go as they please, then it should also allow all people to travel freely across its current borders. If a country provides health care and education for all of its citizens, then it should provide both to whoever passes through its borders. In other words, what such a planetary humanism would look like in practice would include eliminating in policy all hierarchies of personhood tied to civic status. Further, it would mean that currently predominant conceptualisations of obligation, particularly around debt – around who owes whom and why – would need to shift in order to reckon with historical and ongoing (colonial) hierarchies of humanity. A clear example of the need to reframe obligation lies in the fact that Western financial bodies are willing to forgive some of Ukraine's debt but not that of Barbados.[128] These are simple examples of the larger point: the work to be done regarding the concept of humanity includes theorists' clarifying its implications for broader publics, using it to raise political consciousness and explaining how its partial (national, gendered, racialised, etc.) use is always a false use. As Césaire taught us, any 'true' use of 'humanity' must be a universalising one.[129]

In regard to (2) inquiring into the barriers that prevent people from acting upon their understanding of a concept (and to return to Monture), there are moments when the social problem is not that we have an insufficient concept, but that we are not willing to take the risks required in living it out.[130] The example of John Brown remains striking precisely because most of us – while agreeing both that slavery still exists[131] and that it violates our most deeply held principles – do not give up our lives fighting against it. John Brown thus still serves as a touchstone that tests not just how we understand violence and what theology we hold, but also the strength of our will.[132] In other words, sometimes the social problem is not a theoretical or conceptual problem, but rather one of political commitment.

Once we recognise that the problem is not with the concept, then we are able to ask one another the questions that are crucial to transforming the structures in which we live, the kinds of critical questions that Du Bois put on the table in his reading of the life of John Brown, and that Du Bois carried forward into *Black Reconstruction*, as I will suggest in Chapter 1.[133] If we agree that a prison or a pipeline or a for-profit school violates how others around us should be treated as part of humanity, or violates their human rights, or violates our sense of dignity or justice, then what risks are we willing to take?[134] What comforts are we willing to give up?[135] From what are we willing to divest?[136] What public spaces are we willing to reclaim?[137] How will we connect these risks, refusals, divestments and reclamations to ongoing work across borders?[138] How can we remind one another that 'it may be important to pause over the awareness of dissatisfaction just where it starts to seem futile'?[139] What kinds of (queer) kin structures, and ways of taking care of one another, would allow us to take more risks, make these connections and keep going despite our dissatisfaction and alienation?[140] What 'queer forms' and modes of friendship can serve as a bulwark against our desire to belong to an elite ethno-class and thus to abandon the struggle?[141] How can forms of resistance become 'more accessible to people with varying debilities, capacities, and disabilities'?[142] What forms of agency can we outline, given that many of us experience our situations as ones of tremendous constraint (bills to pay, debts racking up, kids to care for) and extremely limited possibility (climate change, police violence, low wages outside of the corporate world)? How can our mobilisations not only make demands on those in power, but also build power in a way that makes a world of decolonised land, as well as of universal health care and education (and so on), a more widely desired and thus a more feasible option?[143] Along the way, how can we see, and explain for wide audiences, what Wynter calls 'the performative enactment of all our roles, of our role allocations as, in our contemporary Western/Westernized case, in terms of, inter alia, gender, race, class/underclass, and, across them all, sexual orientation'?[144] If we understand that all of our roles are 'praxes . . . rather than nouns', then how, concretely, do we practise differently – how do we perform our humanity differently as an affirmation of a different future, no matter the success of each of our mobilisations and demands?[145] Could raising these questions in community and conversation *itself* be part of a larger practice of re-describing humanity and thus living in light of Wynter's task-setting lines that

the struggle of our new millennium will be one between the ongoing imperative of securing the well-being of our present ethnoclass (i.e. Western bourgeois) conception of the human, Man, which overrepresents itself as if it were the human itself, and that of securing the well-being, and therefore the full cognitive and behavioral autonomy of the human species itself/ourselves?[146]

Would this not be, as Wynter reads Glissant, 'a specific mode of uprising, one which calls into question, rising up against, our present mode of being, of subjectivity, of Self'?[147] Finally, what modes of attending to each other, and to the reality of the world around us, do these questions presuppose, such that we would truly be able to ask each other Simone Weil's key ethical question: 'What are you going through?'[148]

Chapter Outline

This book starts where *Choose Your Bearing* left off, with W. E. B. Du Bois, now examining not just his 1940s writings on human rights but starting from his earlier writings that advanced a clear sense of humanity. In Chapter 1, I begin to draw out my opening claim that 'the human' and 'humanity' remain sufficient concepts for decolonial politics today. I look to Du Bois's uses of 'human', 'humanity' and 'human rights' in *Black Reconstruction*, which I suggest were informed by how he came to understand 'humanity' in *John Brown*. I then discuss Du Bois's peace activism, returning to some of his 1940s writings that I discussed in *Choose Your Bearing*, thus rendering it unnecessary for my reader to begin with that book before reading this one.

In Chapter 2, I focus on Édouard Glissant's *Treatise of the All-World*. While the two philosophers Glissant is continually in dialogue with, Aimé Césaire and Frantz Fanon, are frequently read for offering new humanisms, Glissant is not necessarily read as a humanist in the same way, in part because he does not call for a new humanism in as explicit of terms as his Martinican forerunners. Consequently, readings of Glissant's humanism vary greatly. I will suggest that, against his own claim that he offers a 'poetics' but not a 'humanism', Glissant's work maintains a profound sense of humanity such that we could call it a humanism.

Chapters 1 and 2 make up Part I of this book. They proceed through what Hall calls a 'detour through theory', which he describes as 'the necessary delay'.[149] As Hall puts it elsewhere, 'Theory is always a detour on the way to something more important.'[150] Reading the theories of Du Bois and Glissant provided me with both an understanding of the present as an ongoing time of war and a belief in a relational humanism to respond to our context of coercion. Chapters 3, 4 and 5 make up Part II of this book. They proceed through what the feminist scholar and activist AnaLouise Keating calls 'risking the personal'.[151] I start from personal contexts and conversations and then read the work of Sylvia Wynter, Edward Said and Hannah Arendt to think through the practical, lived questions that emerged from them.

In Chapter 3, I turn to Sylvia Wynter's outline for a new humanism. While Wynter poses a daunting task for ethics and politics – recognising and re-performing how we practise human life across *all* of our roles – she also gives us resources for a critical re-fashioning of human life on a collective scale. I draw out these resources by thinking with her 1984 article 'The Ceremony Must Be Found: After Humanism', her 1992 open letter 'No Humans Involved' and her chapter that reflects on her 1984 article, published in 2015, entitled 'The Ceremony Found: Towards the Autopoetic Turn/Overturn, its Autonomy of Human Agency and Extraterritoriality of (Self-) Cognition'. In her writing on humanism, Wynter engages Edward Said, and I follow her lead by returning to Said in my next chapter.

In Chapter 4, I examine sources from Edward Said's archive housed at Columbia University's Rare Book & Manuscript Library. I consider patterns wherein academic institutions in the Global North archive collections from or about the Global South. Thus, this chapter investigates questions of history, responsibility and coloniality in material collection, access and distribution. Beyond these structural questions, and more centrally to the chapter, I situate myself as a participant in these relationships, patterns and questions, and by staying close to Said's archive, I also consider why it was *Orientalism*, and not *The Question of Palestine*, that became the key text of Said's that was mandatory reading for students of postcolonial theory. I conclude this chapter with a reflection on visiting Palestine.

In Chapter 5, I begin from the context of Palestine and return, perhaps surprisingly, to the work of Hannah Arendt. Arendt's ability to see through the categories (and categorial logic) of modernity, coupled with her severe limitations that were decidedly modern (especially around race), provides an example of thinking we can learn from in the present, not least because we have our own limitations as theorists. I stay with both the insights and the limitations that Arendt offers, ultimately finding a relational path forward in her correspondence with Karl Jaspers.

* * *

Overall, this book proceeds in a style somewhere between distanced academic writing and the personal essay. It is a book about how theory travels. While I focus on Du Bois, Glissant, Wynter, Said and Arendt, in no chapter do I simply treat these thinkers alone; instead, I read Du Bois with Wifredo Lam, Glissant with Gilles Deleuze, Wynter with Said, and Said through his interlocutors, including C. L. R. James, Aijaz Ahmad, Wael Hallaq and Sadik Jalal al-'Azm, as well as through the recent commentary of the political theorist Jeanne Morefield. This book has learned from and contributes to ongoing scholarship on the Black Radical tradition or a Black Atlantic tradition, and it would fit in discussions on both what Aaron Kamugisha has called 'the Caribbean intellectual tradition' and, more broadly, what Gary Wilder has called 'traditions of radical universalism and radical humanism'.[152] But if pressed, I would put this book in the tradition that Abdelkebir Khatibi, recalling Du Bois's attention to the problems of each century and the need for planetary inquiry, called 'plural thought':

Only the risk of a plural thought (with several poles of civilization, several languages, several technical and scientific elaborations) can, I think, assure for us the turning of this century on the planetary scene . . . We are still at the dawning of planetary thought. But we have grown up in the suffering that calls for the power of the word and revolt. If I told you, whoever you are, that this work has already begun and that you can hear me only as survivor, maybe then you will listen to the slow and progressive march of all the humiliated and all the survivors.[153]

It will not be lost on my readers that my preference – if I had to locate this very personal book within a tradition – would be to stay with Khatibi, whose 'plural thought' is a decolonial tradition that is also a deconstructive one. This is what I am after in this book, where 'strategy' is only a beginning of a longer and deeper human process. I follow this strategy/process, decolonial/deconstruction tension every time I write 'rights' or 'sovereignty' or 'nation'.[154] We are still at the dawning . . .

* * *

In between these breaks, these ellipses, let me try again to clarify this point, which is perhaps the most important point regarding the method of this book. It has to do with starting from decolonial theory and cultural studies and then running those moves through deconstruction. I agree with the theorist Geoffrey Bennington when he argues, reading Derrida, that 'we have a fundamentally passive relation to the language we speak', *and* I follow Hall in stressing our active responsibility in leveraging this inheritance.[155] I am calling Hall's active use of tradition the decolonial moment, seen in creative uses of self-determination, sovereignty and human rights, to name three examples. That is the necessary reconstructive corrective in our hyper-critical moment; it is also often where the decolonial intervention stops. But I want then and again to return to the insight from deconstruction that 'the Sovereign one is . . . always already overrun by multiplicity, diversity, *to poikilon*, democracy, the politics of politics'.[156] This is what Bennington means in his insight that it is not just that subjects deconstruct texts but that oppositions such as theory/practice are already 'from the start, in deconstruction'.[157] This means that 'sovereignty is, as always, already failing from the start'.[158] Bennington is at pains to avoid a certain normative or moral register, so I will add that, for me, this is a very good thing. This attention to how multiplicity overruns politics gives us an accurate description of political life in this century (as Said's epigraph noted); it reminds us that the contestations and exiles and tensions and plurality that 'haunt politics' – perhaps especially nationalistic and identity politics in their current registers – also provide the most fruitful insights for moving towards another humanity beyond the modern categories we have needed to leverage strategically to conduct the immediate struggles.[159] When we add or acknowledge the deconstructive moment, recognising both the sufficiency of our concepts for strategic purposes and their insufficiency for a wider and slower process, we enter double politics.

* * *

Read one way, this book is an attempt to listen to those survivors of modernity who have advanced the plural and planetary work that, as Khatibi notes, 'has already begun'. Indeed, and before I conclude, it is worth adding that this book has been deeply guided by the methods and contributions not only of Stuart Hall, but also of Simone Weil, Claudia Jones and Hannah Arendt. I mention these contributions here and not later because they informed *how* I read and wrote. While Weil called for discarding claims to rights, she maintained the sufficiency of 'justice' as a concept that does normative philosophical work, and that spirit of writing taught me something about maintaining some orienting terms. When I was struggling with why so much of critical theory has criticised rights claims in the spirit of Marx's 'On the Jewish Question', it was Jones's writings – internationalist and theorising labor, race and gender together – that allowed me to see how rights claims belonged in a project that seeks to talk about our species along different axes of power. (Hall too modelled how to maintain rights claims in his imaginative decolonial project, offering what the poet and Black Studies scholar Brian Meeks has recently called a 'career-long and profoundly humanist engagement with Marxism'.)[160] And Arendt, much more than Weil, had the capacity to tarry with the 'perplexities' of rights as well as other flawed concepts, even if that capacity reflected an adherence to racial and colonial norms more than her champions want to admit; I tarry with the perplexities of 'the human' similarly here.[161] For some, I will be too close to Arendt instead of Weil, Jones and Hall, not only in keeping 'the human' with all its perplexities, but also in that the following chapters proceed 'in the shadow of race', to use McKnight's phrase.[162] This is to say both that race informs every aspect of the following chapters and that after this Introduction I largely leave race behind as my focus or level of analysis. For me, this is the required second move of the 'double politics' I am after. For you, it might read as another book on humanism that runs too quickly from the racial violence contained in that term. In a way, it is both: to be able to choose the degree of my engagement with race does reflect textually what has long been part of living on my side of the Veil, namely, to choose when and how to engage race and when to erase it; at the same time, reading across the Veil is also a textual rejection of 'White sovereignty' (McKnight again) around the question of what it means to be human.[163]

To reiterate one last time what I am suggesting in this Introduction: I could say about race or about 'the human' what Michel-Rolph Trouillot says about the nation state: that it is 'a lived fiction of modernity'.[164] The post-racial or non-racialist position emphasises the fiction, but in this book I am stressing that these modern categories are 'lived' – and so they can be lived differently. Hall reminds us that 'all practices have a discursive aspect', and by reading Du Bois, Glissant, Wynter, Said and Arendt in the following chapters, I focus on different practices – building peace, listening to the landscape, interracial ceremony, rights-based activism, and giving an account of ourselves – in order to draw out their discursive aspects, that is, to allow those practices to re-shape how we think about and thus how we live out what it means to be human and to be part of humanity.[165]

* * *

Having now shared with you the personal and intellectual paths that informed how I got to the questions in this book, I want to stress finally what the political theorist Louiza Odysseos has so helpfully underscored, namely, the need, no matter whether we agree on the sufficiency of 'the human' today in our particular contexts, 'to insist on the *question*' of decolonial ethics.[166] In that spirit, I invite you to think with and against me – with our tensions held together in what I hope will be a longer conversation – as I read five philosophers whose work outlines an answer to Glissant's own insisted-upon questions. As he looked towards a new, increasingly creolised century while watching the sea rise and the wind swirl around him,

Glissant asked: 'Do we have the right and the means to live another dimension of humanity? But how?'[167]

Notes

1. For the argument that race is a consequence of racism, see Karen E. Fields and Barbara J. Fields, *Racecraft: The Soul of Inequality in American Life* (New York: Verso, 2014). For the argument that race is a product of state violence and structural inequality, see Norman Ajari, *Dignity or Death: Ethics and Politics of Race*, trans. Matthew B. Smith (Cambridge: Polity Press, 2023), p. 3. For analysis of ongoing forms of coerced labour, see Jane Gordon, *Statelessness and Contemporary Enslavement* (New York: Routledge, 2020). I borrow my language of war from Joy James. See e.g. her description of Angela Davis's childhood under Jim Crow as 'a war zone' and framing of the United States as 'a war zone of anti-Blackness' (Joy James, *Contextualizing Angela Davis* (London: Bloomsbury, 2024), pp. 10, 54). I simply did not see the present as a time of war until I started to read James's work, upon the recommendation of my friend Mukasa Mubirumusoke.
2. Binyavanga Wainaina, *How to Write about Africa* (London: Penguin, 2024), p. 132.
3. Frantz Fanon, *Les damnés de la terre* (Paris: La Découverte, 2002), p. 180.
4. Theodor Adorno, *Minima Moralia: Reflections from Damaged Life*, trans. Edmund F. N. Jephcott (New York: Verso, 1974), p. 39.
5. Quoted in Anthony Bayani Rodriguez, 'Introduction: On Sylvia Wynter and the Urgency of a New Humanist Revolution in the Twenty-First Century', *American Quarterly* 70, no. 4 (2018): p. 831.
6. My method here combines John Dewey's call to start from and refer back to experience in *Experience and Nature* with Emmanuel Levinas's priority of 'the Other' in *Totality and Infinity* and Enrique Dussel's addition, in *Philosophy of Liberation* and *Ethics of Liberation*, that this Other is excluded by the dominant system and so can offer insights about how to understand and critique that system.

7. The most influential description of this psychological status comes from Du Bois in analysing white workers who, while given a low wage for their work, also received 'a sort of public and psychological wage' that includes deference, titles, access to public services, protection by police forces, and standing in courts. See W. E. B. Du Bois, *Black Reconstruction in America: 1860–1880* (New York: The Free Press, [1935] 1992), p. 700. It is worth noting here that I employ many different and contradictory ideas of 'we' in this book, and maybe you will see yourself in some, and maybe you won't, and that tension itself would make an interesting starting point for further discussion.

8. Édouard Glissant, *Traité du Tout-Monde* (Paris: Gallimard, 1997), p. 21; *Treatise on the Whole-World* (Liverpool: Liverpool University Press, 2020), p. 11. The original French reads: 'N'avons-nous pas droit et moyen de vivre une autre dimension d'humanité ? Mais comment ?' What I will stress in the rest of this book is the verb Glissant selected here: this 'autre . . . humanité' is not just to be theorised or discussed, but to be lived.

9. Zahi Zalloua, *Solidarity and the Palestinian Cause: Indigeneity, Blackness, and the Promise of Universality* (London: Bloomsbury, 2023), p. 30.

10. In *Choose Your Bearing*, I started from rights in order to avoid conflating ethics with how we personally feel about others or with how we understand our own position with respect to another group of people. Starting from rights is a way of cutting through the fog of, for instance, when someone says they 'love' gay people, they are not racist, or they support Indigenous nations, but doesn't show up for queer or racialised people or continues living according to a dispossessive way of life when it allows them to increase their social and professional status. What matters more than what we say (whether an empty pronouncement or an honest misstep) is whether we work and invest ourselves, imperfectly but truthfully as limited creatures, to universalise rights to marriage and mobility, rights to stay and return, rights to land and culture, rights to water and food, rights to pray, migrate, receive health care when sick, and otherwise live as a

human being. In other words, we start from rights in order to name actual conflicts and to see the world as it really is, with all its violations and possibilities. As Edward Said noted about Palestine, 'There is a radical conflict between a view stating that Jews have more rights than non-Jews, and a view – as yet to be formulated with the cogency and power it deserves – stating that all present communities and individuals have civil rights in Palestine, equal in principle' (Edward Said, *The Politics of Dispossession: The Struggle for Palestinian Self-Determination, 1969–1994* (New York: Vintage, 1995), p. 76. See also p. 100). This point also applies to religious communities that deny rights to gay members or universities that exploit workers through extremely hierarchal ranks, to name two other example of radical conflicts that are often covered over by claims to shared principles or a shared pursuit of service and social justice. Overall, the question of human rights moves our focus to the kind of society we are, in fact, in the process of building.

11. Said, *The Politics of Dispossession*, p. 31. See also pp. 67–8.

12. See Patricia J. Williams, *The Alchemy of Race and Rights* (Cambridge, MA: Harvard University Press, 1992). Cf. the important position in Black Male Studies that in the US there is a right to kill Black males. See e.g. Dalitso Ruwe, 'Can Black males be subjects of human rights violations?', *The International Journal of Human Rights* (2024).

13. Said, *The Politics of Dispossession*, pp. xiii, xv.

14. For this reading of the Western tradition, see Pierre Hadot, *Philosophy as a Way of Life: Spiritual Exercises from Socrates to Foucault*, trans. Michael Chase (Malden: Blackwell, 1995); Alexander Nehamas, *The Art of Living: Socratic Reflections from Plato to Foucault* (Berkeley: University of California Press, 2000). See also how the anthropologist David Scott takes up Nehamas to read Stuart Hall in his 2023 lecture 'Universalism & Reparation', https://www.youtube.com/watch?v=BdoPFKPoJTo&ab_channel=ERCMinorUniversality.

15. See Nelson Maldonado-Torres, 'On the Coloniality of Being', *Cultural Studies* 21, no. 2 (2007): pp. 240–70. One result of Maldonado-Torres's thesis has been a proliferation of projects

on the coloniality of x or y. These diagnoses are important, particularly around how the coloniality of law operates. (I thank Mireille Fanon for helping me see this point.) At the same time, to accept the coloniality of being thesis (in general) is to accept the coloniality of x and y (in particular). Other helpful dissertations, articles, books, etc. would offer paths for where to go, that is, how to act, what demands to make, how to mobilise, and so on, *given* the coloniality of x and y.

16. Stuart Hall, 'Race, Articulation and Societies Structured in Dominance', in *Essential Essays, Vol. 1: Foundations of Cultural Studies*, ed. David Morley (Durham, NC: Duke University Press, 2019), p. 234.

17. W. E. B. Du Bois, *Color and Democracy* (New York: Oxford University Press, 2007), p. 241.

18. Zimitri Erasmus, *Race Otherwise: Forging a New Humanism for South Africa* (Johannesburg: Wits University Press, 2017), pp. xxiv; see also p. 38.

19. Ibid. p. xxiv.

20. Ibid. p. 39.

21. The political theorist Utz McKnight suggests moving away from the question 'Why do you think the practice or event has to do with race?' and instead towards 'How is it not racial?' (Utz McKnight, *The Everyday Practice of Race in America: Ambiguous Privilege* (New York: Routledge, 2010), p. 21). In a line that could be helpful in guiding (or starting) our ordinary conversations, McKnight goes on: '[I]t is important to provide a description of the social conditions that are used to elaborate the definition of race for *all* persons. To do otherwise is not an accurate reflection of the real practices of race in this society, but instead represents a social strategy to deflect or obfuscate the persistence of specific forms of mutual racial subjection. We identify racists so we don't have to be implicated ourselves' (ibid. p. 32).

22. Another way of putting this uncertainty is in terms of openness, following Helmuth Plessner. For Plessner, being open or exposed is part of what it means to be human – as both historical and embodied. Plessner offers a striking portrait of human life in his compelling and controversial 1931 essay on this topic, writing,

'The human must lead its life in this openness, uncertain which of its sides is prevalent: life already tells the human about its self, while the body ultimately takes away its independence and exposes it to the course of things' (Helmuth Plessner, *Political Anthropology*, trans. Nils F. Schott (Evanston, IL: Northwestern University Press, 2018), p. 84). To stress the need for everyday conversations, as I do, acknowledges not just the need to talk about politics (frowned upon in social life in the US), but more fundamentally that politics already shapes these conversations – thinking this way works 'to counter the restriction to a so-called political sphere', as Plessner puts it (ibid. p. 55). I follow Plessner to make a more fundamental claim than the personal is political or that the private is public, which draws on the distinction as it challenges it. Plessner avoids the distinction itself in portraying politics as essential, as the ground of human life. As Plessner stresses, 'Politics then is not primarily a field but the state of human life in which it gives itself its constitution and asserts itself against the world, not just externally and juridically but from out of its ground and essence' (ibid. p. 61). To think with and against Plessner, it seems that as a species we have yet to achieve a form of relation in which this openness does not become a struggle for national/particular power, reflected in Plessner's concluding set of claims that we are always already tied to a people. In the present, then, we are already caught up in a politics (as essential), and we are left essaying our way towards a politics beyond the facticity of the nation or of being tied to a people.

23. W. E. B. Du Bois, 'My Evolving Program for Negro Freedom', *Clinical Sociology Review* 8, no. 1 (1990): p. 35. I do think these should be *conversations*, with all the stumbling, mistakes and grace that this word implies, as opposed to something more professionalised, like the current race-relations workshop marketplace, which has long struck me as absurd. I will say a little more about this in my concluding chapter on Arendt.

24. W. E. B. Du Bois, *The Souls of Black Folk* (Boston: Bedford/St. Martin's, 1997), p. 45. See also W. E. B. Du Bois, 'The color line belts the world', 20 October 1906. W. E. B. Du Bois Papers (MS 312).

Special Collections and University Archives, University of Massachusetts Amherst Libraries. You can see the wonderful typescript copy of his essay with this title at the UMass Amherst digital archive's website, https://credo.library.umass.edu/view/full/mums312-b207-i148. To make this point is to side against how Gilroy concludes *The Black Atlantic* and thus sets the terms for his subsequent work in noting that his book contributes 'towards the politics of a new century in which the central axis of conflict will no longer be the colour line but the challenge of just, sustainable development and the frontiers which will separate the overdeveloped parts of the world (at home and abroad) from the intractable poverty that already surrounds them' (Paul Gilroy, *The Black Atlantic: Modernity and Double Consciousness* (Cambridge, MA: Harvard University Press, 1993), p. 223). In this book, I am trying to start from how the colour line shapes that development and has already defined what counts as 'developed'.

25. Steve Biko summarises these responses this way: 'We are collectively segregated against – what can be more logical than for us to respond as a group? When workers come together under the auspices of a trade union to strive for the betterment of their conditions, nobody expresses surprise in the Western world. It is the done thing. Nobody accuses them of separatist tendencies' (Steve Biko, *I Write What I Like* (Chicago: University of Chicago Press, 2002), p. 25). Biko also poses a challenge to my argument by writing that white racism has its 'greatest ally' in 'the refusal by us to club together as blacks because we are told to do so would be racialist', adding that 'while we progressively lose ourselves in a world of colourlessness and amorphous common humanity, whites are deriving pleasure and security in entrenching white racism and further exploiting the minds and bodies of the unsuspecting black masses' (ibid. p. 50). And yet, around the same time Biko was criticising an empty sense of 'common humanity', he also emphasised that Black Consciousness seeks 'some kind of balance – a true humanity where power politics will have no place' (ibid. p. 90). He would conclude that essay by saying, 'We have set out on a quest for true humanity . . . In

time we shall be in a position to bestow upon South Africa the greatest gift possible – a more human face' (ibid. p. 98).

26. Ajari, *Dignity or Death*, p. 3.

27. Utz McKnight, *Race and the Politics of the Exception: Equality, Sovereignty, and American Democracy* (New York: Routledge, 2013), pp. 111, 112.

28. Hall, 'Race, Articulation and Societies Structured in Dominance', p. 239.

29. For commentary on how a CBS News senior foreign correspondent said that Ukraine 'isn't . . . like Iraq or Afghanistan' but instead is 'relatively civilised, relatively European', or for how the BBC hosted a Ukrainian prosecutor who said, 'It's very emotional for me because I see European people with blue eyes and blond hair . . . being killed every day', see Moustafa Bayoumi, 'They are "civilized" and "look like us": the racist coverage of Ukraine', *The Guardian*, 2 March 2022, https://www.theguardian.com/commentisfree/2022/mar/02/civilised-european-look-like-us-racist-coverage-ukraine.

30. Hall wrote in 1980 that South Africa is 'the social formation in which the salience of racial features cannot for a moment be denied' (ibid. p. 199). Cf. Said's comments comparing South Africa and Gaza: Said, *The Politics of Dispossession*, p. 194.

31. Stuart Hall, 'Teaching Race', in *Selected Writings on Race and Difference*, eds. Paul Gilroy and Ruth Wilson Gilmore (Durham, NC: Duke University Press, 2021), p. 132.

32. I borrow this question from how the cultural theorist Mark C. Taylor talks about the influence of religion in *After God*, as well as how McKnight starts from an anecdote where 'nothing was obviously racial' in theorising how race continues to structure democratic life in the US. See McKnight, *Race and the Politics of the Exception*, p. 12.

33. Hall, 'Teaching Race', p. 135. As Black Consciousness activists in Brazil have stressed, one of the ways the myth of racial democracy is maintained is that race is not talked about in public discourse, the mainstream media or in private lives. See Marcia Mikulak, 'The Symbolic Power of Color: Constructions of Race, Skin-color, and Identity in Brazil', *Humanity & Society* 35, nos. 1–2 (2011): pp. 65, 77.

34. Said, *The Politics of Dispossession*, p. 49. He notes about Palestinian feelings and assertions something perhaps useful to keep in mind in these conversations: 'It is not only the historical truth that has been constantly denied but the very experience of the hurt, the very fact of injustice' (ibid. p. 126).

35. Aimé Césaire, 'Letter to Maurice Thorez', trans. Chike Jeffers, *Social Text 103* 28, no. 2 (2010): p. 150.

36. Ibid.

37. Ibid. Cf. Derefe Chevannes, 'The Haitian Revolution and Afromodernity: Political Speech, Euromodernity & Black Universalism', *Theory & Event* 26, no. 2 (2023): pp. 318–44.

38. Rinaldo Walcott, *The Long Emancipation: Moving toward Black Freedom* (Durham, NC: Duke University Press, 2021), p. 5.

39. Césaire, 'Letter', p. 150.

40. See Edward Said, 'Memory, Inequality, and Power: Palestine and the Universality of Human Rights', https://electronicintifada.net/blogs/nora-barrows-friedman/ten-years-edward-saids-passing-listen-his-last-major-speech. For a political rather than juridical sense of universality that resonates with my emphasis on practice, see Massimiliano Tomba, *Insurgent Universality: An Alternative Legacy of Modernity* (Oxford: Oxford University Press, 2019).

41. This is what Ruth Wilson Gilmore calls recitation without rehearsal – a performance of critique without raising the larger question of what we can build together.

42. See Anthony Pagden, *The Fall of Natural Man: The American Indian and the Origins of Comparative Ethnology* (Cambridge: Cambridge University Press, 1986), p. 119. In the North American context, we could read John Wesley Powell alongside Las Casas.

43. W. E. B. Du Bois, *The World and Africa* (New York: Oxford University Press, 2007), p. 50.

44. Walter Mignolo, 'Who Speaks for the "Human" in Human Rights?' *Hispanic Issues On Line* (2009): p. 10.

45. Achille Mbembe, *Necropolitics*, trans. Steven Corcoran (Durham, NC: Duke University Press, 2019), pp. 161, 163.

46. Ayça Çubukçu, 'Thinking Against Humanity', *London Review of International Law* 5, no. 2 (2017): p. 253.

47. Calvin Warren, *Ontological Terror: Blackness, Nihilism, and Emancipation* (Durham, NC: Duke University Press, 2018), pp. 2, 3.

48. Zakiyyah Iman Jackson, *Becoming Human: Matter and Meaning in an Antiblack World* (New York: New York University Press, 2020), p. 1.

49. Ibid.

50. Alberto Moreiras, *Uncanny Rest: For Antiphilosophy*, trans. Camila Moreiras (Durham, NC: Duke University Press, 2022), pp. 103, 101, 102.

51. Kathryn Yussof, *A Billion Black Anthropocenes or None* (Minneapolis: University of Minnesota Press, 2018), pp. 2, 18. For Yussof humanism is ultimately 'a method of erasure' (ibid. p. 57).

52. Norman Wirzba, *This Sacred Life: Humanity's Place in a Wounded World* (Cambridge: Cambridge University Press, 2021), p. xiv.

53. This theoretical line exemplifies what Jonathan Fenderson has described as 'one of the major trends evident in contemporary African American Studies scholarship: the glaring underdevelopment, evasion, and, at times, omission of class analysis – and, more explicitly, political economy – as a fundamental aspect of Black Studies' (Jonathan Fenderson, 'Black Studies Post-Janus', *The Black Scholar* 48, no. 4 (2018): pp. 1–2). For a more existential angle that still attends to political economy and the importance of education, see Kersuze Simeon-Jones, *The Intellectual Roots of Contemporary Black Thought: Nascent Political Philosophies* (New York: Routledge, 2021).

54. Lewis Gordon, *Existentia Africana: Understanding Africana Existential Thought* (New York: Routledge, 2000), p. 160.

55. Ajari, *Dignity or Death*, pp. 16–17.

56. Rei Terada, *Metaracial: Hegel, Antiblackness, and Political Identity* (Chicago: University of Chicago Press, 2023), p. 9.

57. See e.g. Walter Mignolo, 'The Enduring Enchantment: Or the Epistemic Privilege of Modernity and Where to Go from Here', *The South Atlantic Quarterly* 101, no. 4 (2002): p. 934. See Çubukçu's work in *Jadaliyya*, *The Boston Review*, and other outlets, e.g. Ayça Çubukçu, 'Many Speak for Palestine', *Boston Review*, 1 May 2024, https://www.bostonreview.net/articles/many-speak-for-palestine/.

58. Said put it this way: 'What could be more disgraceful an instance of Benda's *trahison des clercs* than the displays of political fervor on the part of intellectuals for "our" side, when so often it has been our side that has been committing the violence in the name of Western virtues, humanism, morality?' (Said, *The Politics of Dispossession*, p. 359).

59. For this phrase, see Rashid Khalidi, *The Hundred Years' War on Palestine: A History of Settler Colonialism and Resistance, 1917–2017* (New York: Picador, 2020). Cf. the South African case in Lebogang Seale, *One Hundred Years of Dispossession: My Family's Quest to Reclaim Our Land* (Johannesburg: Jacana, 2024).

60. Said, *The Politics of Dispossession*, pp. xix–xx. This silence also permeates 'critical' international relations and 'global' human rights circles. For example, I attended an important human rights conference at New York University in early November 2023, during which only one of the many keynote speakers mentioned Palestine – and in that instance only extremely briefly. During the days of the conference, events in Palestine/Israel were on the front page of *The New York Times* each morning, but the silence persisted. Moreover, one of the in-person keynote speakers was supposed to be Volker Türk, the UN High Commissioner for Human Rights, but he had to offer a prerecorded reflection because he suddenly had to travel to the Middle East *because of the ongoing war in/on Palestine*. Still, the general silence remained. When I brought up this silence to one of the conference organisers via email after the conference, he told me that *I did not understand the TED-style format of the conference*.

61. Ibid. p. 143.

62. Ibid. p. 233. Said repeats this idea so many times the citations would be too numerous to recount here. See also his claim – working consistently against a 'military option' – that what Palestine offers is 'a vision' that involves 'respect of nationalities for each other, the right to live within secure and safe borders, and to coexist in a profitable way with other peoples, with differences' (ibid. pp. 312, 313). 'That', Said emphasised, 'is our main weapon' (ibid. p. 313). If you are wondering, by

the way, reader, Said did not have much good to say about Hamas: he criticised their strike strategy and political ideas while also always praising non-violent resistance and drawing our attention to how corrupted the discourse of 'terrorism' has become, not least because it tends to draw our focus away from state violence (see Said, *The Politics of Dispossession*, pp. 197, 403, xlv, 349).

63. Ibid. p. 233.

64. Ibid. p. 143. This is why I consider, for instance, the following books to be about the idea of Palestine: Tiffany Lethabo King, *Black Shoals: Offshore Formations of Black and Native Studies* (Durham, NC: Duke University Press, 2019); Shona N. Jackson, *Beyond Constraint: Middle/Passages of Blackness and Indigeneity in the Radical Tradition* (Durham, NC: Duke University Press, 2024). I thank Rebecca Hankins for recommending the latter.

65. Said, *The Politics of Dispossession*, p. 242.

66. Edward Said, 'Introduction', in *Reflections on Exile* (Cambridge, MA: Harvard University Press, 2000), p. xxviii. The novelist Isabella Hammad has recently summarised Said's humanism as 'a humanism that can evolve and expand beyond its exclusionary, bourgeois European and largely male origins, and that commits itself to crossing boundaries between cultures and disciplines— a humanism that holds the practice of criticism close to heart' (Isabella Hammad, *Recognizing the Stranger: On Palestine and Narrative* (New York: Black Cat, 2024), p. 5).

67. See Nelson Maldonado-Torres, 'Lewis Gordon: Philosopher of the Human', *The CLR James Journal: The Journal of the Caribbean Philosophical Association* 14, no. 1 (2008): p. 103.

68. Lewis Gordon, *Freedom, Justice, and Decolonization* (New York: Routledge, 2021), pp. 5, 6.

69. Paul Gilroy, *Against Race: Imagining Political Culture beyond the Color Line* (Cambridge: The Belknap Press of Harvard University Press, 2000), p. 2.

70. Paul Gilroy, 'Never Again: refusing race and salvaging the human', https://holbergprisen.no/en/news/holberg-prize/2019-holberg-lecture-laureate-paul-gilroy.

71. It is worth noting – given the complications of these traditions and the brevity of this introductory *tour d'horizon* – that some philosophers, such as Joy James, read Afropessimism and human rights together. See George Yancy, 'Reaching beyond "Black faces in high places": An Interview with Joy James', *Truthout*, 1 February 2021, https://truthout.org/articles/reaching-beyond-black-faces-in-high-places-an-interview-with-joy-james/. For Nyong'o's line, see Tavia Nyong'o, 'Black Humanitarianism', in *Retrieving the Human: Reading Paul Gilroy*, ed. Rebecka Rutledge Fisher and Jay Garcia (Albany: State University of New York Press, 2014), p. 187.

72. Paul Gilroy, 'Introduction: Race is the Prism', in *Selected Writings on Race and Difference*, ed. Paul Gilroy and Ruth Wilson Gilmore (Durham, NC: Duke University Press, 2021), p. 2.

73. Gilroy, *Against Race*, pp. 98, 2. See also p. 14.

74. Gilroy, 'A Dialogue on the Human', in *Retrieving the Human*, p. 226.

75. Paul Gilroy, *Postcolonial Melancholia* (New York: Columbia University Press, 2004), p. 57. For further discussion of humanism in feminist philosophy today, see e.g. Ann V. Murphy, 'Corporeal Vulnerability and the New Humanism', *Hypatia: A Journal of Feminist Philosophy* 26, no. 3 (2011): pp. 575–90.

76. See Gilroy, *Postcolonial Melancholia*, p. 54.

77. Gilroy, *Against Race*, pp. 6–7.

78. Ibid. Cf. Alberto Moreiras's analysis of how identity can be commodified in *The Exhaustion of Difference* (Durham, NC: Duke University Press, 2001).

79. Gary Wilder, *Concrete Utopianism: The Politics of Temporality and Solidarity* (New York: Fordham University Press, 2022), p. 4.

80. Ibid. p. 170.

81. Ibid. p. 18.

82. Ibid.

83. For an important critique of strategies that accept this bind, indeed one that influenced Wynter, see Randall Williams, *The Divided World: Human Rights and Its Violence* (Minneapolis: University of Minnesota Press, 2010). For Wynter's citation of Williams, see *Sylvia Wynter: On Being Human as Praxis*, ed. Katherine McKittrick (Durham, NC: Duke University Press, 2015), p. 39.

84. Lewis Gordon, *Fear of Black Consciousness* (New York: Farrar, Straus and Giroux, 2022), p. 158.

85. Stuart Hall, 'The Great Moving Right Show', in *Selected Political Writings*, ed. Sally Davison et al. (Durham, NC: Duke University Press), p. 186.

86. Ibid.

87. Stuart Hall, 'Ideology and Ideological Struggle', in *Cultural Studies 1983*, ed. Jennifer D. Slack and Lawrence Grossberg (Durham, NC: Duke University Press, 2016), p. 143.

88. Honor the Earth, 'Mission + Vision', https://www.honorearth.net/mission-vision.

89. Patricia Monture-Angus, 'Thinking about Aboriginal Justice: Myths and Revolution', in *Continuing Poundmaker and Riel's Quest: Presentations Made at a Conference on Aboriginal Peoples and Justice*, ed. Richard Gosse (Purich: Saskatoon, 1994), p. 230. Thanks to Allison Weir for directing me to Monture's work. Cf. Allison Weir, *Decolonizing Freedom* (Oxford: Oxford University Press, 2024). Cf. bell hooks: 'The importance of verbal communication holds true for the dissemination of feminist ideas. In a door-to-door campaign to reintroduce feminist politics to a wider audience, women would have the opportunity to ask questions, clarify issues, give feedback. If, in a single year, women stopped spending thousands of dollars to organise conferences that are attended by only a select group of individuals, the goal of that year could be mass outreach in every state, with the intention of taking feminism out of the university and into the streets and homes of this society' (bell hooks, *Feminist Theory: From Margin to Center* (New York: Routledge, 2015), p. 111).

90. Monture-Angus, 'Thinking about Agoriginal Justice', p. 230. What Monture teaches resonates with what Hall diagnosed in his 1966 essay 'Political Commitment', namely, that the work of politics needs to 'connect experience with demands in a meaningful relationship' and 'connect awareness of the nature of the system to aspiration, and aspiration for change to the agencies of change' (Stuart Hall, 'Political Commitment', in *Selected Political Writings*, p. 94). Thanks to Bukky Gbadegesin for conversation on this question.

91. Édouard Glissant, *Poetics of Relation*, trans. Betsy Wing (Ann Arbor: University of Michigan Press, 1997), p. 1. I thank Eric Aldieri for conversation about this definition of philosophy. Indeed, the one part of a Levinasian infinite responsibility that I still hold onto is my infinite gratitude for our conversations.

92. See Theodor W. Adorno, *Negative Dialectics*, trans. E. B. Ashton (New York: Continuum, 2007), pp. 17–18, translation modified. Du Bois, *Black Reconstruction*, p. 706.

93. Said, 'Memory, Inequality, and Power'.

94. Ibid.

95. Edward Said, 'Traveling Theory', in *The Selected Works of Edward Said: 1966–2006*, ed. Moustafa Bayoumi and Andrew Rubin (New York: Vintage, 2019), p. 219. My insistence on describing the present as a time of war – as opposed to the more humanitarian newspeak of 'conflict' – could be read as putting me close to Afropessimists who draw on Gramsci's distinction between antagonism and conflict. I would not mind this comparison. Yes, Frank Wilderson III has reiterated what he calls 'the antagonism between Black and Human' (see e.g. Frank B. Wilderson III, *Red, White & Black: Cinema and the Structure of U.S. Antagonisms* (Durham, NC: Duke University Press, 2010), p. 26). While it is obvious that this book approaches the racialisation of the human differently from Wilderson, it is noteworthy that I find this return to the antagonism/conflict distinction helpful in regard to pressing the point of reality, of what is really happening in Palestine and in state surveillance of Black life, and I also find helpful the call (from Jared Sexton) to think libidinal economy alongside political economy – desire, identification, attachments, pleasure and psychic investments do matter very much to who owns land and whether repair is understood as a threat or an opportunity. Where I differ is that, with Glissant, I see this 'antagonism' as occurring within a larger, already-in-process Relation, which is an educational context in which norms, values, desires and goals are shifting and can be shifted by purposive actors. Further, with Stuart Hall (and the epigraph from Said), I would argue that increasingly in this century 'all of us are composed

of multiple social identities . . . we are all complexly constructed through different categories, of different antagonisms, and these may have the effect of locating us socially in multiple positions of marginality and subordination' (Stuart Hall, 'Old and New Identities, Old and New Ethnicities', in *Essential Essays, Volume 2: Identity and Diaspora*, ed. David Morley (Durham: Duke University Press, 2019), p. 78). As aforementioned, in my war/conflict distinction, which troubles claims to the present as a time of peace in North America, I follow Joy James. See Joy James, 'Incarceration (Un)Interrupted: Reclaiming Bodies, Lands, and Communities', talk given at Macalester College, St Paul, Minnesota, 10 October 2019.

96. Hannah Arendt, *The Origins of Totalitarianism* (Boston: Mariner, 2001), p. 299.

97. Ann Laura Stoler, *Duress: Imperial Durabilities in Our Times* (Durham, NC: Duke University Press, 2016), p. 9.

98. In an example of the Afropessimist position, Frank B. Wilderson III writes, 'If, as Afropessimism argues, *Blacks are not Human subjects, but are instead structurally inert props, implements for the execution of White and non-Black fantasies and sadomasochistic pleasures*, then this also means that, at a higher level of abstraction, the claims of universal humanity . . . are hobbled by a meta-aporia; a contradiction that manifests whenever one looks seriously at the structure of Black suffering in comparison to the presumed universal structure of all sentient beings' (Frank B. Wilderson III, *Afropessimism* (New York: Liveright, 2020), p. 15).

99. In this book, I am thinking from but also beyond the Americas. I do not mean to speak for, and I trust that my readers will make connections to, other locations. In pursuing this method, I have in mind Akeel Bilgrami's point that it is 'not only understandable but honorable, if someone speaking and writing in America [he means the US] finds it important to *stress much more* the wrongs of the American governments and its allies and clients . . . rather than speak obsessively, as is so often done, about the wrongs done by Muslim terrorists or Islamic theocratic regimes or, for that matter, Cuba and North Korea' (Akeel Bilgrami, *Secularism,*

Identity, and Enchantment (Cambridge, MA: Harvard University Press, 2014), p. 96). In this context, an interrogation and structural transformation of racialised dehumanisation remains critical 'in the present', Christina Sharpe explains, because of 'the ways that all black people, regardless of sex/gender, but especially the young and poor and working class have become in the United States (but not only in the United States) the symbols of the less-than-Human being condemned to death' (Christina Sharpe, 'Black Studies: In the Wake', *The Black Scholar* 44, no. 2 (2014): p. 62). Césaire noted that such a transformation in thinking alone, a Left theory 'in the service of black peoples', would itself be a 'Copernican revolution' (Césaire, 'Letter', p. 150).

100. Stuart Hall, 'The Empire Strikes Back', in *Selected Political Writings*, p. 206.

101. See Adom Getachew, *Worldmaking after Empire: The Rise and Fall of Self-determination* (Princeton: Princeton University Press, 2019).

102. While my emphasis on political strategy in this book might appear as the opposite of Nikolas Kompridis's call for a more open critical theory, my overall position, beyond the specific intervention here, is very much invested in such a renewed critical theory. In that the human rights claims at Standing Rock were grounded in a larger context of situating ourselves in a way that centred land and ancestral knowledge, I understand Standing Rock as exemplary of a new critical theory that proceeds through a dialectic of strategy *and* receptivity, and thus as resonant with Kompridis's call for 'placing the capacity for receptivity and decentering in an unusually prominent and central normative position' (Nikolas Kompridis, *Critique and Disclosure: Critical Theory between Past and Future* (Cambridge, MA: The MIT Press, 2006), p. 187). I elaborate on Monture's contributions to a 'receptive' critical theory and rights discourse in Benjamin P. Davis, 'The Right to Have Rights in the Americas: Arendt, Monture, and the Problem of the State', *Arendt Studies* 6 (2022): pp. 43–57.

103. Christopher Paul Harris, *To Build a Black Future: The Radical Politics of Joy, Pain, and Care* (Princeton: Princeton University Press, 2023), p. 21. For an important connection between Black Lives Matter and human (political) life, see Derefe Chevannes, 'Black Lives Matter Toward Afromodernity: Political Speech, Barbarism, and the Euromodern World', *Political Research Quarterly* 77, no. 1 (2024): pp. 213–25.

104. Bernard Harcourt, *Cooperation: A Political, Economic, and Social Theory* (New York: Columbia University Press, 2023), p. 15.

105. Hammad, *Recognizing the Stranger*, p. 22.

106. See e.g. John Crabtree and Francisco Durand, *Peru: Elite Power and Political Capture* (Chicago: Zed Books, 2017); Olúfẹ́mi O. Táíwò, *Elite Capture: How the Powerful Took Over Identity Politics (And Everything Else)* (Chicago: Haymarket, 2022).

107. See Maldonado-Torres, 'On the Coloniality of Being'.

108. Joy Harjo, 'Break My Heart', in *An American Sunrise: Poems* (New York: W. W. Norton & Co., 2019), p. 3.

109. Denise Ferreira da Silva, 'Before *Man*: Sylvia Wynter's Rewriting of the Modern Episteme', in *Sylvia Wynter: On Being Human as Praxis*, ed. Katherine McKittrick (Durham, NC: Duke University Press, 2015), p. 101. In colonial contexts, those in power have leveraged race in order to naturalise hierarchical and oppressive divisions of labour, and thus divided humanity. Alexander Weheliye has explained that modernity is constitutively marked by racialisation, meaning 'sociopolitical relations that discipline humanity into full humans, not-quite-humans, and nonhumans' (Alexander Weheliye, *Habeas Viscus: Racializing Assemblages, Biopolitics, and Black Feminist Theories of the Human* (Durham, NC: Duke University Press, 2014), p. 3). Weheliye's concern about 'juridical humanity' and call for highlighting '[t]he problematic of humanity' both suggest that he would take some distance from my return to human rights as well as my suggestion in this book that we leverage *in addition to* problematising 'humanity', even if we are in full agreement that 'black studies . . . is engaged in engendering forms

of the human vital to understanding not only black cultures but past, present, and future humanities' (ibid. pp. 135, 136).

110. Hall, 'Old and New Identities', p. 79.

111. I see the tendency to search for pure concepts as part of the Levinasian inheritance of decolonial philosophy, which, beyond how his specific vocabulary of 'alterity' has been adopted to describe cultural difference, has also led to the impulse to seek out 'the Other' in theory. John Drabinski explains, 'Difference, for Levinas, is only genuinely radical when it is thought *outside* its distinction from, which invariably means *derivation* from, identity' such that 'transmitting Levinas beyond boundaries, borders, and old habits of scholarship *ought* to be quite natural. It is in the very orientation of work dedicated to the Other *to seek out alterity* without the prerogative of conquest' (John Drabinski, *Levinas and the Postcolonial: Race, Nation, Other* (Edinburgh: Edinburgh University Press, 2011), pp. xii, xiv, emphasis mine save on 'derivation'). On those pages, Drabinski also points us to Jacques Derrida's second essay in *Rogues*. There Derrida calls for hospitality and generosity towards 'an event' of *'exceptional singularity'* (Jacques Derrida, *Rogues: Two Essays on Reason*, trans. Pascale-Anne Brault and Michael Naas (Stanford: Stanford University Press, 2005), p. 148; see also p. 149). Derrida asks his reader to think about the becoming of reason in terms of an arrival 'as other, as the absolute exception or singularity of an alterity that is not reappropriable by the ipseity of a sovereign power and a calculable knowledge' (ibid.). In advancing his philosophy and ethics of liberation, Enrique Dussel draws on Levinas, modifying 'alterity' to 'exteriority'. Alejandro Vallega summarises the trajectory this way: 'For Dussel . . . philosophical thought arises in alterity and toward the engagement with alterity . . . a thinking in radical exteriority' (Alejandro Vallega, *Latin American Philosophy from Identity to Radical Exteriority* (Indianapolis: Indiana University Press, 2014), p. 6). In my view, one contribution to critical theory from Caribbean philosophers – such as Édouard Glissant (in his concept of 'entanglement') and Stuart Hall (in how he

sees the world as becoming increasingly diasporic) – is to call into question the possibility of a Levinasian 'event' or 'encounter' or 'rupture' of alterity in a globalised/colonial world where languages, norms, values and concepts are already shared, overlapping and mixed. If these philosophers are correct, then a person on the search for exteriority will never find what they seek, because it does not exist in modern/colonial conditions. Instead, we are left with what Paul Gilroy called 'another, more difficult option: the theorisation of creolisation, métissage, mestizaje, and hybridity', leading to a series of 'strategic choices' (Gilroy, *The Black Atlantic*, pp. 2, 19). The task of decolonial philosophy and decolonial ethics becomes not to find concepts *outside of* the contaminations of capitalism, colonialism and neoliberalism, but to leverage strategically the always already contaminated concepts that we have in order to make political gains. Thinking with Hall and Gilroy (as well as with Du Bois, as I suggest in the following chapter), I find this point to be not at all an admission of defeat, but rather a point that liberates us from worrying about whether we found an 'exterior' concept and whether that concept can become co-opted (we did not; and it can, because all concepts can, because politics does not come with guarantees).

112. My reading of Du Bois in this Introduction and in my first chapter is less of a contribution to Du Bois scholarship and more of a suggestion for critical theory. The method I call for here is less a new intervention and more in search of a renewal; it is an echo of the method of Caribbean critical theory, with Aimé Césaire's new humanism in *Discourse on Colonialism* being perhaps the most famous, and in my view still the standard-setting, example. This method was arguably part of not just Césaire's theory but also his practice. In his resignation from the French Communist Party, he wrote that in light of Stalin's brutalities, he expected from the Party 'not a renunciation, but a new and solemn departure' (Césaire, 'Letter', p. 146). This method (departure but not renunciation) is why Césaire can say later in that letter, without contradicting himself, that 'the time has come

to abandon all the old ways, which have led to fraud, tyranny, and murder' while still calling for a new universal, 'a universal enriched by every particular' (ibid. pp. 150, 152).

113. Several readers of this Introduction have commented that I do not sufficiently define 'we' and 'our' in this paragraph. I have in mind those of us who think of ourselves as on the Left. My lack of definition reflects, I think, the state of an un-formed New Left in the present. For Hall, as he discussed in *Familiar Stranger*, the New Left hinged on the events of 1956: it needed to be democratic (because of Hungary), anti-imperialist (because of Suez), and anti-war (because of nuclear prolifera-tion). The question of what our new Left would hinge on today remains largely unanswered, but my sense is that it would still be all of these things, with an additional focus on receptivity to our shared environment, and in this sense planetary as much as international. I thank Paget Henry for emphasising the need for a (new) New Left today in conversation.

114. Stuart Hall, 'Culture, Resistance, and Struggle', in *Cultural Stud-ies 1983*, pp. 183–4. For the line about re-articulating 'black', see Hall, 'Old and New Identities', p. 75.

115. Hall, 'Culture, Resistance, and Struggle', p. 184.

116. Ibid.

117. See Clare Foran, 'Hillary Clinton's Intersectional Politics', *The Atlantic*, 9 March 2016, https://www.theatlantic.com/politics/archive/2016/03/hillary-clinton-intersectionality/472872/.

118. Stuart Hall, 'Race, the Floating Signifier: What More Is There to Say about "Race"?', in *Selected Writings on Race and Difference*, ed. Paul Gilroy and Ruth Wilson Gilmore (Durham, NC: Duke University Press, 2021), p. 372. For Hall's earlier formation of politics without guarantees, see Stuart Hall, 'The Problem of Ideology – Marxism without Guarantees', *Journal of Communi-cation Inquiry* 10, no. 2 (1986): pp. 28–44.

119. I thank an anonymous reviewer for *Philosophy & Global Affairs* for noting that this kind of humanism is the significance of this passage. This was not my original reading; it is really their contribution to this Introduction.

120. See Edward W. Said, *Beginnings: Intention & Method* (New York: Columbia University Press, 1985), esp. pp. xv–xvii. See also Bedour Alagraa's wonderful attention to beginnings in Bedour Alagraa, 'The Underlife of the Dialectic: Sylvia Wynter on Autopoeisis and Epistemic Rupture', *Political Theory* 51, no. 1 (2023).

121. Hall's attention to responsibility across societies is exemplified in his famous line 'I am the sugar at the bottom of the English cup of tea' (Hall, 'Old and New Identities', p. 70).

122. Aijaz Ahmad noted that one consequence of the rise of post-structural methods has been 'greatly extending the centrality of *reading* as the appropriate form of politics, and how theoretical moorings tend themselves to become more random, in this proliferation of readings, as much in their procedures of inter-textual cross-referentiality as in their conceptual constellations' (Aijaz Ahmad, *In Theory: Classes, Nations, Literatures* (New York: Verso, 1992), pp. 3–4).

123. More interestingly, as some leading theorists have suggested, it might be that concepts – perhaps (on my Glissantian misreading) as a way of naming shifting realities by beings who are themselves always changing – are always deconstructing themselves in the first place. Geoffrey Bennington has noted the following about deconstruction: 'In those early uses, where the term deconstruction is closely linked to Heidegger's notion of destruction, Derrida tends to present it as a task, a philosophical task, a way that we need to recognize and measure up to the tradition from which we inherit . . . In some of his later works he tends to suggest that it is perhaps a less willfully operated task than some of those early formulations might suggest, so I think he would tend to say, in slightly later work, that metaphysics is in deconstruction from the start, always already; it is not that there was metaphysics doing its ontology, doing its metaphysical thing for many centuries, and then at a certain point somebody deconstructed it – that sounds like a rather subject-object, instrumentalized version of events. So I think he would say . . . that metaphysics was always already

in deconstruction from the start' (Alberto Moreiras and Geoffrey Bennington, 'On Scatter, the Trace Structure, and the Opening of Politics', *Diacritics* 45, no. 2 (2017): p. 40). By now I trust it is rather clear that I have no problem with a subject-object approach, instrumental as it may be, as we use concepts strategically.

124. In my view, various liberation theologies provide examples of working within a given terrain – the predominant moral vocabulary of a situation – to achieve a more just society.

125. This, as we will see, is a decidedly humanist reading of Hall, a reading that, in his own terms on two paradigms in cultural studies, he would locate as much more culturalist than structuralist. See Stuart Hall, 'Cultural Studies: Two Paradigms', in *Essential Essays, Volume 1: Foundations of Cultural Studies*, ed. David Morley (Durham, NC: Duke University Press, 2019), p. 64.

126. For my first articulation of this idea, see Benjamin P. Davis, 'On Conceptual Sufficiency: Humanity in Du Bois's *Black Reconstruction* and *John Brown*', *Philosophy & Global Affairs* 3, no. 1 (2023).

127. As Adolph Reed explains, 'ascriptive status' is 'status defined by what you supposedly are rather than what you do'; this status, he further argues, was foundational for 'a rigidly hierarchical social order like that of the segregationist South' (Adolph Reed, *The South: Jim Crow and Its Afterlives* (New York: Verso, 2022), p. 75).

128. '[B]y failing to fully account for how the exceptional costs of climate change affect national wealth, the I.M.F. and the World Bank have wound up driving countries in need toward profit-reaping hedge funds and banks, to borrow billions of dollars, often at credit-card-like interest rates. Throughout, the debts have been collected. They were collected as the shadow of the 2008 financial crisis lingered and as a pandemic decimated tenuous health care systems and tourist-reliant economies. They continue to be collected despite a climate crisis that is caused almost entirely by the copious fossil fuels that those

same creditor nations burned to industrialize and achieve their own wealth, the very wealth that undergirds the I.M.F. Caribbean nations are being asked, in a sense, to pay not only their own debts but the rest of the world's debts, too, for all the progress it made while leaving the Caribbean behind . . . Debt is written off in Ukraine, as it was for Germany after World War II. Other countries, though, the ones subjugated throughout history, have seen their humanitarian crises ignored . . . Perhaps the suggestions that lenders forgive debt isn't about kindness but about obligation – about seeing it as a kind of back tax that they owe to society and to frontline societies, in particular' (Abrahm Lustgarten, 'Oceans of Debt', *The New York Times Magazine* (31 July 2022): pp. 31, 49, 47).

129. See Aimé Césaire, *Discourse on Colonialism* (New York: Monthly Review Press, [1950] 2001), p. 73.

130. A related problem, and a personal pet peeve, is when we trade on the radicality of a concept or a figure without ourselves taking on even a scintilla of risk in our work (such as citing Said but not writing and speaking about Palestine or, in other contexts, citing Du Bois but not writing and speaking about race, naming white supremacy, and teaching about Black dignity, refusal and philosophy). Perhaps the most common example is when intellectuals draw on Gramsci, but it also happens when we trade on the main figures of our religious traditions, many of whom (like Gramsci) spent much of their lives in prison or exile – or facing the violence of the state. Black Studies has kept alive this sense of intellectual risk more than any other field, or perhaps alongside Indigenous Studies, though for all of us there always remains the temptation towards respectability, professionalism, and a level of abstraction that, as Glissant says opening *Poetics*, withdraws into a 'a dimensionless place'.

131. See Gordon, *Statelessness and Contemporary Enslavement*.

132. For commentary on Brown as a 'touchstone', see Ted Smith, *Weird John Brown: Divine Violence and the Limits of Ethics* (Stanford, CA: Stanford University Press, 2014), pp. 15–39.

133. To bring my position into further relief by way of another comparison, I am overall quite invested in how concepts, in Stoler's words, 'do work and work on us to authorize some questions, to reconfigure what questions are worth asking, and, not least, to foreclose others' (Stoler, *Duress*, p. 173). However, in this book I am suggesting that critiquing concepts can become autotelic, such that *the critical approach can itself foreclose questions about practice*, including those I list following the work of James, Salaita, Monture, Revilla, TallBear and others.

134. For a discussion of 'risk-taking commitments' in service of 'communal goals for social and cultural freedoms, economic sufficiency, and radical democracy', see Joy James, *Resisting State Violence: Radicalism, Gender, and Race in U.S. Culture* (Minneapolis: University of Minnesota Press, 1996), p. 243. See also Steven Salaita, 'My Life as a Cautionary Tale: Probing the Limits of Academic Freedom', *The Chronicle of Higher Education*, 28 August 2019, https://www.chronicle.com/article/my-life-as-a-cautionary-tale/.

135. In regard to the self-determination of Indigenous peoples in the settler state of Canada, Patricia Monture-Angus writes, 'Self-government requires the significant letting go of Canadian government power over the lives of Aboriginal citizens. I do not doubt that the release of power is a difficult thing' (Monture-Angus, 'Thinking about Aboriginal Justice', p. 230).

136. Maybe we could connect these eventful divestments, these refusals, to more daily practices of repair, where '[r]epair, like refusal', the anthropologist and dancer Deborah Thomas writes, 'is practice-oriented and quotidian; it is non-eventful and deeply historical and relational. Like its nominal counterpart [reparation], repair urges us to interrogate the multiple scales of entanglement that have led us to where we are now. But where reparation seeks justice through the naming of names, the exposure of public secrets, and the articulation of chains of causality, repair looks for something else. It demands an active listening, a mutual recognizing, an acknowledging of complicity at all levels – behavioral evidence of profound

interior transformations that are ongoing' (Deborah Thomas, *Political Life in the Wake of the Plantation: Sovereignty, Witnessing, Repair* (Durham, NC: Duke University Press, 2019), p. 212).

137. Here, because the context I am familiar with is the Americas, I am thinking of Occupy, Idle No More, Standing Rock, and the Movement for Black Lives. My reader likely has in mind different examples based on the movements they are a part of. I also wonder here how we can build and make and perform what María Pía Lara calls a 'wider space' and a 'more complicated' space, how we might reclaim public space while acknowledging that '[t]he feminist social imaginary is a wider space than the public sphere, which, as a political institutional device, made women invisible' (María Pía Lara, *Beyond the Public Sphere: Film and the Feminist Imaginary* (Evanston, IL: Northwestern University Press, 2021), pp. 3, 5, 170).

138. Cf. the poet No'u Revilla's concept of 'generative refusal' as tied to a practice of centring land: 'The Land is the Center', https://www.poetryfoundation.org/podcasts/158639/the-land-is-the-center.

139. Rei Terada, *Looking Away: Phenomenality and Dissatisfaction: Kant to Adorno* (Cambridge, MA: Harvard University Press, 2009), p. 200.

140. See Kim TallBear, 'Making Love and Relations Beyond Settler Sex and Family', in *Making Kin Not Population*, ed. Adele E. Clarke and Donna Haraway (Chicago: Prickly Paradigm Press, 2018). See also Alexis Pauline Gumbs et al., eds, *Revolutionary Mothering: Love on the Front Lines* (Oakland, CA: PM Press, 2016).

141. See Ramzi Fawaz, *Queer Forms* (New York: New York University Press, 2022), especially the concluding discussion of friendship in dialogue with Arendt. Thanks to Helen Kinsella for this suggestion and for friendship.

142. Jasbir Puar, *The Right to Maim: Debility: Capacity, Disability* (Durham, NC: Duke University Press, 2017), p. xiii.

143. I have in mind Walter Mignolo's continued emphasis that decolonisation is an 'option' among other options. In my view, this framing suggests the *increased* importance of theoretical

and discursive work that can explain widely why this option is both just and desirable. See Walter D. Mignolo, *The Darker Side of Western Modernity: Global Futures, Decolonial Options* (Durham, NC: Duke University Press, 2011).

144. Sylvia Wynter and Katherine McKittrick, 'Unparalleled Catastrophe for Our Species?: Or, to Give Humanness a Different Future: Conversations', in McKittrick, *Sylvia Wynter*, p. 33.

145. Ibid.

146. Sylvia Wynter, 'Unsettling the Coloniality of Being/Power/Truth/Freedom: Toward the Human, After Man, its Overrepresentation – An Argument', *The New Centennial Review* 3, no. 3 (2003): p. 260.

147. Sylvia Wynter, 'Beyond the Word of Man: Glissant and the New Discourse of the Antillies', *World Literature Today* 63.4 (1989): p. 640.

148. Simone Weil, 'Reflections on the Right Use of School Studies with a View to the Love of God', in *Waiting for God* (New York: G. P. Putnam's Sons, 1959), p. 115. This is why it is ethically and politically important to write by hand, avoid many forms of social media, and live a life that is not oriented by dings and notifications; these are efforts to keep alive our capacity to think and relate to one another in our time of the predatory attention economy, with its algorithmic forms of governance and ecologically destructive pursuit of 'efficiency'.

149. Stuart Hall, 'Cultural Studies and Its Theoretical Legacies', in *Essential Essays, Volume 1: Foundations of Cultural Studies*, ed. David Morley (Durham, NC: Duke University Press, 2019), p. 81.

150. Hall, 'Old and New Identities', p. 64.

151. AnaLouise Keating, 'Risking the Personal: An Introduction', in Gloria Anzaldúa, *Interviews/Entrevistas* (New York: Routledge, 2000).

152. See Aaron Kamugisha, *Beyond Coloniality: Citizenship and Freedom in the Caribbean Intellectual Tradition* (Indianapolis: Indiana University Press, 2019); Wilder, *Concrete Utopianism*, p. 57. See also Cedric Robinson, *Black Marxism: The Making of the Black Radical Tradition* (Chapel Hill: University of North Carolina Press, 1983); Gilroy, *The Black Atlantic*.

153. Abdelkebir Khatibi, *Plural Maghreb*, trans. P. Burcu Yalim (London: Bloomsbury, 2019), p. 5.

154. Working through these tensions, especially in terms of how we relate to land and to sea, remains, in my view, the most politically important way that we are still learning to live, in Reiner Schürmann's wonderful phrase, 'under the sign of Proteus' (Reiner Schürmann, *Broken Hegemonies*, trans. Reginald Lilly (Bloomington: Indiana University Press, 2003), p. 514.

155. Geoffrey Bennington, *Scatter 2: Politics in Deconstruction* (New York: Fordham University Press, 2021), p. 2.

156. Ibid. p. 203.

157. Ibid. p. xi.

158. Ibid. p. 249.

159. Ibid. p. 259. For how deconstruction/*Destruktion* offers a three-step method of reading for positive possibilities, limits or concealments, and questions opened or provoked – a method that is part of how I strategically read 'the human' and 'humanity' in the following chapters – see Sean D. Kirkland, *Heidegger and the Destruction of Aristotle: On How to Read the Tradition* (Evanston, IL: Northwestern University Press, 2023), pp. 27–8. 'Rather than simply generating arbitrary neologisms in order to think in excess of the inherited metaphysical tradition', Kirkland continues in outlining a method I follow, 'Heidegger feels compelled to take on the traditional vocabulary and press it into service, radicalizing it and amplifying some of its underdeveloped tendencies' (ibid. pp. 44–5). The key methodological difference between what I am advancing and deconstruction, it seems to me, is that I am (obviously) very instrumental in how I want to use concepts, seen in my sense of the first (strategic) move in double politics, which is very different from Heidegger's goal: what Kirkland describes as 'a nonconceptual mode of thinking' (ibid. p. 33). But again: learning to do both – to leverage concepts that inevitably 'grasp' the world in our necessary struggles (we might need 'sovereignty' to stop a pipeline), while remaining receptive to the disclosures of the world – remains of critical importance for an ethical/political attunement equal to the challenges of this century.

160. Brian Meeks, *After the Postcolonial Caribbean: Memory, Imagination, Hope* (London: Pluto Press, 2023), p. 114.

161. See e.g. Simone Weil, 'Human Personality'; Claudia Jones, 'An End to the Neglect of the Problems of the Negro Woman!'; Stuart Hall, *Cultural Studies 1983*; Hannah Arendt, *Origins of Totalitarianism*.

162. McKnight, *Race and the Politics of the Exception*, p. 93.

163. See e.g. ibid. p. 109.

164. Michel-Rolph Trouillot, *Global Transformations: Anthropology and the Modern World* (New York: Palgrave MacMillan, 2003), p. 85.

165. Stuart Hall, 'The West and the Rest: Discourse and Power', in *Essential Essays, Volume 2: Identity and Diaspora*, ed. David Morley (Durham, NC: Duke University Press, 2019), p. 155.

166. Louiza Odysseos, 'Prolegomena to Any Future Decolonial Ethics: Coloniality, Poetics and "Being Human as Praxis"', *Millennium: Journal of International Studies* 45, no. 3 (2017).

167. Glissant, *Traité/Treatise*, p. 21/11.

PART I: DETOUR THROUGH THEORY

1 W. E. B. Du Bois's Anti-War Humanism

In reading Du Bois in this chapter, I will ultimately argue that 'humanity' remains a sufficient concept for organising (at least in the US) today because of: (1) its normative ability to work against fabricated hierarchies of our species created by concepts such as race; (2) the universality of its scope, calling for species-wide rights and expectations; and (3) how it has functioned historically, and continues to function, to invite people to realise or achieve the universalism it outlines. To provide an illustration of how to leverage a concept understood as sufficient, I look to Du Bois, because, in an exemplary fashion, he re-described some inherited concepts for liberatory ends. As the political theorist Inés Valdez has argued, Du Bois's transnationalism 'helps us recover forms of cosmopolitan engagement that can work with – rather than against – self-definition'.[1] In Du Bois's critique of imposed, Eurocentric hierarchies of humanity but maintenance of a self-defined humanity and claims to human rights in his 1935 *Black Reconstruction*, which I will suggest was informed by his reading of 'humanity' in his 1909 *John Brown*, I see an exemplary mode of critique that is also constructive, a mode of critical theory more valuable than the ontological approaches that are increasingly popular today.[2] Du Bois not only criticised his world but also tried to produce or create an alternative one.

I read Du Bois's leveraging of the concept 'human' as turning its noun form into a verb, that is, not simply as invoking 'the human' as a given universal, but as pragmatically calling for his audience to respond with actions that would realise the universalism that the concept ostensibly – but rarely in historical practice – outlines.[3]

Du Bois's Use of 'Humanity' in *Black Reconstruction* and *John Brown*

Before I turn to Du Bois's work in detail, I will note why I am beginning from *Black Reconstruction* and *John Brown* instead of Du Bois's writings from the 1940s, such as *Color and Democracy* (1945) and his unpublished manuscript 'Human Rights for All Minorities' (1947). Indeed, aren't *those* the places where Du Bois took on the question of the human and human rights most directly? The context of those texts informs why I am starting from his earlier writings and only then turning to his work from the 1940s. Du Bois wrote *Color and Democracy* as a specific intervention into the formation of the United Nations and, more broadly, into the post-war global order that Western powers were founding on still-colonial and capitalist lines despite their ultimately false rhetoric of democracy, equality, freedom and humanity.[4] Because Du Bois was intervening into this specific discourse, he had to take on the language of human rights and humanity in those 1940s writings.[5] But that was not the context or problematic to which he needed to respond in writing *Black Reconstruction*. He did not have to speak of humanity in the epic terms he chose to use in telling the story of Reconstruction; he did not have to invoke the concept at all (much less capitalise it!). He could have limited the scope of his analysis to a national context. He could have presented the consequences of that period with respect only to one race, to one class, or to one place. Instead, he connected that period in US politics not only to an international labour struggle, but also to the fate of our species itself and even to how we would be judged by the world and the divine. ('God wept . . . The world wept because within the exploiting group of New World masters, greed and jealously became so fierce that they fought for trade and markets and materials and slaves all over the world until at last in 1914 the world flamed in war.')[6] Further, as he himself acknowledged, he did not need to write *John Brown*; he noted at the beginning of the book that there were already plenty of good biographies on Brown. On my reading, then, both *Black Reconstruction* and *John Brown* reflect not only Du Bois's particular political interventions, but also his overarching *constructive vision* of a universalising *practice* of humanity, a universalising practice that, as the work of LaRose Parris reminds us, must start from the emancipation of unfree labourers and the abolition of the structures that deny their freedom.[7]

* * *

In the December 1934 prefatory remarks of *Black Reconstruction*, Du Bois embeds the story he is telling into a larger one of 'human culture', asks his reader to consider the Black person as 'an average and ordinary human being', and says he will tell his story assuming that Black people are 'ordinary human beings, realizing that this attitude will from the first seriously curtail my audience'.[8] Early in the book, he describes the system of slavery as 'the absolute negation of human rights',[9] and he diagnoses the racialised global division of industrial labour as 'the kernel of the problem of Religion and Democracy, of Humanity', such that the resulting political task is to achieve '[t]he emancipation of man', meaning 'the emancipation of labor . . . the freeing of that basic majority of workers who are yellow, brown and black'.[10] Later on, when presenting '[t] he decisive battle of Reconstruction' in 1867, he explains that '[a]bolition-democracy demands for Negroes physical freedom, civil rights, economic opportunity and education and the right to vote, as a matter of sheer human justice and right'.[11] He goes on to describe the connection between democracy and humanity in ethical terms:

The current theory of democracy is that dictatorship is a stopgap pending the work of universal education, equitable income, and strong character. But always the temptation is to use the stopgap for narrow ends, because intelligence, thrift and goodness seem so impossibly distant for most men. We rule by junta; we turn Fascist, because we do not believe in men; yet the basis of fact in this disbelief is incredibly narrow. We know perfectly well that most human beings have never had a decent human chance to be full men. Most of us may be convinced that even with opportunity the number of utter human failures would be vast; and yet remember that this assumption kept the ancestors of present white America long in slavery and degradation. It is then one's moral duty to see that every human being, to the extent of his capacity, escapes ignorance, poverty and crime.[12]

And in his final chapter, he writes in poetic terms about a future where 'we are going . . . with regard to all social problems, to be able to use human experience for the guidance of mankind'.[13] From these few but representative examples – Du Bois employs 'human' so much in *Black Reconstruction* that you can almost open a page at random and find it[14] – we see the different ways in which Du Bois invokes the concept of humanity not simply as a universal already in existence so much as to call for universalising practice: invoking 'humanity' can put a historical event in the perspective of our species; it can ask his reader to see someone who looks different from oneself as part of the same species, and thus worthy of fair treatment and possessive of rights; it can be used negatively, as a standard to condemn social structures that violate human rights and, specifically, to call for the abolition of (racial) capitalism; it can be used positively, as an aspirational standard, the reaching of which would require new social, economic and political organisation (e.g. an expanded system of public education, a universal right to vote); it can be used to describe our shared fallibility and vulnerability while challenging undemocratic assumptions and rejecting any form of organising a polity that maintains ignorance and poverty; and it can remind its reader that there are moral duties we've always owed one another.

Writing from Atlanta in the 1930s about Reconstruction, Du Bois was more than aware of insidious uses of 'human' and 'humanity' that maintained hierarchies over time ('Something died in me that day', he said about bearing witness to the loss of Sam Hose).[15] Many of his writings, from *Souls* to *The World and Africa*, could be read as tracking the fallacies that are part and parcel of any racialised hierarchisation of our species. Nevertheless, different from many contemporary critics, he did not see violence and oppression as intrinsic to, or domination a sure result of, the operation of 'the human'. Rather, he maintained the concept in *Black Reconstruction*, leveraging it alongside the focus on class and labour he gained from his 1933 turn to Marx, who also maintained a sense of species-being.[16] Given these methodological moves, we can ask: Why would Du Bois maintain a term that he knew, first-hand and historically, has contributed to hierarchy, violence and terror? I suggest that one answer can be found in Du Bois's biography of John Brown.

* * *

In his short Preface to *John Brown*, Du Bois notes that the only reason he is conducting yet another study of Brown is to put emphasis on a different element of his life.[17] In the final chapter, he cites both a letter of Brown's that says 'I cannot believe that anything I have done, suffered, or may yet suffer, will be lost to the cause of God or of humanity', and another letter Brown wrote to his younger children, 'I feel just as content to die for God's eternal truth and for suffering humanity on the scaffold as in any other way.'[18] Du Bois then summarises Brown's conceptual influences:

Was John Brown simply an episode, or was he an eternal truth? And if a truth, how speaks that truth to-day? John Brown loves his neighbor as himself. He could not endure therefore to see his neighbor, poor, unfortunate or oppressed. This natural sympathy was strengthened by a saturation in Hebrew religion which stressed the personal responsibility of every human soul to a just God. To this religion of equality and sympathy with misfortune, was added the strong influence of the social doctrines of the French Revolution with its emphasis on freedom and power in political life. And on all this was built John Brown's own inchoate but growing belief in a more just and a more equal distribution of property. From this he concluded, – and acted on that conclusion – that all men are created free and equal, and that the cost of liberty is less than the price of repression.[19]

In making his moral judgements, Brown was influenced by a variety of sources, his faith probably the most important. But then again, as the theologian Ted Smith has noted, perhaps it is '[b]ecause commentators have not seen him as fighting for "his own" people' that 'his religious motives come into sharper focus'; in other words, too often commentators miss the fact that 'Brown . . . sincerely regarded enslaved people as his sisters and brothers.'[20] Du Bois saw in Brown someone who embraced 'suffering humanity' as his own people. One lesson Du Bois drew from his study of Brown – and that I am suggesting he carried into *Black Reconstruction* – is that a belief in shared humanity over and against using race to create divisions of labour and distributions of property was, for Brown, sufficient not only to conclude that the state-sanctioned violence of his time needed to be challenged but also to personally act on that conclusion.

Moreover, this sense of 'humanity' was sufficient for those Brown inspired, especially the multiracial group that carried out the illegal raid with him – 'not men of culture or great education', Du Bois says of the group, but 'intellectually bold and inquiring' and 'skeptical of the world's social conventions'.[21] Ultimately, for Du Bois, in matters of 'vast human import', there is a 'great parting of the ways – the one way wrong, the other right, in some vast and eternal sense'.[22] In regard to the matter of slavery, Du Bois says, 'John Brown was right.'[23] And one concept that led Brown to the right position was humanity. (Said echoed this point about Palestine: 'I am strongly convinced that there is indeed justice and injustice . . . there is a truly profound, irreducible injustice for which the injured side needs to get institutional recognition.')[24]

To connect this chapter to the Introduction, we could say that Du Bois's maintenance of 'the human' illustrates Hall's idea of a politics without guarantees. For those who came to the conclusion that their society was unjust and acted upon it by raiding Harper's Ferry at the cost of their lives, 'humanity' was what Hall called '*that* term'. On my reading, one reason Du Bois maintained a vocabulary of 'human', 'humanity' and 'human rights' in *Black Reconstruction* is that he knew, from his earlier study of John Brown's raid, how a notion of humanity inspired Brown and how it could inspire others.[25] It was a term that Du Bois would maintain into the 1940s as he imagined a new, more human order for the world.

Du Bois's Use of Human Rights in the 1940s

In response to ongoing colonisation, the Holocaust, the atomic bomb, and the conclusion of another World War, many artists in the 1940s strove to create work that tapped into a wide sense of humanity. Wifredo Lam looked to African-based religions in Cuba for inspiration, and he portrayed human, animal and other natural life as deeply and complexly entangled. 'In a society where money and the machine have immeasurably increased the distance between Man and things', Aimé Césaire said of Lam's art, 'Wifredo Lam fixes on canvas the ceremony through which everything exists.'[26] Mark Rothko rejected the easel-sized canvas in favour of a much larger surface. Barnett Newman also chose to make artworks of a size that better reflected his immense ambitions. 'I hope that my own painting', Newman said, 'has the impact of giving someone as it did me the feelings of his own totality, of his own separateness, of his own individuality, and at the same time his connection to others.'[27] As these artists encouraged a wider vision of human connection, political actors advanced new conceptions of human rights.

Eleanor Roosevelt contributed to the hopeful spirit of the mid-1940s. The legal scholar Mary Ann Glendon describes Roosevelt as a woman of political commitment – that despite her elite background seen in her 'trademark fox furs', she was a 'political activist and popular journalist' known 'to champion progressive causes'.[28] At the end of 1945, Roosevelt sailed to London for the first meeting of the United Nations General Assembly. One of the only women at the General Assembly meeting, she raised her voice effectively, and consequently she was elected chairman of the Commission of Human Rights, which in January 1947 began its task of drafting an international bill of rights. Glendon summarises Roosevelt's politics this way:

Eleanor Roosevelt's feminism was ardent but pragmatic and subordinate to her broader social concerns. She credited women's suffrage with having forced governments to take more interest in human welfare, and she tried to demonstrate through her own efforts that increased participation by women in political and economic life could make a difference. To her, that chiefly meant lending a helping hand to those who were still politically and economically marginalized – women and men alike, especially blacks in the southern states, the unemployed, the rural poor, and urban slum dwellers. As First Lady she had used the prestige of her position to draw attention to the causes of racial equality and decent housing, health care, and education.[29]

Echoing Glendon's laudatory account of Roosevelt's commitments, the theorist Alexandre Lefebvre has argued that Roosevelt is a powerful example of carrying out the ethics of human rights, especially in her critique of conformity; Lefebvre presents Roosevelt as practising human rights 'in terms of a way of life'.[30] Importantly, however, Roosevelt's commitments to human rights also included a series of compromises, perhaps most notably her unwillingness to use her international platform to speak back to her own country's failure to live up to its self-proclaimed human rights ideals regarding democracy, colonisation and racism. When these historical notes are accounted for, that is, when a contemporaneous Black Atlantic archive of human rights is recognised alongside the predominant liberal archive she represents, Roosevelt appears as more of a conformist than some of her champions argue.

As the United Nations (UN) was taking shape, the US called out the Soviet Union for repressing political speech. In turn, the Soviet Union highlighted ongoing racial discrimination in the US; the Soviets argued that the US was not a true humanitarian country because it permitted racial discrimination.[31] Feeling that her official position meant that she could not voice her private beliefs, Roosevelt did not thoroughly address the material conditions that made the Soviet rebuttal accurate and damning. Ultimately, and as I will elaborate upon below, in the terms of her nightly prayer asking God to 'show us a vision of a world made new', the new world order Roosevelt promoted maintained colonialism.[32] For that reason, I suggest in this chapter that the example we have the most to learn from regarding the question of peace today – the example of an activist who best embodied the post-war artistic sentiment of imagining wider human connections – is not Eleanor Roosevelt but W. E. B. Du Bois. In making this suggestion, I am following the recent work of the sociologists José Itzigsohn and Karida Brown, who have argued that Du Bois asks his readers to think not just of modern progress but of 'racialized modernity'; I also draw on the long-standing scholarship of the historian Gerald Horne, who describes the 'prescience of his vision' in Du Bois's 1940s writing on colonisation and peace.[33]

Before I elaborate on Du Bois's inspiring example, I would like to clarify some of the stakes of my argument. Whether we follow the path that Roosevelt or Du Bois offers – whether we own up to our positions as elite or radical, liberal or decolonial, capitalist or Marxist, or somewhere overlapping or in between – matters for how we pursue peacebuilding today. To a large extent, in practice these are mutually exclusive paths, even if they share some values and are on the same side on a political spectrum (towards the Left, what Glendon calls 'progressive'). This clarification speaks to the field of Peace Studies today.

With John Paul Lederach, a leading voice in Peace Studies, I agree that '[t]ranscending violence is forged by the capacity to generate, mobilize, and build the moral imagination.'[34] Violence can be transcended, Lederach continues, when what he calls 'the moral imagination' moves through four dimensions. He explains the moral imagination as follows:

[T]he moral imagination requires the capacity to imagine ourselves in a web of relationships that includes our enemies; the ability to sustain a paradoxical curiosity that embraces complexity without reliance on dualistic polarity; the fundamental belief in and pursuit of the creative act; and the acceptance of the inherent risk of stepping into the mystery of the unknown that lies beyond the far too familiar landscape of violence.[35]

Both Roosevelt and Du Bois built a moral imagination that fits within Lederach's capacity-based definition. Both were inclusive in their projects, sustained curiosity towards the world, acted creatively again and again, and took on risks in political life, including making stands in a US public sphere not accustomed to listening to women or Black people; in their own ways, both remain exemplary. Yet the paths that Roosevelt and Du Bois offered were, in the final instance, decidedly different, because our moral imaginations are always already conditioned by our political commitments. Lederach's own book reflects this point. It exhibits tremendous imagination. It is a personal book, compelling and beautiful in its story. Its thematic focus is more about art than about political economy (meaning how resources are extracted, who labours towards those ends, and who enjoys the fruits of that labour). Black Marxists, including Du Bois after 1933, have long worried that insufficiently addressing colonial political economy *as part of morals and culture* will ultimately result in an *anaesthetic* position, because '[p]erhaps the greatest disaster' of colonial political economy, Du Bois suggested regarding peoples across the world, is 'the ruthless and ignorant destruction of their cultural patterns'.[36] Empire, Du Bois teaches, always results in a 'slave trade in human rights'.[37] If Du Bois is right in these lines – and I think he is – then to transcend violence or to affirm art, to affirm human creation in a brutal world, we must first transcend capitalism and colonialism.[38] In other words, Du Bois calls for a re-valuing of life, a new ethics and aesthetics, that breaks from colonial values, which systematically suppress questions of labour.[39]

Like Lam, Rothko and Newman, in the 1940s Du Bois creatively asked his audience to engage the world in terms more expansive than those to which they had become accustomed. In 1944 Du Bois said of colonisation, 'This is the problem to which I propose to devote the remaining years of my life.'[40] That same year, he left his post at Atlanta University to return to the NAACP, where he enlarged its focus from domestic legal questions and advocacy for civil rights to international law and human rights. In his own words reflecting on his decision, he returned to the NAACP 'specifically for the purpose of concentrating on study of colonial peoples and peoples of Negro descent throughout the world, and to revive the Pan-African Congresses'.[41] He also continued his research and writing. Frustrated by the failure of the Allied Powers to confront at Dumbarton Oaks the contradiction between their claims to democracy and their colonial holdings, he wrote *Color and Democracy: Colonies and Peace*, which appeared amidst the conference to institute the United Nations in San Francisco in 1945.[42]

To consider peacebuilding in the present, it is worthwhile to consider in detail Du Bois's intervention in *Color and Democracy*, not just to see what he said, but also because the nascent international institutional order to which Du Bois was responding remains the structuring order of the present. Just as the founding of the UN failed to remedy its constitutive contradiction of claiming democracy while maintaining colonisation, so too did the writing of the UN's Sustainable Development Goals in 2012 sideline historical and ongoing colonisation as the goals tried to speak about ending poverty and generating 'sustainable development' by 2030. That strategy has simply failed. The sociologist Gurminder Bhambra puts it this way: 'As we approach the third decade of the twenty-first century, climate change, military aggressions, settler colonial projects, resource extraction and dispossessory debt mechanisms – the primary causes of mass expropriation and displacement – remain active across the globe.'[43]

As I discussed in *Choose Your Bearing*, Du Bois's *Color and Democracy* quickly became, as Horne puts it, 'the Bible for anticolonial advocates in the United States'.[44] In that book, which reflects what the political scientist Adolph Reed calls Du Bois's 'normative presumption of the unity of scholarship and activism', Du Bois offers a critique of colonisation not simply on the abstract grounds that it is unjust, but for the concrete reason that it causes war, and that it does so in two ways.[45] '[O]ne of the vast paradoxes of human nature', Du Bois teaches, 'is that no matter how degraded people become, it is impossible to keep them down on a large scale and forever.'[46] Colonialism causes war (uprisings) within the colonies by declaring the colonised inferior and forcing them to labour in unsafe conditions and without life-sustaining compensation. That is, colonialism causes war by trying, through a system 'based on racial repulsions as well as on greed for wealth and power', to keep the colonised down on a large scale and forever.[47] Second, because colonialism involves competition for land, resources and cheap labour among colonial powers, it causes war as colonial powers fight to possess colonies.[48] 'If colonialism has caused war for a century and a half', Du Bois concludes his chapter titled 'Peace and Colonies' in *Color and Democracy*, then '[i]t can be depended upon to remain as a continual cause of war in the century to come.'[49]

The implication of Du Bois's argument is that, if Dumbarton Oaks and the founding UN conference do not promote a plan for decolonisation, then they are planning not for peace, but for war. By not getting rid of a colonial world order, what Dumbarton Oaks in truth proposed was 'a peace resting on force'.[50] In sum, *Color and Democracy* argues that by not rectifying racism, imperialism and militarism, Dumbarton Oaks offered an 'organized pacifism' that showed its true colours as 'pacifism designed "for white people only"'.[51] This limited sense of peace and pacifism could have been rectified in San Francisco, Du Bois argued, if we 'beware how far we build the new world upon military force and ignore such known and existent causes of war'.[52] What a more expansive understanding of peace during the founding of the United Nations in San Francisco would have required was not just a new, global institution made up of agreeable nation states but also decolonisation. Quite simply, Du Bois writes, 'So long as colonial imperialism exists, there can be neither peace on earth nor goodwill toward men.'[53]

Part of the reason Western powers have failed to address the root causes of war – the by-then Marxist Du Bois continues in *Color and Democracy*, echoing his claim in *Black Reconstruction* – is that they have failed to understand and resolve the larger conflict behind colonisation, namely, 'the battle between capital and labor in the modern economy'.[54] On Du Bois's analysis, until 1914 diplomacy was largely successful 'in keeping most European nations from each other's throats in armed rivalry for the proceeds of investment in Africa and Asia'.[55] But World War I 'left the colonial question with only token settlement'.[56] In other words, after World War I, the colonies remained 'a method of investment yielding unusual returns', profit that has been 'the foundation of much modern wealth, luxury, and power', competition over which 'led to the First World War and was a prime cause of the Second World War'.[57] If the West was finally to learn its lesson in San Francisco, Du Bois stresses, then it would additionally have to promote more than formal decolonisation; it would also have to transition away from the 'stage in which we are today', namely, a capitalist stage in which '[p]olitical domination changed . . . to domination through invested capital'.[58]

In 1946 Du Bois asked the NAACP board of directors if he could pen a petition to the UN; he wanted to publicise human rights violations against Black people in the US. 'At a time when Washington was seeking to indict Moscow on similar charges', Horne comments, 'this petition was not accepted with equanimity in the Oval Office – or in the inner sanctums of the NAACP.'[59] Introducing his petition, Du Bois notes the 'restricted legal rights' of Black people in the US. He discusses strategies that are still used in right-wing political organising today, such as logics of racial inferiority that function to divide working-class people of all backgrounds. He also frames the disenfranchisement of Black people as part of a wider effort to prevent white masses from voting.[60] '[W]hile this nation is trying to carry on the government of the United States by democratic methods', he states, 'it is not succeeding because of the premium which we put on the disfranchisement of the voters of the South.'[61] On his analysis, because the US disenfranchises Black people, and because white women are not yet accustomed to having the vote, the US is in fact more aristocratic than it is democratic. Given these anti-democratic policies, the real enemies of the project of the United States might come from within: 'It is not Russia that threatens the United States', he explains, 'so much as Mississippi.'[62]

Taken together, Du Bois's 1945 *Color and Democracy* and his co-drafted *Appeal*, which would be submitted to the UN in October 1947, sketch the contours of what Du Bois called in *Color and Democracy* 'a new conception of human responsibility'.[63] Du Bois would elaborate on that sense of responsibility further in his April 1947 speech 'Human Rights for All Minorities'. What unites the minorities of the world – cultural, religious and racial minorities within each nation state – Du Bois argues there, is not some 'logical or functional unity' but that their rights have been denied.[64] He further contends that the myth that poverty is a natural result of resource scarcity and not a social product of unjust resource distribution serves a larger 'denial to faiths, nations, groups and races of any rights or privileges which infringe or threaten the status of the privileged'.[65] 'Whenever at any time a wave of sentiment, or surge of conviction or even scientific hypothesis starts to challenge this basic and widespread belief of mankind', he observes, 'immediately violence, hate and intolerance break forth and we have increased denial to men of basic human rights.'[66] Du Bois's attention to state repression should not be lost on his reader. One brutal reality he describes is that challenges to the racialised order of the modern nation state (whether those challenges be social scientific, philosophical or manifested in marches) are met not just with counterclaims, but also with the full force of the police state. In the US context in recent years, this force has looked like Governors of Maryland, North Dakota and Minnesota invoking states of emergencies against Black and Indigenous activists marching (as well as singing, dancing, praying and laughing) as part of the Movement for Black Lives and at Standing Rock.[67]

In 'Human Rights for All Minorites', Du Bois further echoes his point in *Color and Democracy* about the need for increased economic literacy, including how that literacy is tied to understanding how wealthy countries and individuals leverage hierarchies of humanity to control labour, and how, when such control exists, democracy does not. On Du Bois's analysis, by 1947, capitalism is akin to a crime against humanity. It is a 'new economics' that 'regarded all labor black, brown, yellow and white as a commodity. It trafficked the bodies of men in the slums of London as well as the plantations of Virginia.'[68] All the while 'the dominant majority, which calls itself the world, wants to believe to justify its acts', Du Bois continues with great attunement to the psychic life of exploitation and oppression, meaning that humans who oppress others tend to offer some kind of conceptual justification for their actions.[69]

In order to highlight the voices of minorities within these structures of domination (capitalism and colonialism), Du Bois conceptualises democracy in a way different from how the colonial powers contemporaneously framed the ideal.

'Democracy is not merely a distribution of power among a vast number of individuals', he writes.[70] It should not be limited to 'merely majority rule, based on the fact that the majority has the physical force to prevail'.[71] In a more robust or fundamental sense, for Du Bois democracy means 'when we have proven knowledge, interpreted through the experience of a large number of individuals, it is possible through this polled knowledge and experience, to come to decisions much more fundamental and much more far-reaching than can be had in any other way'.[72] Such a definition recalls both the potential and the pitfalls of Dumbarton Oaks and of the San Francisco conference. In both cases, the world powers denied the knowledge and experience of the world; attending democratically to this experience would have required fostering an expansive sense of freedom and rights for humankind. Instead, dominant majorities – victorious colonial powers – created an institutional structure that was, in comparison with the vision of world knowledge Du Bois draws our attention to, decidedly unimaginative. A world made new by elites who call themselves the world ends up looking like an old world.

In his 1947 speech, Du Bois then explicitly connects economics to ethics. Describing the colonial land seizures of the twentieth century, he maintains that these 'are not something we can consider at our leisure but [are] rather a part of our own present local economic organization'.[73] There are at least two reasons such colonial control of land in far-away places can be better understood as close to home. The first is that colonial methods of creating racial hierarchies of personhood to control labour are applied 'at home'. '[W]e must remember', Du Bois writes,

that also in the organized and dominant states there are groups of people who occupy the quasi-colonial status; laborers who are settled in the slums of large cities; groups like Negroes in the United States who are segregated physically and discriminated against spiritually in law and customs . . . All of these people occupy what is really a colonial status and make the kernel of the problem of minorities.[74]

In this line, Du Bois is clear that racism is a colonial method applied domestically; that is, racism can challenge civic status to function in a way that in effect renders racialised minorities as having a 'colonial status'.[75]

Du Bois's next call to remember continued colonial conditions of labour, his second reason for understanding the connection between colonisation abroad and life at home, rings even more loudly and remains worth re-visiting at length:

Remember today that we depend upon colonial and quasi-colonial workers for coffee, tea and cocoa; for sugar, rubber, and the increasingly valuable vegetable oils; for minerals like gold, diamonds, uranium, copper and tin; for fibers like cotton, hemp and silk; for rice, spices, quinine and gum Arabic. Indeed for a mass of material which are so inextricably part of our modern life that it would practically be impossible for us to get on without them. Yet all of these materials are raised by labor which does not receive in return enough income to keep it healthy, trained or effective, or even physically to reproduce itself. In order to force this labor to work it is systematically deprived of ownership of land and of a share in the free bounty of nature. It is kept in ignorance, first because intelligence would bring active or passive revolt against these conditions; and secondly because the cost of education would reduce the profits which are pouring into the coffers of the investors and into the mounts and on our backs. This means that every civilized man is part and parcel of the colonial system and is depending for his welfare and convenience, not to mention his luxury, upon the degradation of the majority of man.[76]

Here Du Bois focuses on the distribution of land, how the victorious countries in the 1940s continue to give themselves title to land that they acquired through colonisation (and thus perpetuate war). In this way, nation states naturalised their theft of Indigenous land throughout Africa, Asia, Australia and the Americas. Du Bois says this violates Indigenous peoples' right to live from the 'free bounty of nature'.[77] Further, instead of aspiring to 'civilisation' – and much like Césaire, Fanon and Glissant after him – Du Bois links civilisation to colonisation, such that being 'civilised' is not his guiding ethical or political goal. Third, although Du Bois's sense of social change has shifted through his reading of Marx and Freud, as well as through his extensive travels, it is noteworthy that he maintains his early belief in education as radical, as containing the potential to 'bring active or passive revolt'.

By the 1940s structures of labour the world over were such that it was not only the wealthy with their luxury goods – we might think of Roosevelt's furs here, products of a trade that dispossessed thousands of Indigenous peoples across Turtle Island – whose everyday life was shaped by colonial conditions of labour, but also, as Du Bois puts it, the everyday citizen's 'welfare and convenience'. In other words, all people in what we would now call the Global North are (differentially) entangled in still-colonial patterns of resource extraction and unequal distribution. Refusing to consider the possibilities of what is today called 'ethical consumption' under these conditions, Du Bois calls this what it is: the 'the degradation of the majority' of humanity.[78] By showing how entangled even well-meaning social life has become with degrading violence via a global division of labour, Du Bois teaches that decolonisation and international socialism need to go hand in hand if peace is to be achieved. If we say we want to uphold human rights or that we believe in humanity, Du Bois argues, then we should work to reform how land is owned (and perceived as something that can be owned in the first place). In this way, the measure of ethics both starts from and is evaluated by political transformation.

* * *

Du Bois then returned his focus to advancing the *Appeal*. He noted in a 14 October 1947 letter to William Stoneman, an advisor to the UN Secretary General, that '[a]lready some twelve delegations have asked to read it, and it is receiving publicity from the press'.[79] 'The case of American Negroes is not going to be kept from knowledge by denial of the right to petition', Du Bois went on, 'no more than in the past slavery could bolster itself by silence.'[80] Thus, the *Appeal* offered the UN a chance to take its first step in accordance with its own principles: 'We are going to give world-wide publicity to our complaint; but first, we would like to proceed by regular process and lay this petition before the United Nations publicly and in such a manner as their Secretariat suggests.'[81]

But the UN did not take Du Bois up on this chance. Because his *Appeal* called attention to rights violations in the US, it was understood as advancing the Soviet side of the Cold War. Indeed, the Soviet delegate to the UN Committee on Human Rights, in December 1947, proposed to get the submitted petition on the Committee's agenda. In the face of further efforts from India, Haiti and Liberia, the US defeated the proposal.[82] Du Bois's biographer David Levering Lewis observed, 'Du Bois's petition was an early casualty of the new cold war civil rights politics.'[83] For her part, Roosevelt told Walter White she had concerns regarding Du Bois's continued public advocacy for *An Appeal*.[84] Moreover, she personally asked Du Bois to meet with her in the US offices to the UN on Park Avenue, which he agreed to, and they met on 30 June 1948. At that meeting, Du Bois again asked that the US use its influence to get the petition on the UN agenda. After all, that would show that the US did indeed promote free speech and other political rights (or negative rights), receiving criticism from its citizens as its Constitution suggested. But Roosevelt objected.[85] By that time in 1948, White too sided with Roosevelt. He believed that the petition would serve as an embarrassment to the US.

On 1 July 1948, Du Bois sent White a memo regarding his meeting with Roosevelt. While Du Bois noted that the US State department had severe reservations about putting the petition on the next GA's agenda, he also painted a picture of Roosevelt's opposition. He said she believed that if 'the matter [of state-sanctioned human rights violations of Black people in the US] was discussed in the Assembly, she and her colleagues would be put in the unpleasant position of having to defend the United States'.[86] Du Bois kept a close eye on these developments. He saw that the Department of State's objectives were moving along and thus that 'the Declaration of Human Rights . . . would come up at that session and be discussed and possibly assented to'.[87]

To summarise these events differently, we could say that Du Bois's 1947 petition was part of a moral imaginary that was an alternative to the one that not only moved along but also took hold in the 1948 Universal Declaration, which failed to recognise the self-determination of the colonies and therefore failed to address the ongoing 'colonial problem'. For all her ardent advocacy, in the final instance and when it really mattered, Roosevelt proved correct a point Du Bois had made in a different 1947 letter, namely, that 'no people who consciously or unconsciously is oppressing another is going to agree upon a proper time when they are willing to listen to protest'.[88]

That said, in May 1948 Du Bois published an article in the *Chicago Star* called 'The Case for the Jews'. He titled his draft for that article 'The Ethics of the Problem of Palestine'. Early in the draft, he follows John Locke in asserting that, 'as Americans ought to know, the question of possession of a land is in the long run the question of the use to which the land is put'.[89] As Du Bois goes on, he maintains positions that not only further Indigenous dispossession but that also, more specifically, are clearly Zionist. For instance, still on the first page of the draft, he writes, 'Among the million Arabs there is widespread ignorance, poverty and disease and a fanatic belief in the Mohammedan religion, which makes these people suspicious of other peoples and other religions.'[90] These prejudicial words reveal Du Bois's limitations, especially around Indigeneity, Islam and Palestine, at the same time as he was making more imaginative decolonial arguments around labour and land in the US. The argument of this book – against an ethics of purity – is that these lines do not discount Du Bois's contributions to theorising war in the present; at the same time, reading Du Bois for his contributions does not mean we get to avoid his claims that discursively aided and abetted Indigenous dispossession. Instead, we should clearly and publicly repudiate his problematic claims even as we think continue to think with him. For Du Bois himself kept thinking. Indeed, he would somewhat change his position on Israel in 1956, arguing in favour of Nasser's attempt to nationalise the Suez Canal Company and denying Israel legitimacy in Egypt.[91]

Notes towards a Du Boisian Politics

In this chapter, I have presented Eleanor Roosevelt as a foil to the politics, ethics and sociological method – to the expansive moral and political imagination – that Du Bois exemplifies. But I do not mean for my critical analysis of Roosevelt's fur-based fashion, for instance, to be petty; such everyday acts reflect our political imaginaries and commitments in a deep way.[92] If we begin our social analysis from political economy, then – as the long paragraph I quoted above from 'Human Rights for All Minorities' demonstrates – we necessarily return to everyday life, to the ordinary life that was Du Bois's focus in opening *Black Reconstruction*.[93] We return to the fact that most of us, myself included, do not know where and by whom the shirt we are currently wearing was made, where and by whom the beans for the coffee we are drinking was picked, and what is the history of the land on which we sit, dwell, settle, read and teach – a fact that is a result of ideological victories and the naturalisation of colonial life. In this colonial context, to have, as Glendon said of Roosevelt, an 'ardent but pragmatic' politics in which that ardency is expressed primarily through 'lending a helping hand' and that pragmatism is seen in maintaining colonial structures is no longer sufficient, and indeed never has been – that was Du Bois's point in criticising philanthropy (what we would now call 'elite capture') in the 1940s.[94]

One of the reasons Du Bois's sociological analysis remains compelling for envisioning peaceful institutions today is that he addresses, but does not simply remain on, the level of the personal and the local. As the political scientist Adom Getachew has outlined, Du Bois's project in the late 1940s was ultimately one of demanding that the post-war settlement address and rectify 'the global color line'.[95] His return to the NAACP at a time when he was also organising around Pan-Africanism represents his multifaceted method, seen in his contributions to the Fifth Pan-African Congress, held in Manchester in October 1945. Informed by Kwame Nkrumah's socialism and George Padmore's anti-imperialism, the Fifth Pan-African Congress attended to questions of labour more directly than the inter-war Congresses that Du Bois organised. Planned in part as a response to, and thus as an alternative to the limitations of the imaginary of, the San Francisco founding of the UN, the Fifth Pan-African Congress demanded, as Du Bois's final resolution to the Congress summarised, the 'autonomy and independence' of Black Africa.[96] '[W]e are unwilling longer to starve while doing the world's drudgery', Du Bois stated in the penultimate paragraph of the resolution. 'We condemn monopoly of capital and the rule of private wealth and industry for private profit alone', he continued. 'We welcome economic democracy as the only real democracy.'

These lines – which could be heard as an echo of his call for 'abolition-democracy' in *Black Reconstruction* – continue to speak strongly to those of us trying to make peace a reality in this century. They assert with great clarity that an only slightly modified global capitalism means the perpetuation of degrading labour along racialised lines. They underscore that the failure of the UN to end poverty is the result *not* of the fact that there are no adequately imaginative paths to do so, but that colonial countries and their citizens and representatives, in every thinkable way, continue to reject the ethical and political implications of a sufficiently expansive imaginary, namely, the Black Atlantic anti-colonial project stretching into the present. For many of us – and I will let my readers positions themselves inside or outside of this 'us' – the first step for social theory and life regarding institutional capacity in the present, then, might be not the mere application of what we have learned on our way to our prestigious PhDs, but a renewed, self-critical study of the archives our fields of study have rejected, a concerted effort to learn from the oral histories that we have dismissed, and an imaginative willingness to begin not from the institutional re-designs we claim are 'possible' given the official responsibilities we say we have to uphold, but from the often still-unpublished manuscripts and oft-concealed practices that have long asserted, usually in the face of great repression, our fundamental and far-reaching connection with every other human being on the planet we share.[97] By orienting us to this starting point, we might say of Du Bois's page what Césaire said of Lam's canvas – it invites us to 'the ceremony through which everything exists'.

* * *

In 1950 Du Bois was elected the chairman of the Peace Information Center, which organised internationally against war and for the outlawing of nuclear weapons. The US Department of Justice pressured the organisation such that it disbanded.

In 1951, for his work with the Center, Du Bois was indicted as an 'unregistered foreign agent'. In response, he toured the country to raise the money necessary for his defence: 'It had not occurred to us how costly justice in the United States is', he reflected in his recollection of his indictment and trial, the 1952 *In Battle for Peace*.[98] 'It is not enough to be innocent in order to escape punishment. You must have money and a lot of it.'[99] Speaking to an audience of 15,000 at the Coliseum of Chicago in 1951, Du Bois nevertheless sidelined his personal plight in order to speak to wider social needs. He proceeded through what he later called a 'clear thesis': 'There is no way in the world for us to preserve the ideals of a democratic America, save by drastically curbing the present power of concentrated wealth . . . There must come vast social change in the United States; a change not violent, but by the will of the people.'[100] When he reflected on that speech in 1952, he wrote, 'I wanted to dispel in the minds of government and of the public any lingering doubt as to my determination to think and speak freely on the economic foundation of the wars and the frustration of the twentieth century.'[101] Amidst the frustrations of the twenty-first century, it remains up to those of us who still stand for peace to change the economic foundations that continue to generate war.

Notes

1. Inés Valdez, 'Cosmopolitanism without National Consciousness Is Not Radical: Creolizing Gordon's Fanon through Du Bois', *Philosophy and Global Affairs* 1, no. 2 (2021): p. 295.

2. We might also call this mode Romantic. Walter Benjamin wrote that 'for the Romantics and for speculative philosophy, the term "critical" meant objectively productive, creative out of thoughtful deliberation' (Walter Benjamin, 'The Concept of Criticism in German Romanticism', in *Walter Benjamin: Selected Writings*

Volume 1 1913–1926, eds. Marcus Bullock and Michael W. Jennings (Cambridge, MA: The Belknap Press of Harvard University, 1996), p. 142).

3. At the risk of being wildly misunderstood, I will note here that the method I have in mind for critical theory regarding the judgement of when a concept is sufficient is in fact a pragmatic method, but not the kind of pragmatism Glendon says Roosevelt exemplifies. I see my own claims as resonant with John Dewey when he writes that while 'a withdrawal is necessary', the fact is that '[t]hinkers often withdraw too far'; he goes on by noting that '[o]ver-specialization and division of interests, occupations and goods create the need for a generalized medium of inter-communication, of mutual criticism through all-around transla-tion from one separated region of experience into another. Thus philosophy as a critical organ becomes in effect a messenger, a liaison officer, making reciprocally intelligible voices speaking provincial tongues, and thereby enlarging as well as rectifying the meanings with which they are charged' (John Dewey, *Experi-ence and Nature* (Carbondale: Southern Illinois University Press, 2008), p. 306). Du Bois himself acknowledged the importance of Pragmatism (especially that of James, his teacher, more than that of Dewey) to his project: 'I went forward to build a sociol-ogy, which I conceived of as the attempt to measure the element of Chance in human conduct. This was the Jamesian pragma-tism, applied not simply to ethics, but to all human action' (Du Bois, 'My Evolving Program', p. 48). In a connection worth not-ing but ultimately beyond the scope of this essay, Césaire is per-haps the most instructive example of such a radical pragmatism, meaning an experimental and always political orientation to concepts understood more as verbs than nouns – that political ideas should always start from and return back to local contexts and practical ramifications. For this reading of Césaire, see Gary Wilder, *Freedom Time: Negritude, Decolonization, and the Future of the World* (Durham, NC: Duke University Press, 2015), p. 21. Finally, I would like to say that whether my reader agrees with the con-tent of my thesis might not be significant, because the overall

contribution of this essay lies in the form of the thesis: one skill for connecting critical theory to practice today is our ability to acknowledge when a concept does sufficient normative work, such that the resulting political task is not to perpetually debate the limitations of the concept, but to organise around it. Some might justifiably wonder whether my claim that my contribution lies in form more than content is in fact a defence mechanism for this book in its entirety. And perhaps it is. But I also have a larger point in mind. I am trying to say: my readers (even if they are limited to my friends) might be in Cairo, Tokyo, Gqeberha, Melbourne, Santiago de Chile or Santiago de Cuba. In my particular context in the Midwest of the US, following Hall's setting our task as 'strengthening and deepening the oppositional elements of already existing cultural forms', one concept worth strategically engaging is 'humanity' and one instructive history related to this context is Du Bois's reading of John Brown, who carries historical significance not just out East where he died, but also and perhaps especially in Kansas, Missouri and Iowa, where he fought against the creation of states that supported slavery (Stuart Hall, 'Culture, Resistance, and Struggle', in *Cultural Studies 1983: A Theoretical History*, eds. Jennifer Daryl Slack and Lawrence Grossberg (Durham, NC: Duke University Press, 2016), p. 189). Writing from the US, I am trying to acknowledge that I do not know which concepts have, or could have, the most purchase in the places where my reader finds themselves, but that my reader and I share a need for concepts we can organise around in order to make international political gains.

4. For an incisive critique of this moment of human rights rhetoric, a critique that was important to Caribbean critical theorists such as Sylvia Wynter, see e.g. Randall Williams, *The Divided World: Human Rights and its Violence* (Minneapolis: University of Minnesota Press, 2010). For Wynter's citation, see McKittrick, ed. *Sylvia Wynter: On Being Human as Praxis* (Durham, NC: Duke University Press), p. 39.

5. For a summary of how race and empire played into the 1948 Universal Declaration of Human Rights, see Emma Mackinnon,

'Declaration as Disavowal: The Politics of Race and Empire in the Universal Declaration of Human Rights', *Political Theory* 47, no. 1 (2019): pp. 57–81.

6. Du Bois, *Black Reconstruction in America: 1860–1880* (New York: The Free Press, 1992), p. 634.

7. See LaRose T. Parris, *Being Apart: Theoretical and Existential Resistance in Africana Literature* (Charlottesville: University of Virginia Press, 2015).

8. Du Bois, *Black Reconstruction*, p. xix.

9. Ibid. p. 8. One of the reasons slavery was 'cruel and hideous', Du Bois says on the first page of *John Brown*, is that 'it gradually built itself on a caste of race and color, thus breaking the common bonds of human fellowship and weaving artificial barriers of birth and appearance . . . The result was evil, as all injustice must be' (W. E. B. Du Bois, *John Brown: A Biography* (New York: Routledge, [1909] 2015), p. 1).

10. Du Bois, *Black Reconstruction*, p. 16. For how this claim goes beyond a Marxist tendency to focus on Europe, see Parris, *Being Apart*, p. 86.

11. Du Bois, *Black Reconstruction*, p. 325.

12. Ibid. pp. 382–3.

13. Ibid. p. 722.

14. I did this exercise, and I found the following: '[I]n general, it is true that there is scarcely a bishop in Christendom, a priest in the church, a president, governor, mayor, or legislator in the United States, a college professor or public school teacher, who does not in the end stand by War and Ignorance as the main method for the settlement of our pressing human problems' (ibid. p. 678).

15. Du Bois, 'My Evolving Program', p. 44.

16. Du Bois's biographer David Levering Lewis describes Du Bois as 'self-instructed' in Marxism – his 1933 self-study was 'Marx in months, not years' (David Levering Lewis, *W.E.B. Du Bois: A Biography* (New York: Henry Holt and Company, 2009), pp. 624, 549).

17. Du Bois, *John Brown*, p. xxv.

18. Ibid. pp. 187–8, 188.

19. Ibid. p. 190. Teju Cole raises these ethical questions in a planetary context today, asking 'Who is my neighbor?' and 'Who is kin to me?' on the cover of his book; Fazal Sheikh's photographs focus on the dispossessed and displaced across the world, suggesting a non-linear, non-filial sense of responsibility. Cf. Teju Cole and Fazal Sheikh, *Human Archipelago* (Göttingen: Steidl, 2021).

20. Ted A. Smith, *Weird John Brown: Divine Violence and the Limits of Ethics* (Stanford, CA: Stanford University Press, 2014), pp. 8, 161.

21. Du Bois, *John Brown*, p. 144.

22. Ibid. p. 172.

23. Ibid.

24. Edward Said, *The Politics of Dispossession: The Struggle for Palestinian Self-Determination, 1969–1994* (New York: Vintage, 1995), pp. 126–7.

25. My sense is that some contemporary philosophers who maintain a radical humanism do so based on a similar historical understanding of how the concept has functioned: Paul Gilroy's call for a 'planetary humanism' informed by Black Atlantic political struggles – including the rights claims of David Walker, Frederick Douglass and Ida B. Wells – comes to mind, as does Lewis Gordon's maintenance of a humanism based on his reading of Frantz Fanon and Sylvia Wynter's foundational reconstruction of the human that draws on Césaire, Fanon and Michel Foucault. See Paul Gilroy, *Against Race: Imagining Political Culture beyond the Color Line* (Cambridge, MA: The Belknap Press of Harvard University, 2000); Lewis Gordon, *What Fanon Said: An Introduction to His Life and Thought* (New York: Fordham University Press, 2015); David Scott, 'The Re-enchantment of Humanism: An Interview with Sylvia Wynter', *Small Axe* 8 (2000): p. 121. Such *constructive* or *re-imaginative* practices of reading and conceptualisation are, in my view, examples worth following today, because our movements still very much need tools to make judgements and demands as well as to build more just societies.

26. Quoted in Samantha A. Noël, *Tropical Aesthetics of Black Modernism* (Durham, NC: Duke University Press, 2021), p. 87.

27. Wall text. Museum of Modern Art.

28. Mary Ann Glendon, *A World Made New: Eleanor Roosevelt and the Universal Declaration of Human Rights* (New York: Random House, 2001), pp. 25, 22.

29. Ibid. p. 90. It is worth noting that Glendon's colloquial use of 'pragmatic' is drastically different from Du Bois's pragmatic sociology in the spirit of William James. See n. 3 above.

30. Alexandre Lefebvre, *Human Rights and the Care of the Self* (Durham, NC: Duke University Press, 2018), p. 2; see also p. 189.

31. See Glendon, *World Made New*, p. 100.

32. For this line from Roosevelt's prayer, see ibid. p. x.

33. See José Itzigsohn and Karida Brown, *The Sociology of W. E. B. Du Bois: Racialized Modernity and the Global Color Line* (New York: New York University Press, 2020); see Gerald Horne, 'Introduction' in W. E. B. Du Bois, *Color and Democracy* (New York: Oxford University Press, 2007), p. 237. The literature on Du Bois is so extensive as to make a summary endnote impossible. For an analysis of Du Bois's wider cultural imagination, see Arnold Rampersad, *The Art and Imagination of W. E. B. Du Bois* (Cambridge, MA: Harvard University Press, 1976). For the limits of Du Bois's own 'false consciousness' regarding a Western ideology of progress and the distinction between 'backward' and 'advanced' peoples, see Adolph Reed Jr, *W. E. B. Du Bois and American Political Thought: Fabianism and the Color Line* (New York: Oxford University Press, 1997), pp. 78–9. For more on Du Bois's relationship to sociology, see e.g. Aldon Morris, *The Scholar Denied: W. E. B. Du Bois and the Birth of Modern Sociology* (Berkeley: The University of California Press, 2017). For the question of how far sociology and the academy have to go in regard to taking Black Studies seriously, see Christina Sharpe, 'Black Life, Annotated', in *The New Inquiry* (8 August 2014), https://thenewinquiry.com/black-life-annotated/; and Christina Sharpe, 'Black Studies: In the Wake', *The Black Scholar* 44, no. 2 (2014): pp. 59–69.

34. John Paul Lederach, *The Moral Imagination: The Art and Soul of Building Peace* (New York: Oxford, 2005), p. 5. For an indication that such an aesthetic framing of peace carries wide social purchase, see e.g. Krista Tippett's *On Being* episodes that feature Lederach, including the 2012 'The Art of Peace', https://onbeing.org/programs/john-paul-lederach-the-art-of-peace/; and the 2018 'The Ingredients of Social Change', https://onbeing.org/programs/america-ferrera-john-paul-lederach-the-ingredients-of-social-courage/.

35. Lederach, *The Moral Imagination*, p. 5.

36. Du Bois, *Color and Democracy*, p. 269.

37. Ibid. p. 329.

38. Part of what I am trying to suggest is that lying behind the often frustrated and deeply critical tone of Marxist analysis is an equally profound aesthetic and peaceful sensibility. Following the recent work of Mihaela Mihai, we can think of Du Bois's 1940s writings and the tradition of Marxism of which he is a part as exemplifying an 'aesthetics of care'. Such an aesthetics, Mihai teaches, involves acknowledging a 'generalized complicity' with systemic violence while 'sabotag[ing] reductive historical scripts and prosthetically enabl[ing] spectators to see the world in its complexity, from different points of view'; ultimately, these artworks 'could open up a space for remembering and imagining differently' (Mihaela Mihai, *Political Memory and the Aesthetics of Care: The Art of Complicity and Resistance* (Stanford, CA: Stanford University Press, 2022), pp. 4, 46). It is the argument of this chapter that Du Bois's late 1940s texts are such artworks, with *The World and Africa* remembering history differently and *Color and Democracy* imagining a different institutional order. To cite just one example, in *The World and Africa*, Du Bois provides a history of global labour struggles different from many accounts that start from European and white working classes. He writes, 'The slave revolts were the beginnings of the revolutionary struggle for the uplift of the laboring masses in the modern world' (W. E. B. Du Bois, *The World and Africa* (New York: Oxford University Press, 2007), p. 38).

39. A telling example of both the strengths and limitations of Lederach's approach is found in how Arianne Zwartjes uses a line from *The Moral Imagination* – about the artist allowing us to find something new – as the epigraph to her book *These Dark Skies*. While it is strikingly unfair to judge a work by how someone else takes it up, I am interested here in the perceived resonance between the projects. Zwartjes uses Lederach to ask about the power of art 'to break us open, to change our thinking, to teach us things emotively' while posing additional questions such as '*why are we, as a species, so prone to violence?*' (Arianne Zwartjes, *These Dark Skies: Reckoning with Identity, Violence, and Power from Abroad* (Iowa City: University of Iowa Press, 2022), pp. xiv–xv, 26). My view is that this 'we' can remain too abstract; that the problem of violence is not a species problem so much as a problem of capitalism and colonialism (and so tied to racism, whiteness and its aspirations, and a property logic), as Du Bois will highlight in his analysis of war.

40. Quoted in Horne, 'Introduction', p. 238. Elsewhere Horne summarises Du Bois's late 1940s work as reflective of his insistence that 'the greatest single question facing humanity was the ending of colonialism' (Gerald Horne, *Black and Red: W. E. B. Du Bois and the Afro-American Response to the Cold War, 1944–1963* (Albany: State University of New York Press, 1985), p. 25).

41. W. E. B. Du Bois, *In Battle for Peace: The Story of My 83rd Birthday* (New York: Oxford University Press, 2007), p. 7. 'From this plan', he went on, 'came the Fifth Pan-African Congress in England, 1945; and my book, *The World and Africa*, in 1947' (ibid.). For the radical elements of Du Bois's social theory and practice during this time, see Charisse Burden-Stelly, 'In Battle for Peace during "Scoundrel Time": W. E. B. Du Bois and United States Repression of Radical Black Peace Activism', *Du Bois Review: Social Science Research on Race* 16, no. 2 (2019): pp. 555–74.

42. It is arguable that *Color and Democracy* follows Du Bois's argument in his May 1915 *Atlantic Monthly* article 'The African Roots of War'.

43. Gurminder Bhambra, 'Theory for a global age: From nativism to neoliberalism and beyond', *Current Sociology Monograph* 68, no. 2 (2020): p. 138.

44. Horne, *Black and Red*, p. 38.

45. Reed, *W. E. B. Du Bois and American Political Thought*, p. 43.

46. Du Bois, *Color and Democracy*, p. 301.

47. Ibid. p. 246; see also p. 309.

48. See ibid. pp. 309, 310.

49. Ibid. p. 311.

50. Ibid. p. 246.

51. Ibid. p. 305.

52. Ibid.

53. Ibid. p. 304.

54. Ibid. p. 275.

55. Ibid. p. 304.

56. Ibid. p. 308.

57. Ibid. p. 275.

58. Ibid. p. 281. Du Bois argues in *Color and Democracy* that the social sciences have an important role to play in struggles to change colonial structures of land and labour. Against the 'propaganda' and 'caricature' of colonial powers and their official histories, the social scientist can challenge the inaccurate premises that 'give an entirely unfair picture of the colonial world' (ibid. p. 258). Following Du Bois's implicit humanism in *Color and Democracy*, the social scientist can also provide evidence to challenge racist stereotypes that posit people of colour as inferior to white people in intelligence or culture. Following Du Bois's Marxism, the social scientist can highlight that such stereotypes are not natural but functional – they serve to justify resource extraction from the colony to the metropole, from the South to the North, and from the racialised poor to the wealthy within a given country. Since the founding of the United Nations in 1945, we have witnessed movements for a new economic order: e.g. the Bandung Conference, the American Indian Movement and the Black Power movement. These and other social movements influenced the academy, leading to the creation of Peace Studies in the late 1940s and Black Studies and Native Studies in the late 1960s. Taken together, these movements and fields of inquiry have consistently affirmed that claims to 'peace' cannot be valid if colonisation structures planetary social life. The fact that these

fields remain on the margins of academic discourse reflects institutional roadblocks for students attempting to understand how to build a true peace in the present. Students of social theory in North America remain much more likely to read Max Weber's *The Protestant Ethic and the Spirit of Capitalism* than they are to read Walter Rodney's *How Europe Underdeveloped Africa*. Much work remains to be done if the social sciences today are to heed Du Bois's call 'to attack the economic illiteracy, the ignorance of economic facts and developments, now deliberately encouraged in our schools and colleges, in our press and periodicals and in our books' (Du Bois, *Color and Democracy*, p. 318). One institution contributing to literacy today is the project around global social theory. See https://globalsocialtheory.org. While global social theory has over time used different language to describe how colonial structures have persisted after formal, political decolonisation – from the Ghanaian leader Kwame Nkrumah's 'neo-colonialism' to the Peruvian sociologist Aníbal Quijano's concept of 'coloniality' – it has consistently shed light on the re-installations and afterlives of colonial structures that extend into the present. See Kwame Nkrumah, *Neo-colonialism: The Last Stage of Imperialism* (London: Thomas Nelson & Sons, 1965); Aníbal Quijano, 'Colonialidad y modernidad/racionalidad', *Perú Indígena* 13, no. 29 (1992).

59. Charisse Burden-Stelly and Gerald Horne, *W.E.B. Du Bois: A Life in American History* (Santa Barbara: ABC-CLIO, 2019), p. 158.

60. W. E. B. Du Bois, *An appeal to the world*, pp. 4, 8. W. E. B. Du Bois Papers (MS 312). Special Collections and University Archives, University of Massachusetts Amherst Libraries.

61. Ibid. p. 9.

62. Ibid. p. 12.

63. For the line about a new responsibility, see Du Bois, *Color and Democracy*, p. 327.

64. W. E. B. Du Bois, 'Human Rights for All Minorities', p. 1. W. E. B. Du Bois Papers (MS 312). Special Collections and University Archives, University of Massachusetts Amherst Libraries.

65. Ibid. p. 2.

66. Ibid.

67. Cf. Siddhant Issar, 'Listening to Black Lives Matter: Racial Capitalism and the Critique of Neoliberalism', *Contemporary Political Theory* 20, no. 1 (2021): pp. 48–71. See also Tiffany L. King, *The Black Shoals: Offshore Formations of Black and Native Studies* (Durham, NC: Duke University Press, 2019).

68. Du Bois, 'Human Rights for All Minorities', p. 3.

69. Ibid.

70. Ibid.

71. Ibid.

72. Ibid. p. 4.

73. Ibid. p. 5.

74. Ibid. p. 4–5.

75. The liberal position accepts a version of this point even if it avoids the language of colonisation. See e.g. Richard Rothstein, *The Color of Law: A Forgotten History of How Our Government Segregated America* (New York: Liveright, 2017).

76. Du Bois, 'Human Rights for All Minorities', p. 6.

77. Cf. Adom Getachew, *Worldmaking After Empire: The Rise and Fall of Self-Determination* (Princeton, NJ: Princeton University Press, 2019), p. 83.

78. The above long passage can be read as the fruit of years of analysis, combining the sociological eye of *The Philadelphia Negro*, the psychological attunement found in *Souls*, and the Marxism of *Black Reconstruction*. For a summary discussion of Du Bois's 1920–40 writings regarding the question of land, race and title, see Ella Myers, 'Beyond the Psychological Wage: Du Bois on White Dominion', *Political Theory* 47, no. 1 (2019): pp. 6–31. This is not to say that Du Bois's trajectory is entirely consistent; like that of the rest of us, his human-all-too-human work contains what Reed calls an 'apparent ambivalence' seen, for instance, in his 'alternation of extravagant pro-Bolshevik rhetoric and effusion over debutante balls in the pages of the *Crisis*' (Reed, *W. E. B. Du Bois and American Political Thought*, pp. 65–6).

79. W. E. B. Du Bois, *The Correspondence of W. E. B. Du Bois: Volume III: Selections, 1944–1963*, ed. Herbert Aptheker (Amherst: University of Massachusetts Press, 1978), p. 181.

80. Ibid.

81. Ibid.

82. Manfred Berg, 'Black Civil Rights and Liberal Anticommunism: The NAACP in the Early Cold War', *The Journal of American History* 94, no. 1 (2007): p. 83.

83. Levering Lewis, *W.E.B. Du Bois: A Biography*, p. 673.

84. Ibid. p. 676.

85. Ibid.

86. Du Bois, *The Correspondence*, p. 189.

87. Ibid.

88. Du Bois, *The Correspondence*, p. 186. The tension between Du Bois and White/Roosevelt, which I am reading as exemplifying a broader difference between decolonial and liberal approaches to human rights, was larger than just a single incident. By 1948, Du Bois was increasingly critical of the United States as an evolving power, and in that year, he supported the Progressive Party candidate Henry Wallace, a position that put him against both Walter White and the NAACP board (including Roosevelt) who supported Truman and deliberately distanced themselves from communism. Du Bois thought that Truman's liberal sympathies for human rights were not radical enough given that he dropped an atomic bomb on Japan, that he provided aid to Europe but not the colonies, and that he required a loyalty oath in his administration. Cf. Horne, *Black and Red*, pp. 100–1.

89. W. E. B. Du Bois, 'The ethics of the problem of Palestine, ca. 1948', p. 1. W.E.B. Du Bois Papers (MS 312). Special Collections and University Archives, University of Massachusetts Amherst Libraries.

90. Ibid. Thanks to Janine Jones for pointing me to this source.

91. See Nadia Alahmed, 'From Black Zionism to Black Nasserism: W. E. B. Du Bois and the Foundations of Black Anti-Zionist Discourse', *Critical Sociology* 49, no. 6 (2023): pp. 1053–64.

92. In his 1966 essay 'Political Commitment', Stuart Hall describes politics as 'the form in which the connexions are made between lived experience and the demands made upon the system' (Stuart Hall, 'Political Commitment', in *Selected Political Writings*, eds. Sally Davison et al. (Durham, NC: Duke University Press, p. 94). As I mentioned in *Choose Your Bearing*, both Roosevelt's and Du

Bois's moral imaginations and practices could follow from this description, which is why Hall's next sentences are so important: 'Certain kinds of politics will connect experience with demands in a meaningful relationship, will connect awareness of the nature of the system to aspiration, and aspiration for change to the agencies of change. But there are also false ways of connecting lived experience to the agency of change. And in the absence of the right kind of politics, the false connexions become the stabilizing myths of society' (ibid.). Roosevelt's ardent but elite liberalism ultimately promoted a vision of human rights that served as one more myth stabilising capitalist and colonial society.

93. I have written about such a return in dialogue with Édouard Glissant's concept of 'entanglement'. See Benjamin P. Davis, 'Human Rights and Caribbean Philosophy: Implications for Teaching', *Journal of Human Rights Practice* 12, no. 4 (2021): pp. 1–9.

94. The narrow point of my criticism admittedly addresses the norms of academic and professional life today. To throw on the Zegna blazer and make a case for political rights at the four-star conference hotel without implicating oneself in, and attempting to redress, the conditions of labour that created that blazer and the settler history of the land on which the hotel sits, is today's analogue to Roosevelt's wearing fox furs on the international stage. Du Bois's analysis asks us to call ourselves to account on this level of everyday life, which is always already entangled with the degradation of workers in the Global South as well as racialised workers within a given country. Decolonial social movements today speak to this level of ordinary life. Commenting on the norms at Standing Rock, the photography Larry Towell noted, 'The rules were simple: No cursing. No alcohol. No drugs. No weapons (rare for North Dakota). Dress modestly.' At Standing Rock, in other words, norms were put in place to rectify the everyday degradation of the humanity of others that is the presentation of social class. Du Bois himself made this point in 1952: '[T]he huge profits of industry go not to [the comparatively poor] but to the

financiers who as middle-men handle their funds, giving them 2% in savings banks while this wealth in foreign trade often reaps 50%. Small wonder Big Business fights and schemes and drafts the 18-year-old youth. Profit is thicker than blood. This has led many a social thinker to point out that capital for all real human want and improvement could easily be taken from production and leave sufficient income for all consumers, provided, of course, that individual consumption was so limited that no man had cake if any man lacked bread; that mink coats for the rich were not allowed if the poor had no shoes. And of course here's the rub. This compulsion, which socialism proposed long before Lenin as the only way to decent human life, raises shrieks of protest if hinted at today in the United States' (Du Bois, *In Battle for Peace*, p. 118). In terms of human rights discourse today, Du Bois's point is not far from Sam Moyn's argument in *Not Enough: Human Rights in an Unequal World*.

95. Getachew, *Worldmaking After Empire*, p. 84.
96. W. E. B. Du Bois, 'Fifth Pan-African Congress final resolution, ca. October 1945'. W. E. B. Du Bois Papers (MS 312). Special Collections and University Archives, University of Massachusetts Amherst Libraries.
97. Reflecting on the late 1940s, Du Bois argued that 'the hope of the future of the Negro race in America and the world lies far more among its workers than among its college graduates, until the time that our higher training is rescued from its sycophantic and cowardly leadership of today, almost wholly dependent as it is on Big Business either in politics or philanthropy' (Du Bois, *In Battle for Peace*, p. 52). As tenured faculty keep quiet in the face of increasing contingent academic labour, as administrators refuse to divest from fossil fuels, and as some of our best students go to law school to work in defence of corporations that pollute rivers, surely these lines remain true today.
98. Ibid. p. 64.
99. Ibid.
100. Ibid. pp. 70, 71.
101. Ibid. p. 70.

2 Édouard Glissant's Relational Humanism

While the two fellow Martinicans and philosophers Édouard Glissant is continually in dialogue with and compared to, Aimé Césaire and Frantz Fanon, clearly offer new humanisms, it is less clear whether there is a humanism in Glissant's corpus.[1] Readings of Glissant's stance towards humanism vary greatly, from the literary critic (and his translator) Celia Britton's contextualising his work as broadly critical of humanism to the City University of New York's celebration of his 'humanistic project' upon his death.[2] In an interview in Paris in 2005, Glissant explicitly responded to the question of whether he proposes a new humanism. Given the importance of these words to my inquiry in this chapter and in this book itself, I will quote Glissant's response at length. He said about his work:

I would not say that it is a new humanism because the very notion of humanism has something of a system of thought that does not please me: I would say that it is perhaps a new approach to humanities [*une nouvelle approche des humanités*], as they are lived today in the contemporary world, but not a new humanism. I do not claim to arrive at humanism because, whatever one may say, there is in the notion of humanism once more a dimension of morals [*une dimension de morale*] that does not appear necessary to me . . . I am resolutely optimistic but that is not to say that I am founding a new system of humanism. Optimism is confidence in the effectiveness of the interrelations [*des interrelations*] between many systems: systems of cultures, of languages, of landscapes, of countries. It is not a humanism, it is a poetics [*Ce n'est pas un humanisme, c'est une poétique*].[3]

Notwithstanding Glissant's own understanding of his work, might it be the case that the very reasons for which Glissant says his work does *not* offer a humanism – his avoidance of systematic thought, his emphasis on a new approach to (worldly) humanities, and his attempt to create not yet another '-ism' but rather a poetics – together form his contribution to a new humanism for today? That will be the thesis of this chapter.[4]

The Importance of Poetry

If I refer to Glissant's 'humanism' before proving that he indeed has something of one, it is only to begin connecting the ideas that when seen together, I want to say, make up the constellation of what I will call his 'relational humanism'. Following Gilles Deleuze and Félix Guattari, themselves in dialogue with Glissant, we might first call Glissant's humanism a 'minor humanism', not only because it is understated, but because it exemplifies the three main characteristics Deleuze and Guattari associated with 'minor literature': deterritorialised language, politics and collective value.[5] Glissant's engagement with humanist discourse is written in French (from the 'problem-space' of Martinique), from a Caribbean angle, and with a view towards regional (and ultimately planetary) solidarity.[6] But it is also a humanism, I will suggest, that ultimately decentres humanity and complicates any native/foreigner sense of belonging, and thus it is, in Deleuze and Guattari's terms, 'appropriate for strange . . . uses'.[7] Following Edward Said, we might also say that Glissant's is an example of the 'different kind of humanism' Said insisted the world needs, one that would begin from the recognition that there are always 'other humanities' – an urgent new humanism that would proceed by resisting *idées reçues*, disclosing the present and avoiding Eurocentrism.[8] Ultimately, I will read Glissant's humanism as he reads Césaire's – that is, as combining 'political activity' and 'poetic creation'.[9] I will underscore that, for Glissant, poetics influences, and at times calls into question, politics.

To read Glissant's 'minor humanism' as a poetics, as a theory of poetry or a text containing poetic feelings, has a number of important implications for how we make sense of and evaluate it. If we understand Glissant's contributions as coming from the place of the poet more than the place of the lecturer – he is interested not just in theorising modernity but in disclosing 'the question of lived modernity'[10] – then we need to proceed with our readings accordingly. That means that we would read with a set of expectations about how to take up his work that is different from the traditional approach to philosophy in the Western academy; this difference in approach applies even if we follow Deleuze and Guattari's claim that philosophy is about creating concepts.[11] Certainly Glissant is a writer in dialogue with tradition – but which one? A tradition of Western literature? Of Continental philosophy? Of anti-colonial humanism? Of situating himself within the land by way of stories told in dialogue with others, as he learned from accompanying his father to work in Martinique's cane fields, where he heard storytellers crafting Creole? If all of these at once, then how can we think with Glissant's mode of concept creation?

To begin, ambiguity in conceptualisation would not necessarily be a limitation; we would drop our expectation that the philosopher define their terms. Instead, ambiguity places the burden on (or offers an opportunity to) the reader to give a new sense to, or to re-conceptualise, the term in question. I have in mind here Glissant's concepts of opacity, Relation and trace – all of which I will discuss further in what follows. Second, poetry does not always make deductions or move 'logically' to conclusions; it often moves expansively, with every word, pause or echo pointing beyond itself. Third, by keeping in mind that Glissant is a poet, the question of voice also comes to the fore, because the poet is not always writing in their own voice, but rather is often giving voice to someone, something, some feeling, some event – or even to multiple (and perhaps contrasting) perspectives. Indeed, in Glissant we have a conversation across voices: the notion of the rhizome might recall conversations in Paris with the psychoanalyst Félix Guattari or ginger plants in Martinique; the image of the cave could suggest a dialogue with Plato or gesture towards a Maroon hideout; the presence of a tree could indicate a sign of knowledge and life in the West, the spectacle of murdering enslaved people, shade on a hot day, or an active witness to history – and likely, precisely in its ever-signifying incompleteness, the figure of the tree in Glissant points to all of these elements at once.[12] Finally, I will suggest that Glissant in *Caribbean Discourse* gives voice to a shared struggle for self-determination in the Caribbean; in *Poetics of Relation* gives voice to the increasing creolisation of the world;[13] and in *Treatise of the All-World* gives voice to the landscapes or ecological contexts that become increasingly important to his understanding (and situation) of human community and culture in his later work.[14]

'The Human' across Glissant's Theoretical Work

Glissant discussed humanism from his early work forward. His humanism starts from the lived realities of the Caribbean. 'The Caribbean', he writes, 'may be held up as one of the places in the world where Relation presents itself most visibly, one of the explosive regions where it seems to be gathering strength.'[15] Due to ongoing colonial histories of labour as well as variety and openness in relations – that is, due to both the heteronomous impositions of colonial regimes and the autonomous agency of colonised, formerly colonised and postcolonial subjects – the Caribbean is a region of intense cultural intermixture, of complex and mutually informing ways of being human.[16]

In his 1981 *Caribbean Discourse*, Glissant criticises humanism but, to some extent following Césaire's 1950 *Discourse on Colonialism*, he does not necessarily jettison the concept. Instead, he underscores the need to transcend a Western, imposed humanism:

> We are aware of the fact that the changes of our present history are the unseen moments of a massive transformation in civilization, which is the passage from the all-encompassing world of cultural Sameness, effectively imposed by the West, to a pattern of fragmented Diversity, achieved in a no less creative way by the peoples who have today seized their rightful place in the world. The tug of Sameness, which is neither uniformity nor sterility, interrupts the efforts of the human spirit to transcend that universal humanism that incorporates all (national) particularities.[17]

Like Césaire in *Discourse*, Glissant here acknowledges and criticises how a pseudo-universal humanism can function to deny cultural ('national') particularities. He too describes resistance to such an imposition in terms of a 'dialectical process of opposition and transcendence'.[18] Against colonial hierarchies of personhood, the downtrodden need to *seize* their place creatively in the world. In other words, Glissant affirms Césaire's point – as well as Eric Williams's regarding the abolition of slavery in *Capitalism and Slavery* – that such a 'human' place is not *given* in humanitarian charity.[19]

In part to challenge an exclusionary European humanism, in *Caribbean Discourse* Glissant also articulates the concept of Relation, itself built on a right to opacity.[20] In doing so, he does not abandon the ideal of humanity, even if one of its predominant articulations comes out of the context of the French Revolution, whose ostensible universalism was quickly proven provincially circumscribed by race when Haitians lived it out.[21] Glissant writes:

To develop everywhere, in defiance of a universalizing and reductive humanism, the theory of specifically opaque structures. In the world of Relation, which takes over from the homogeneity of the single culture, to accept this opacity – that is, the irreducible density of the other – is to truly accomplish, through diversity, a human objective. Humanity is perhaps not the 'image of man' but today the evergrowing network of recognized opaque structures.[22]

Humanity is in the plural for Glissant, even when he employs the term in the singular. It is changing through exchanges, constantly in process ('evergrowing'). If it has a *telos* – and for Glissant, it probably does not, because such a *telos* as a final cause could pre-determine its trajectory – the *telos* would lie in further exchanges.[23] If Glissant's sense of humanity is not per se teleological, then, it might still be an end or a goal, as his language of accomplishment and objective suggests.[24] In other words, for Glissant such a plural sense of humanity still needs to be lived out; it remains to be 'performed', we might say with Wynter in mind.[25]

One of the reasons we can argue that there is, in the spirit of Césaire and Fanon, a decolonial politics in Glissant's re-construction of humanity, is that he explicitly ties the concept to memory and land. He writes:

This practice of cultural creolization [*métissage*] is not part of some vague humanism, which makes it permissible for us to become one with the next person. It establishes a Relation, in an egalitarian and unprecedented way, between histories that we know today in the Caribbean are interrelated. The civilization of cassava, sweet potato, pepper, and tobacco points to the future of this Relation; this is why it struggles to repossess the memory of its fragmented past [*reconquérir la mémoire de ses histoires raturées*].[26]

The above connection between memory and land, culture and cultivation, follows Glissant's claim, which he will echo in *Treatise of the All-World*, that multilingualism is not quantitative so much as it is an orientation and a politics. Humanity in Glissant, as I am beginning to read it here, is similar: it is a cultural practice of forming relationships based on acknowledging histories that are already entangled in modern/colonial life.[27] The Relation Glissant invites us to practice in this passage is 'unprecedented' precisely because it would be 'egalitarian'. Modern/colonial life, including through its imposing, vague Humanism – what Wynter calls the over-represented 'Man' – is based on exploitation that leveraged an artificial hierarchy of our species through the concept of race. Glissant's humanism confronts this history to envision (through a process of fragmented recollection) cultural exchanges where human social life is characterised not by impositions or attempts to become (like) others so much as by sharing, growing and struggling with others. What this fragmented recollection looks like, and how it should proceed, remains ambiguous. Perhaps its reconquest or re-overcoming lies in seeing what the art theorist and curator Ariella Azoulay has recently called the 'potential history' that parts of the past disclose.[28] Perhaps it lies in modifying or toppling colonial conquests of public memory, as when Martinicans behead the statue of the Empress Joséphine in Fort-de-France or when student activists throw buckets of filth on the statue of Cecil Rhodes in Cape Town.

If Glissant's affirmation of Relation sounds too lofty, too Pollyanna, too much like ethical platitudes removed from political economy, we only have to recall that the cultivation of tobacco and sugar in the Caribbean (or wild rice on Anishinaabe land in Minnesota from where I drafted this chapter), proceeded through forced labour and remains largely controlled by US and European capital (in the case of tobacco and sugar today) or remains threatened by the construction and spills of oil pipelines (in the case of wild rice today). To start from agriculture is one of Glissant's ways of speaking to material conditions and historical inheritances of social life in our still-colonial present.[29] Further, in that early text he advances several clearly decolonial arguments with respect to land. For instance, regarding Palestine in his opening chapter on dispossession, he writes, '[T]he return of the Palestinians to their country is not a strategic maneuver; it is an immediate struggle [*un combat immédiat*]. Expulsion and return are totally contemporary. This is not a compensatory impulse but a vital urgency.'[30]

* * *

In his 1990 *Poetics of Relation*, Glissant once again criticises an imposed and standardising humanism, what he calls there 'a lukewarm humanism, both colorless and reassuring'.[31] In this 'colorless' we can hear what we might now call a post-racial humanism, a humanism that avoids questions of race, that avoids history. It is 'reassuring' because it offers (for some) 'the correct version of humanism', with this 'correct' gaining official sanction from a European source, such as those who have appointed themselves guardians of the French language, Glissant's example here.[32]

Glissant goes on to criticise the language of a singular, correct or official humanity, avoiding an appeal to 'a universal model, a sort of archetype of humanity'.[33] Once again he is concerned with a narrative that flattens cultural particularities; he calls such a metanarrative 'the History of Humanity', using capitalisation to highlight the importance such a narrative arrogates to itself. One example of such a narrative is the Christian division of time into before and after Christ. Glissant explains that when he invokes Relation, he has in mind modes of life that developed in American Plantations – 'within this universe of domination and oppression, of silent or professed dehumanization', he writes, 'forms of humanity stubbornly persisted'.[34] He is clear that our clock time remains conditioned by structures the Plantation inaugurated, but he also sees more possibility amidst the cultural exchange of the present. If he is against a vague humanism, he nevertheless holds on to what he calls an 'overly vague idea: that Relation diversifies forms of humanity according to infinite strings of models infinitely brought into contact and relayed'.[35] The shift he has in mind is one that would pluralise; it would be a movement 'referring not to Humanity but to the exultant divergence of humanities'.[36]

But it needs to be said that if Glissant maintains the idea of humanity and especially of humanities in *Poetics*, he also remains largely critical of humanism in that book, or at least of what he calls, with the history of Martinique in mind, a 'cooperative humanism'.[37] The specific target of his criticism here is, as it is so often, the elite in Martinique, and in particular their willing assimilation into French values, a practice Glissant describes as 'a masked colonization'.[38] This process is ongoing. 'Wouldn't it be best just to go along with it?' he asks rhetorically – that is, 'Wouldn't it be a viable solution to embellish the alienation, to endure while comfortably receiving state assistance, with all the obvious guarantees implied in such a decision?'[39] It is in this context of assimilation that he locates humanism as a conceptual justification for 'going along with it', which he sees as a way of re-installing colonial forms of life. The problem is that such an assimilation means a certain positioning for Martinicans and so many others, namely, 'having to consume the world without participating in it, without even the least idea of it, without being able to offer it anything other than a vague homily to a generalizing universal'.[40] As in *Caribbean Discourse*, Glissant's worry remains that Martinique does not produce what it, and the Caribbean it is a part of, needs to survive – or, put better, to thrive on its own terms with 'the right and the means' of self-determination. Colonially conditioned desire, here the desire to participate in an imposed and inherited form of what it means to be human – in terms of language, fashion, diet and transportation[41] – prevents a regional participation and leads to little more than repetitive, passive consumption. Perhaps it is with this analysis in mind that, by his 1993 *Tout-monde*, he condemns 'the great churn of humanism' as a practice of affirmation that does not risk something itself.[42]

* * *

It is in his 1997 *Treatise of the All-World* that Glissant poses the questions that serve as the guiding questions for this book: 'Are we reduced to these impossible choices? Do we have the right and the means to live another dimension of humanity? But how?'[43] On the previous page, he qualified what I am reading as an invitational 'we' here to something more localised: 'When we – I mean the Antilleans – rush into these traces of our under-valued histories, it is not in order to quickly outline a model of humanity that we would then oppose, in a ready-made fashion, to those other models that are forcibly imposed on us.'[44] For Glissant, a new 'model' is still too constraining; he is after something more hesitant. If in *Poetics* it is opacity and the right to opacity that link actors to Relation, in *Treatise* it is the concept of the trace.[45] Trace here is not just retrospective, marking a fragmented history or a history in ruins (as opposed to the clarity of an 'outlined' history). It is also prospective, suggesting a way or a path – we can hear 'trace' as 'track' in *Treatise*, as well as suggesting the action or process of carving a path.[46] 'Trace' is also a concept that Glissant cites to bring back an element of universality into the first-person plural. '[T]he thought of the *trace*, as opposed to systematic thought, acts as a wandering that guides us', Glissant continues. 'We know that the trace is what puts us, all of us, wherever we come from, in Relation.'[47]

But a few pages later he leaves us again with an ambiguous relation to humanism. His concern with a claim to a stable identity – Négritude included – comes up once again here:

> In a world where so many communities find themselves mortally denied the right to any identity, it is paradoxical to propose the imagination of an identity-relation, an identity-rhizome. I believe however that this is indeed one of the passions of these oppressed communities, to believe in this moving beyond identity and to carry it along with their sufferings. No need to bleat about a humanist vocation to understand this, quite simply.[48]

We are left wondering: What is this 'moving beyond identity' that also moves beyond, or simply does not perform, a claim to humanism?

And yet, Glissant returns (again and again) to the idea of the human. He presses against the loss, for everyone, that standardised forms of life cause, imposed through colonialism and capitalism, which come together in what is today called 'globalisation'. The loss is for everyone. It is felt on the level of our species: 'For with every language that disappears a part of the human imaginary is lost forever: a part of the forest, of the savannah or the crazy sidewalk. The taste of tin plates, the flavour of food. The price of hunger.'[49] What are the modes of 'the human' in this imaginary that Glissant wants to maintain? We know that it is not the Christian model that Europeans carried with them to assert on cultures. He explains that 'medieval faith remains the detour whereby these cultures through massacres and violent deaths, tried to bring about the progress, or simply the salvation, of the individual, so that he could accede to the dignity of the human person'.[50] Even if challenging this model and sense of linear time, as he also argued in *Poetics*, has fallen 'to diversifying thoughts, mad poets and heretical relativists', it is necessary to challenge an imposed dimension of humanity on the grounds of defending particularity, such as languages, *for the sake of the whole world*.[51] The modes of human life Glissant endorses are necessarily abstract and ambiguous, not only because he wants to leave room for unexpected outcomes instead of falling into the trap of repeating a prescriptive model, but also because he insists that human life can be otherwise, that we can live out a Relation more beautiful and imaginative, and he wants to leave room for that creation to occur not in a book, which would itself become a kind of mythical text, but in the lived relations themselves. Leaving room for the unexpected is not just what happens in the creolisation of languages, for Glissant, but it is also a methodological principle in his work. It is seen for instance when he writes, 'To study contacts between cultures means one has already decided that there is no lesson to be learnt from them, since the nature of such contacts is to be fluid and unexpected.'[52] Once again, if there is a goal here, it is more exchange on egalitarian terms – Césaire's attention to power relations in false or genuine 'contacts' among cultures in *Discourse* returns to our minds here. As Glissant puts it, 'That the being is relation, and it goes everywhere.'[53] 'That human cultures exchange while living on, change without losing themselves: that this becomes possible.'[54]

Importantly, by his 1997 *Treatise of the All-World*, for Glissant there is not just a sense of being human but also a humanism that he praises. It emerges when he discusses the work of the sociologist and ethnographer Jacques Berque, particularly his scholarship on Islam.[55] Berque, Glissant writes, 'saw in Islam its rationality but also its mystique. What does this mean, if not that he believed that every conceptualization has its corresponding poetics.'[56] Berque taught about 'the often conflictual but always enriching encounter of orality and writing, in . . .

the Arabic language for example, but also in the context of modernity' – and he taught us about this encounter 'without any manifesto, with rectitude and clarity'.[57] Glissant goes on:

> This clarity, in the structure of his thought and also in its expression, is close to what we could call a humanism. A clarity that is forever questioning. That of the pioneer, who clears the ground, or the ploughman. It is therefore also accompanied by an appeal to that which is blurred, to mystery, and by an anxious attention to whatever is weaving itself in the underside of the real, by an approach to the incomprehensible, the ineffable. Which does not detract from its clarity.[58]

Glissant's poetic method comes to the fore in this description of Berque's humanism: an attention to what is mysterious, to what is weaving itself, which we know from *Poetics* includes languages, peoples and places as they become increasingly creolised. Perhaps in 'forever questioning' Glissant has in mind the final lines of Fanon's *Black Skin, White Masks*, and perhaps we could say that in praising a humanism that is 'blurred' Glissant brings to mind Fred Moten's recent discussion of blackness, which drew on Glissant from its title onward.[59] In any case, we gain here a qualified humanism, something close to a humanism, something both clear and blurred, something questioning yet clear – and something Glissant endorses.

In sum, in reading 'humanity' and 'the human' across three of Glissant's more theoretical texts, I have tried to paint a picture of an ambivalent humanism in Glissant. We might also call this a poetic humanism, a negative humanism (à la negative theology), or, in keeping with Deleuze and Guattari, a 'minor humanism'. We are left wondering about whether this (like Césaire's and Fanon's) is a decolonial humanism, and moreover we are left wondering about whether we can fairly say of Glissant's humanism that he brings together poetics and politics.

Returning to the Ancestors

It is not just that Glissant leaves us with a humanism that focuses on what remains unanticipated, such that we have to find a way to live it out – though of course we do. It is also that he asserts a clarity. As he says of Berque: 'He has always conceived of the approach to the Other *in* a vision of solidarity with the world.'[60] Here, as he follows Berque, Glissant comes close to directly situating his ethics (how to approach, engage and learn from others) in a politics (solidarity and standing with).[61] Like Du Bois – and in a point to which I will return in my conclusion – here Glissant offers an ethics of responsibility that is, and must be, situated in a politics, in 'a vision of solidarity'.

To start ethics from within politics in this way leads to more than just the critiques and affirmations he makes late in *Treatise*: critiques of consumption, of tourism, of shortsighted political plans, of assimilations to the standards of Europe, and even of a reliance on cars; and affirmations of taking time to read slowly, of thinking of and using time differently from how advertisements suggest, and of acknowledging and seeking out entanglement with the whole world.[62] In regard to this final point, he writes, 'To speak of one's surroundings, one's country: to speak of the Other, of the world.'[63] In addition to these practical points, Glissant's vision is also normative: he teaches us to understand that amidst the uneven entanglements of the world, we live in 'common modernities' as well as a modernity that continually begins anew;[64] that amidst the speed of modernity we are faced with a deficit, that speed itself is a kind of lack; and that '[i]n our increasingly accelerated dealings with the diversity of the world, we need pauses, times for meditation, where we step aside from the flood of information that is provided for us so that we can start putting some order into our accidental encounters'.[65] Finally, he teaches us that amidst the market logic we all inhabit, we need new aesthetic standards, what he calls 'a new kind of beauty in the world and a new health for contemporary human communities'.[66] But it is not with critiques or affirmations of an explicitly practical kind that Glissant concludes *Treatise*.

Perhaps surprisingly given his disagreements with Négritude, which he said in *Poetics* can come with an 'essentialist coloration',[67] Glissant concludes *Treatise* with a regionally focused yet outward-facing return to his African ancestors:

We fight the oppressions in our own place, we also open onto the neighbouring islands, and onto all lands. This does not mean leaving our ancestors, either known or unknown. Those who sank to the bottom of the Immense Waters during transportation [*pendant la Traite*], those who smothered the fruit of Plantations, who marooned in the hills. We must bring them with us as we enter into the renewal of all things. Give a meaning to what they were, which it is so difficult for us to imagine. Look in the face of those desperate times that haunt us. Is it necessary to summon up these times? Yes, to open them up. And not to fall back on the old definitions . . . Every archipelagic thought is a thought of trembling, of non-presumption, but also of openness and sharing.[68]

For those Glissant is addressing, how do they bring with them known and unknown ancestors? What does it mean to open up a haunting past? What does it mean not just to summon but also to open desperate times? What are the 'old definitions' Glissant wants to move past? (How could 'humanism' gain a new definition? How could it be re-enchanted?)[69] Considering these lines allows us to bring Glissant's humanism into further relief.

* * *

What can we say, if it is still not yet clear that Glissant, following Césaire and Fanon, is even a humanist? Despite Glissant's critique of humanism, I suggest we can say that Glissant maintains a humanism for two reasons. The first is that, by employing the terms 'humanity', 'humanities' and 'human communities', as Glissant does so frequently in *Treatise*, he insists on thinking our species together. I am reading Glissant here in a way similar to how Paul Gilroy takes him up in *Against Race*: to insist on a 'planetary humanism', what we might call a *tout-monde* humanism, is to think along the contours race has outlined but also to offer an exercise in thinking beyond them; such a humanism starts from the landscape, the realities of the people, but it also refuses to adopt the old definition of race, the constructed colonial vocabulary that, often very effectively, tries to naturalise its structure of labour and landholding.[70] Glissant's focus on openness, sharing and Relation speaks, as Gilroy reads him, to 'a concern with what has been relayed together with a critical interest in relative and comparative approaches to history and culture and attention to what has been related in both senses of that word: kinship and narration'.[71] Could there also be a way, paradoxically, that Glissant's focus on African ancestors is not simply an example of the kind of assertions of identity that Gilroy worries about, but instead or also is a particular mode of reckoning with history? And in offering that mode, could Glissant be envisioning a future (one where a wider sense of kinship is narrated into being) as well as reconstructing a history? We could read Glissant here as – to reiterate this point – Rinaldo Walcott offers his recent project in Black Studies: 'This is not an exceptionalist argument on behalf of Black people', Walcott says, 'but an accounting of the ways that Black people's dispossession and its possible rectification would require global reordering, rethinking, and remaking; such an accounting would mean a reorientation of the planet and all modes of being human on it.'[72]

The second reason I suggest we can talk about Glissant's humanism is that, as we have seen throughout his work, he brings together ethical, political and aesthetic modes of our species. Importantly, he situates those modes within a larger ecological context. In doing so, Glissant's humanism places us in something much larger than ourselves – it is thus a humanism for 'strange uses', in Deleuze's terms, a humanism that, like a poem, in remaining incomplete figures beyond itself.

* * *

In his section on Martinique towards the end of *Treatise*, Glissant makes a point that I want to contemplate in closing this chapter in the spirit of his appeal to the open and to the world entire. He writes:

Let's run this risk. Our responsibility in this matter is collective, and our action should be so too. We must make our place immeasurable, that is, link it up with the Immeasurability of the world. Let's also look at its beauty. My hope lies in this voice of the landscapes [*J'espère en cette parole des paysages*].[73]

And in the overture to the last 'theoretical' text he would write, *Philosophie de la Relation*, Glissant went on to link a poetics back to land and human life, saying of a kind of primordial poem of the world, 'It was before all humanity [*C'était avant toute humanité*].'[74] By situating human life within landscape, Glissant, especially in his late work, again refuses to fall back on the 'old definitions'. Glissant's 'poetics of landscape', the geographer Katherine McKittrick explains, 'creates a way to enter into, and challenge, traditional geographic formulations without the familiar tools of maps, charts, official records, and figures'; it is through 'a poetic-politics', McKittrick continues, that Glissant 'conceptualizes his surroundings as "uncharted," and inextricably connected to his selfhood and a local community history'.[75]

Yet at the end we still must ask: What have we gained over-all from this 'detour through theory', to borrow Hall's phrase?[76] I suggest that from Glissant we gain not a Promethean human-ism, where humans defy the gods through exemplary actions, nor a Protagorean humanism, where man is the measure of all things, nor a Marxist humanism, where our species is defined by labour. If, unlike Césaire, Glissant does not find a 'political programme' to be 'suitable or convincing',[77] his minor, critical, negative humanism nevertheless remains close to Césaire's call for a 'true humanism', one finally made to the measure of the world, what Glissant calls the *tout-monde*. But – and this is deci-sive – for Glissant humans are a small part of that *tout-monde*, a part relative to an expanse and situated in a place.[78] It is per-haps for these reasons that Glissant's humanism cannot speak to (or runs into its limits in addressing) class struggle, Indig-enous rights, gender politics and how to structure a society on the level of policy. Thinking on these levels is not the strength of his theory, of how he 'degrades' Césaire's humanism, to bor-row from Said's sense of how theory travels.[79] Still, Glissant's humanism carries with it, if not exactly a politics, then some-thing of an ethics.

The ethics of Glissant's humanism is an ethics of response, of responding to a cry, which is how he describes *Treatise* as a whole:

This is a cry, quite simply a cry. Of a realizable Utopia. If the cry is taken up by some or by all, it becomes speech. A common song. The cry and speech work together to lift up the possibilities, and also what we have always believed to be the impossibilities, of our countries.[80]

Glissant's words portray an ethics of responsibility based on a certain kind of music. He underscores the need to hear the cries of the downtrodden and to make those cries speech, to turn them into public demands and uplifting claims. And he says these public claims are not so much stated as sung.

But the other cry Glissant's humanism asks us to hear is that of the land, which he understands as having a voice. And it is for this reason that I think Glissant is exemplary in offering what the cultural theorist Alexander Weheliye calls a 'speculative blueprint for new forms of humanity'.[81] It is for this reason that I think Glissant makes a real contribution to those of us thinking with 'the human' and 'humanity'. He allows (perhaps *invites*) us to remember that our more specific ethical projects are always situated in something larger, not just in solidarity but also in landscape. Thus, Glissant's *hesitant* humanism resonates with the spirit of recent prayer camps that have located themselves within a larger pursuit of right relations to land, where resistance to a pipeline is part of a way of honouring water as sacred. And so if Glissant asks us to situate any narrow sense of response ethics within a solidarity, he also asks us to situate our politics within, or relative to, a larger way of understanding the place of our species in an unfolding world. He offers not a counter-humanity but an open humanity, a vision of our species that, like Wifredo Lam's paintings, listens to land – cassava, sweet potato, pepper, tobacco. This is a humanism not just for but also *of* the future, in that humans have yet to live out this 'right and means'. But it might be better to specify that humanity *in general* or *as a whole* or *within and across societies* has yet to live out this 'right and means', because such a specification would allow us to acknowledge that many people at many times have lived out not so much this 'new' as this 'other' dimension of humanity. For is it not the arrogance of modernity to see only future 'progress' as promising, thus rejecting the beauty and the example of what our ancestors have passed down and performed as examples? And doesn't such a valuation of the future also miss the present, a key site of Glissant's poetics, what I am calling his humanism, a humanism that will certainly not emerge from a single event like a mystical experience or revelation, nor one that is thoroughly secular. For Glissant's, following Césaire's, is a humanism that will come into full relief through *genuine, true* contacts among cultures that are already underway, including contacts among peoples and traditions that have been influenced by different mystical experiences and revelations. And so ultimately, of all the ways I have described Glissant's humanism – ambiguous, poetic, decolonial, negative and strange – his is a *relational* humanism, a humanism that places us as responsive to not just one another but also to the past, to land and to water, and as relative to and reliant on that land and water, which in the floods and the earthquakes and the fires as much as in the winds and the waves and the rain, cries out to us now.

Notes

1. For Césaire's humanism, see Aimé Césaire, *Discours sur le colonialisme* (Paris: Éditions Présence Africaine, 1955), p. 54; *Discourse on Colonialism* (New York: Monthly Review Press, 2001), p. 73. For Fanon's humanism, see Frantz Fanon, *Les damnés de la terre* (Paris: Éditions La Découverte, [1961] 2002), p. 305; *The Wretched of the Earth* (New York: Grove Press, 1963), pp. 254–5. One important reader of Glissant as a humanist is Sylvia Wynter. See Sylvia Wynter, 'Beyond the Word of Man: Glissant and the New Discourse of the Antilles', *World Literature Today* 63, no. 4 (1989): pp. 637–48. I will return to some of Wynter's readings of Glissant in the following chapter.

2. See Celia M. Britton, *Edouard Glissant and Postcolonial Theory: Strategies of Language and Resistance* (Charlottesville, University of Virginia Press, 1999), p. 5. See also 'Édouard Glissant's Tout-Monde', https://www.gc.cuny.edu/Page-Elements/Academics-Research-Centers-Initiatives/Centers-and-Institutes/Center-for-the-Humanities/Events/Open-to-the-Public/2018/Edouard-Glissant-s-Tout-Monde-Transnational-Perspectives.

3. Édouard Glissant, *L'imaginaire des langues* (Paris: Gallimard, 2010), pp. 84–5. Translation mine.

4. In *Poetics of Relation*, Glissant criticises a hierarchical concept of 'Humanity [*l'Humanité*]' and affirms instead other 'humanities [*humanités*]' woven together by relayed (hi)stories [*histoires*]. His concern with the singular, capitalised 'Humanity' is that such an ideal covers over the myriad ways humans live their lives. His favouring the plural 'humanities' can be read as affirming non-ideal, ordinary and contradictory practices that make up human life across the world. See Édouard Glissant, *Poétique de la Relation* (Paris: Gallimard, 1990), p. 45; *Poetics of Relation*, trans. Betsy Wing (Ann Arbor: University of Michigan Press, 1997), pp. 32–3. Henceforth PR/PO.

5. See Gilles Deleuze and Félix Guattari, *Kafka: Toward a Minor Literature*, trans. Dana Polan (Minneapolis: University of Minnesota Press, 1986), especially Chapter 3, 'What is a Minor Literature?' Edward Said commented in an interview, 'I think that the concept, that Delueze and Guattari mobilize in the whole business of minor literature, turns out to be a description of a much larger and more influential phenomenon than they suspected . . . we have to change the landscape from a discussion of dominant to peripheral literatures. A series of assembled peripherals is really what we have, peripherals that work in an elaboration that is simply unceasing. I think what we have is a new perspective, and we're able to see all literatures working in that way instead of major versus minor, which is the theory. You understand, I don't think that the dichotomy is really operable' (Cindi Katz and Neil Smith, 'An interview with Edward Said', *Environmental and Planning D: Society and Space* 21 (2003): pp. 647–8).

6. For the idea that Glissant's 'problem-space' could be Martinique even (and especially) when writing from France and the US, see the concept that David Scott first outlined in *Refashioning Futures: Criticism after Postcoloniality* (Princeton, NJ: Princeton University Press, 1999).

7. Deleuze and Guattari, *Kafka*, p. 17.

8. Edward Said, *Humanism and Democratic Criticism* (New York: Columbia University Press, 2004), p. 11. See also pp. 3–4, 22, 43, 61 and 73.

9. Édouard Glissant, *Philosophie de la Relation* (Paris: Gallimard, 2009), p. 132. Translation mine. Henceforth PhR. Paget Henry describes these two modes as the historicist and poeticist modes of Caribbean philosophy. While he locates Glissant more in the latter, Henry also stresses that the Caribbean intellectual tradition features a combination of both modes. See Paget Henry, *Caliban's Reason: Introducing Afro-Caribbean Philosophy* (New York: Routledge, 2000).

10. See Édouard Glissant, *Le discours antillais* (Paris: Gallimard, 1997), p. 441; *Caribbean Discourse*, trans. J. Michael Dash (Charlottesville: University of Virginia Press, 1991), p. 148. Henceforth DA/CD.

11. See Gilles Deleuze and Félix Guattari, *What Is Philosophy?*, trans. Hugh Tomlinson and Graham Burchell (New York: Columbia University Press, 1994), p. 5.

12. 'Trees that live a long time exude mystery and magic . . . we don't see trees until we have situated them in their history, until they have spoken to us in our language . . . In this country, Martinique, the ones telling the story pass it on to those who look for it without knowing who they will be. At the edge of the world this is how we move forward' (Édouard Glissant, *Mahogany*, trans. Betsy Wing (Lincoln: University of Nebraska Press, [1997] 2020), pp. 3, 5).

13. He writes, for instance, that he has 'auscultated the hot spots' of the world (PR 225/PO 209).

14. Peter Hallward and Nick Nesbitt have argued that Glissant's work becomes increasingly de-politicised after *Caribbean Discourse* (see Peter Hallward, *Absolutely Postcolonial: Writing between the singular and the specific* (Manchester: Manchester University Press, 2002), p. 105; Nick Nesbitt, *Voicing Memory: History and Subjectivity in French Caribbean Literature* (Charlottesville: University of Virginia Press, 2003), p. 184). In slight contrast, Celia Britton argues that Glissant's late emphasis on sustainability and on cultures instead of nations does not necessarily preclude political action

(Celia M. Britton, 'Globalization and Political Action in the Work of Edouard Glissant', *Small Axe* 13, no. 3 (2009): p. 11). Valérie Loichot contends that 'Glissant resists the easy temptation of turning ecology into an ideological, if not mystical, claim to the territory' (Valérie Loichot, 'Between Breadfruit and Masala: Food Politics in Glissant's Martinique', *Callaloo* 30 no. 1 (2007): p. 129). Yet, for Loichot, there is in Glissant, especially by *Philosophie de la Relation*, a 'relational ecological sacred', what Glissant calls 'another sacred' (see Valérie Loichot, *Water Graves: The Art of the Unritual in the Greater Caribbean* (Charlottesville: University of Virginia Press, 2020), p. 50; see also PhR 148). Loichot sums up her reading of Glissant's political trajectory this way: 'While I agree with Peter Hallward and Nick Nesbitt that the anticolonial ideology of an early Glissant is gone in his late work, I contend that the object of his politics has shifted. Glissant's late work takes not an apolitical turn, but rather a new political turn, an ecopoetic turn, a sacred-political turn, which becomes more and more concerned with what numerous biologists, chemists, geographers, environmentalists, economists, and cultural critics . . . have identified and theorized as the Anthropocene, an age in which the presence of human animals on earth has had enough of an impact to constitute a geological-scale epoch' (Loichot, *Water Graves*, p. 61). In reading Glissant as a poet who places a humanism within larger ecological contexts, I am to some extent following Loichot's insight that Glissant takes an 'ecopoetic turn, a sacred-political turn'. That said, I do not want to conflate Glissant's invocations of the sacred or the ecological as political per se. I prefer to describe Glissant's humanism as ultimately helpful for questions of ethics, that is, questions of how to relate to one another and to the world around us, as opposed to helpful for mobilising around shared issues and making demands as a project of building power. That we maintain these distinctions is important lest everything become 'political'.

15. PR 46/PO 33.
16. Alexander Weheliye writes, 'I construe race, racialization, and racial identities as ongoing sets of political relations that require,

through constant perpetuation via institutions, discourses, practices, desires, infrastructures, languages, technologies, sciences, economies, dreams, and cultural artifacts, the barring of non-white subjects from the category of the human as it is performed in the modern west' (Alexander Weheliye, *Habeas Viscus: Racializing Assemblages, Biopolitics, and Black Feminist Theories of the Human* (Durham, NC: Duke University Press, 2014), p. 3). He goes on, 'If racialization is understood not as a biological or cultural descriptor but as a conglomerate of sociopolitical relations that discipline humanity into full humans, not-quite-humans, and nonhumans, then blackness designates a changing system of unequal power structures that apportion and delimit which humans can lay claim to full human status and which humans cannot' (ibid.).

17. DA 326/CD 97.

18. Ibid.

19. See Eric Williams, *Capitalism and Slavery* (New York: Penguin, 2022).

20. For my first reading of 'the right to opacity' in Glissant, see Benjamin P. Davis, 'The Politics of Édouard Glissant's Right to Opacity', *The CLR James Journal: The Journal of the Caribbean Philosophical Association* 25, no. 1 (2019): pp. 59-70. For an elaboration, see my first chapter in Benjamin P. Davis, *Choose Your Bearing: Édouard Glissant, Human Rights, and Decolonial Ethics* (Edinburgh: Edinburgh University Press, 2023).

21. DA 328–9/CD 99.

22. DA 418/CD 133. Translation modified.

23. In a recent book, Samantha Noël describes Glissant's view of exchanges/relations in terms that suggest they are essential to our species: 'As Édouard Glissant explains, the human spirit yearns for a cross-cultural relationship without universalist transcendence, and diversity requires the presence of people with the intention of creating a new relationship' (Noël, *Tropical Aesthetics of Black Modernism* (Durham, NC: Duke University Press), p. 51).

24. Glissant would later stress the connection between imagination and practice in a memorable line from *Traité*: 'What Relation gives us to imagine, creolization has given us to live out'

(Édouard Glissant, *Traité du Tout-Monde* (Paris: Gallimard, 1997), p. 25; *Treatise on the Whole-World*, trans. Celia Britton (Liverpool: Liverpool University Press, 2020), p. 14), translation modified. Henceforth TTM/TWW.

25. Cf. Sylvia Wynter and Katherine McKittrick, 'Unparalleled Catastrophe for Our Species?: Or, to Give Humanness a Different Future: Conversations', in *Sylvia Wynter: On Being Human as Praxis*, ed. Katherine McKittrick (Durham, NC: Duke University Press, 2015), p. 33.

26. DA 794/CD 249. Translation modified.

27. For Glissant 'histories', which he endorses (in the lower case and plural), and which in the French more clearly include 'stories', are opposed to an official, singular, usually written, capital-H History.

28. See Ariella Azoulay, *Potential History: Unlearning Imperialism* (New York: Verso, 2019).

29. In an instructive summary of Glissant's relationship to Césaire's humanism in *Le discours antillais*, Natalie Melas writes, 'Glissant traces . . . pathologies across a large number of areas (labor, the family, language, history, space), arguing that the condition of assimilation under departmentalization is an unconscious and unacknowledged extension of the pathologies of slave society . . . The project of disalienation involves a turn away from the anticolonial critique of Eurocentrism and its prominent polarization of colonizer and colonized, and a turn inward to the excavation and reinvention of the specificity of localized resistance and cultural expression on the island. The writer's daunting ontological change is directed at the specificity of place . . . Such a practice requires what Glissant calls "the risk of enclosure," an attentiveness to the native land in its Antillean context that is very clearly set in opposition to negritude's assertion of Africanity and to the vast reaches of diasporic humanism in Césaire's *Notebook*' (Natalie Melas, *All the Difference in the World: Postcoloniality and the Ends of Comparison* (Stanford, CA: Stanford University Press, 2007), pp. 198–9). It is arguable that by the end of his life, Glissant was thinking more about diaspora.

For instance, in the 2009 film 'Edouard Glissant: One World in Relation', about five minutes in, Glissant stresses that Africa was the source of multiple diasporas: the first diaspora that gave birth to humanity, the diaspora imposed by slavery, and today's diaspora imposed by poverty.

30. DA 44/CD 16–17.
31. PR 125–6/PO 111.
32. PR 127/PO 113.
33. PR 36/ PO 24.
34. PR 79/PO 65.
35. PR 174/PO 160.
36. PR 204/PO 190. By 'exultant' perhaps Glissant means mutually informing praise for beauty and critique of domination. In *Treatise* Glissant repeats his line from *Caribbean Discourse* and *Poetics of Relation*: 'We believe in the future of small countries' (TTM 226–7/TWW 141). Even if the vision he presents in all of these books is wider than one based on the nation (evidenced after all in the titular ideas of *discours antillais*, *Relation*, and *tout-monde*), he does, for instance, write in defence of Martinique and Palestine in *Treatise*. Such a defence is related to, and perhaps even based on, what he calls 'a new kind of beauty in the world and a new health for contemporary human communities' (TTM 226–7/TWW 141).
37. PR 159/PO 145. Cf. Celia Britton, *Edouard Glissant and Postcolonial Theory*, pp. 19, 92.
38. PR 159/PO 144.
39. PR 159/PO 144–5.
40. PR 159-160/PO 145.
41. See his footnote in PR 159/PO 145.
42. Édouard Glissant, *Tout-monde* (Paris: Gallimard, 1993), p. 435.
43. TTM 21/TWW 11.
44. TTM 19–20/TWW 10.
45. Just as he echoed the right to opacity in *Poetics* from *Caribbean Discourse*, in *Treatise* he says, 'I claim for everyone the right to *opacity*, which is not the same as closing oneself off' (TTM 29/TWW 16).

46. Cf. PhR 36. I thank Valérie Loichot for helping me understand the multiple resonances of *la trace*.

47. TTM 18/TWW 9.

48. TTM 22/TWW 12.

49. TTM 85/TWW 52. Translation modified.

50. TTM 97/TWW 59.

51. TTM 105/TWW 64.

52. TTM 132/TWW 80.

53. TTM 178/TWW 110. Alexandre Leupin argues that Glissant is the only philosopher to make 'relation' the central and key concept to his work. See Alexandre Leupin, *Édouard Glissant, philosophe* (Paris: Hermann, 2016), p. 221.

54. TTM 178/TWW 110.

55. Said noted that Berque was 'in some minds the most audacious Western thinker about the Arabs' (Said, *The Politics of Dispossession*, p. 15). For more of Said's respect for Berque, see also ibid. p. 306.

56. TTM 184/TWW 113.

57. TTM 184/TWW 113.

58. TTM 184/TWW 113. Translation modified.

59. See Fred Moten, 'to consent not to be a single being', *Poetry Foundation*, 15 February 2010, https://www.poetryfoundation. org/harriet-books/2010/02/to-consent-not-to-be-a-single-being.

60. TTM 183/TWW 112.

61. Situating ethics in politics matters to larger decolonial debates because, to a considerable extent, the line of Latin American philosophy that is increasingly called decolonial philosophy maintains a Levinasian ethical vocabulary and impulse, which implies that ethics is the *arche* and the *telos* and politics is avoided so as not to diminish alterity/exteriority.

62. TTM 226–32/TWW 141–5.

63. TTM 252/TWW 156.

64. TTM 186/TWW 114.

65. TTM 172/TWW 105.

66. TTM 227/TWW 141.

67. PR 149/PO 135.

68. TTM 230–1/TWW 143.

69. David Scott, 'The Re-Enchantment of Humanism: An Interview with Sylvia Wynter', *Small Axe* 8 (2000): pp. 119–207.

70. Paul Gilroy, *Against Race: Imagining Political Culture beyond the Color Line* (Cambridge, MA: The Belknap Press of Harvard University Press, 2000), pp. 6–7.

71. Ibid. p. 6.

72. Ibid.

73. TTM 232/TWW 144.

74. PhR 11.

75. Katherine McKittrick, *Demonic Grounds: Black Women and the Cartographies of Struggle* (Minneapolis: University of Minnesota Press, 2006), p. xxii.

76. Stuart Hall, 'Through the Prism of an Intellectual Life', in *Essential Essays, Volume 2: Identity and Diaspora*, ed. David Morley (Durham, NC: Duke University Press, 2019), p. 310.

77. TTM 233/TWW 145.

78. For a discussion of 'the expanse' in Glissant, see Miguel Gualdrón Ramírez, 'Resistance and Expanse in *Nuestra América*: José Martí, with Édouard Glissant and Gloria Anzaldúa', *Diacritics* 46, no. 2 (2018): pp. 12–29.

79. Edward Said, 'Traveling Theory', in *The Selected Works of Edward Said: 1966–2006*, eds. Moustafa Bayoumi and Andrew Rubin (New York: Vintage), p. 204.

80. TTM 233/TWW 145.

81. Weheliye, *Habeas Viscus*, p. 14.

PART II: RISKING THE PERSONAL

3 Sylvia Wynter's Ceremonial Humanism

In the summer of 2022, I drove north for a few hours to join a gathering at the headwaters of the Mississippi River, in rural northern Minnesota. I grew up along the Mississippi in central Minnesota, and perhaps it was because of that connection, as much as any sense of political commitment or ethical responsibility, as much as any desire to participate in a social movement, that caused me to go that day, in response to a call put out by the organisation Honor the Earth.

About twenty of us ended up at the headwaters together, all part of overlapping groups that had protested the Line 3 pipeline, which then and now brings Alberta oil across northern Minnesota to Superior, Wisconsin – along the way crossing Anishinaabe lands held according to nineteenth-century treaties, crossing Lake Superior's watershed, and crossing under the Mississippi River. Importantly, we were at the headwaters *after* our efforts to stop the pipeline had failed. It was a pipeline that Minnesota Governor Tim Walz, a Democrat, supported, just as he supported and activated the National Guard to quell protests in the wake of the murder of George Floyd. In rural Minnesota, people both for and against the pipeline had hoped that Line 3 would *not* become another Standing Rock – the supporters meaning that it would be 'renovated' quickly and without event, the water protectors meaning that it could be stopped, and stopped without facing state violence. My thought along the river that morning was that it *certainly* wasn't Standing Rock – again, there were only about twenty of us there, and I didn't see anyone from the media. For a while we stood in a circle in silence. Then a few Anishinaabe men played the drums. Some of us exchanged names. And then we left.

Since that day, I have often reflected on what we were doing there, our efforts so futile and our gathering so fleeting. And I have largely been left at a loss, until I returned to Glissant's *Treatise of the All-World*, in which he describes 'opacity' – his term for cultural and personal difference and part of what he would demand in calling for the 'right to opacity' – in highly unusual terms. He says about opacity, 'Let it be a ceremony.'[1]

But as is his fashion, Glissant does not elaborate on what he means by opacity as a ceremony, even if in *Poetics* he had situated himself with great honesty, reflecting on the Old Testament and the *Odyssey*, as

wondering if we did not still need such founding works today, ones that would use a similar dialectics of rerouting, asserting, for example, political strength but, simultaneously, the rhizome of a multiple relationship with the Other and basing every community's reasons for existence on a modern form of the sacred, which would be, all in all, a Poetics of Relation.[2]

But today it sounds strange to talk about human rights – whose traditional field is the United Nations or the international courtroom – as a ceremony. If modernity has led to what the philosopher Charles Taylor calls 'a secular age', then how could we talk about 'a modern form of the sacred'?[3] Perhaps it makes more sense to talk about cultural difference as a ceremony, such as when we hear calls to 'celebrate difference'. Glissant means that, but he also means much more than that. So as usual with Glissant's key concepts, it is up to us to gain a sense of it together, and to live it out. For some help doing so, in this chapter I am going to think with Sylvia Wynter's two essays, more than a quarter century apart, on ceremony and humanism. Because the question of the secular is so important to Wynter in those pieces, I will then take a brief detour through Edward Said and Wael Hallaq's debate on secularism and religion as related to criticism and politics, and finally – reading through the lens of Wynter, Said and Hallaq – I will return to Glissant, ultimately trying to flesh out a little more about how an approach to difference and a claim to rights could also be a ceremony.

'The Human' in Wynter

I begin from what the Black Studies scholar Joshua Myers has called Wynter's 'Human Project', even if Myers and I have a different 'we' in mind when he writes, 'What Wynter is after and what we must be after is a Human Project that is an invitation to ourselves, that re-initiates us into what we were doing before we were so rudely interrupted by the present order of knowledge, the plantation regime that inaugurated the modern world-system'.[4] I draw upon how Xhercis Méndez and Yomaira C. Figueroa have read Wynter with a view towards 'the making of fully realized and complex human futures'.[5] This is a reading of what Zimitri Erasmus calls Wynter's 'theory of the human' as a counter-European humanism instead of a post-humanism.[6] This is a reading of Wynter's 'new humanism' as a 'politics of possibility'.[7]

In her 1984 article 'The Ceremony Must Be Found: After Humanism',[8] Sylvia Wynter criticises contemporary academic modes of knowledge. As we increase in our specialisation, she says, our knowledge of the world and our place in it recedes. Before she calls for a new approach to knowledge, she traces how we got to our current mode of self-understanding as a species. For her, two pivotal moments were Renaissance humanism and the emergence of liberalism as tied to capitalist economics. Wynter traces how the Christian medieval conception of knowledge argued 'that God had ordered the world according to certain principles, and the role of fallen man was to decipher these principles and abide by them, but not seek to question or have knowledge of things celestial which, unaided, his corrupted human knowledge could not encompass'.[9] Such a medieval conception was itself a kind of ceremony or ritual, using 'oppositional codes' to 'orient the parameters of . . . behaviors of the order'.[10] Renaissance humanists challenged this medieval conception not for anti-Christian reasons, but to return to the holy texts themselves. 'The category of the celestial', Wynter summarises, 'was being submitted to the activity of the *humanista*, bearers of the inferior mode of knowledge, a mode which had now begun to constitute itself as a new *ordo* or *studium*.'[11]

In offering a new order or form of study, which departed from the authority of the Catholic Church, the humanists committed a heresy, which Wynter wants to follow as the key precedent for what she calls in that essay 'an overall rewriting of knowledge, as the re-enacting of the original heresy of a *Studia*, reinvented as a science of human systems'.[12] She adds that this rewriting of knowledge will come from the 'New Studies'[13] of that moment, meaning Black Studies, ethnic studies and women's studies. The shift here is that the new heresy 'proposes the long processes of the self-making . . . as the proper sphere of the *humanitas*, now conceived as . . . the global human rather than with merely its Indo-European expression'.[14] It is a heresy not regarding a theological order or regarding a God, but regarding an over-represented form of being human. The new study is heretical in the sense that it departs from a Eurocentric (or any nationalistic) understanding of what it means to be human. On the philosopher Elisabeth Paquette's reading, 'the

New Studia is not established through ceremony', but rather 'the New Studia makes it so that ceremony can be found'.[15] Wynter goes on: '[T]he *studia* must be reinvented as a higher order of human knowledge, able to provide an "outer view" which takes the human rather than any one of its variants as a subject.'[16] This 'outer view' would allow us 'to attain the position of an external observer, at once inside/outside the figural domain of our order', that is, to the laws and behaviours that guide human life in the present.[17] The promise of this outer view is that it offers a new space for us to make ourselves again.

* * *

Following the acquittal of the policemen who beat Rodney King, Wynter returned to the question of the human on different terms, now through a May 1992 open letter to her colleagues at Stanford. With characteristic nuance, Wynter questions how not just a specific group of police officers, but also a white suburban jury and 'the juridical officers of Los Angeles' could unreflexively (or rather in that other, knee-jerk sort of reflexivity) adopt as if by nature the category of 'N.H.I.', meaning 'No Humans Involved', to describe cases in which young Black men had their rights denied.[18] She asks:

How did they [those working in the judicial system] come to conceive of what it means to be both *human* and *North American* in the *kinds of terms* (i.e. to be White, of Euroamerican culture and descent, middle-class, college-educated and suburban) within whose logic, the jobless and usually school drop-out/push-out category of young Black males can be *perceived*, and *therefore behaved towards*, only as the *Lack* of the human, Conceptual Other to being North American?[19]

This is a striking question for several reasons. First, it suggests that people understand what it means to be part of our species in specific terms, meaning that there is a not a universal sense of what it means to be human and suggesting a scepticism towards claims to our species. Second, these terms around 'the human' set up a 'logic', meaning that the governing terms lead to some conclusions being understood as true and false, valid and invalid. Third, this logic affects not just what we might call reason, but also what we perceive. And based upon these perceptions, we act in certain ways towards others. In this way, the conception of what it means to be human, the terms that guide what is an 'ideal' human in some place at a given time, affect how individuals understand humanity *as an ethical practice 'towards' others*. In response to this acknowledgement of the terms/logic/praxis of being human, how can we observe this 'classifying logic' that shuts some racialised/criminalised people out of the realm of moral obligation, such that we take on an 'outer view' regarding it? And what is the connection between *recognising* that this is an anti-Black, anti-poor logic and *practising* our humanity differently? Indeed, where might Wynter's observation – that this is indeed a logic 'clearly having genocidal effects with the incarceration and elimination of young Black males by ostensibly normal, and everyday *means*' – lead us if we sit with it, if we – those of us who need this corrective – allow such an observation to bear on us?[20]

Wynter's answer lies partly in how in the US – or at least among those who would write the acronym N.H.I. – there exists a group of people who 'mistakes the representation for the reality, the map for the territory' regarding what it means to be human.[21] This mistake is buttressed by an academic verification of status inferiority that teaches and socialises students into seeing racial and jobless others as inferior not just by culture but also by nature. To see through this element of our culture, we need first to recognise precisely the cultural (and not natural) element in status hierarchy in order to begin to see larger processes of knowledge production (logic, terms) at play. For Wynter, the status of the poor and jobless 'embodies a plight, which like that of the ongoing degradation of the planetary environment, is not even *posable*, not to say *resolvable*, within the conceptual framework of our present order of knowledge'.[22] She refers to the 'inner eyes' of the current predominant conceptual framework, a phrase that can be fruitfully read in contrast with the need for an 'outer view' that she stressed in the earlier article.[23]

Towards the end of 'No Humans Involved', Wynter returns to the 1984 essay, framing that essay in explicitly epistemological terms, with the role of New Studies to be 'that of rewriting knowledge' starting from the uprising-based knowledge that 'challenged the "Truth" of our present *episteme*'.[24] Having already stressed that this logic bears out in a granting or denial of *obligation*, Wynter then closes with an explicit move towards ethics: 'The eruption of the N.H.I./liminal category in South Central Los Angeles has again opened a horizon from which to spearhead the speech of a new frontier of knowledge able to move us toward a new, correlated human species, and eco-systemic, ethic.'[25] It is because of this line more than any other in this open letter that I maintain it is fair to read 'No Humans Involved' for a humanism and for one with an ethical dimension (of obligation and practice), even one that maintains a positive sense of thinking through humanity as a species. Wynter then expands on the language of the human and a sense of species being, emphasising our task

to understand the rules governing our human modes of perception and the behaviors to which they lead – as in the case of the *misrecognition of human kinship* expressed in the N.H.I. acronym, in the beating, and the verdict, as well as in the systematic condemnation of all the Rodney Kings, and of the global Poor and Jobless, to the futility and misery of the lives they live, as the price paid for *our* well-being. It is only by this mutation of knowledge that we shall be able to secure, as a species, the full dimensions of our human autonomy with the respect to the hitherto systemic and always narratively outside of our conscious awareness and consensual intentionality.[26]

Perhaps echoing Glissant, Wynter here returns to a responsible 'we' ('*our* well-being'), an ethics of obligation tied to living out 'the full dimensions' of our human lives. At the same time, and as Myers summarises, for the Black men criminalised and brutalised by the police, those who could be labelled 'N.H.I.' and 'thus not existing in the category of the protected', for them, 'the idea of Man was not metaphorical'.[27] And so it would also be fair – to think with another one of Myers's concepts – to note that Wynter's humanism, as much as Glissant's, still remains a *hesitant* one, one that takes time first 'to pause and to consider' before it moves forward with an unexamined concept.[28] Wynter nevertheless would return to humanism, in part because, as she also recognised in 'No Humans Involved', White/Black segregation served powerful social divisions until the civil rights movement in the same way as Noble/Peasant divisions served to verify domination until 'the intellectual revolution of humanism'.[29] In this analysis, she hints at the need for a combination of intellectual and activist practice – what she called, citing her predecessor in Afro-American Studies at Stanford, St. Clair Drake, the need for both 'street tasks' and 'intellectual tasks' – to re-signify the dimensions available to perform our humanity anew.[30] I read this move as part of how Wynter, as McKittrick argues reading a different essay, works towards 're-presenting the grounds from which we can imagine the world and more humanely workable geographies'.[31]

* * *

In a 2015 book chapter entitled 'The Ceremony Found', Wynter revisits her 1984 essay. In between her two writings on ceremony, Wynter had made several important contributions to the question of the human – contributions that both trouble and use the category given and despite considerations of race, labour and state violence – such as not just her open letter but also her interview with David Scott, published in 2000, entitled 'The Re-enchantment of Humanism', and the 2003 article 'Unsettling the Coloniality of Being'. In her 2015 chapter, she now contextualises the 1984 essay as 'written in the lingering afterglow of what had been the dazzling, if brief cognitively emancipatory hiatus that had emerged in the wake of the social uprisings of the 1950s and 1960s'.[32] The problem of Renaissance humanism, she says, was to institute what she calls '*Man(1)*', which created a division between Western humans understood as a political human, *homo politicus*, and 'all the other humans now classified and subordinated as the West's ostensible *irrational Human Others*'.[33] Thus, from the beginning of humanism, 'the human' was in fact not a universal category but a 'negation of our co-humanity as a species'.[34] Liberal humanists would make a similar division between what she calls '*Man(2)*', Western economic man, *homo oeconomicus*, and the racialised Other. In other words, both Renaissance and liberal humanisms offered a negation of humanity, presenting a sense of the human, yes, but also defining clearly what was 'not' human in terms of what was not Western, using the concept of 'race' to divide our species. As the philosopher Rafael Vizcaíno summarises:

[T]he secular humanist revolution maintained the symbolic space of the non-Christian, inherited from the previous theocentric order. Only now, the space became that of the racialized other in secular modernity, one that conceives the Black and the Indigenous as the 'others' upon which Man is able to achieve his newfound humanity . . . Secularization thus *concurrently* established the modern racial order while it de-centered medieval Christendom.[35]

Wynter's 1984 contribution, she says retrospectively, was to offer 'the *negation* of the above forms of co-human negation'.[36]

To be clear, Wynter celebrates the humanist accomplishments of Renaissance and liberal humanism as veritable gains, what she calls 'dazzling natural and techno-scientific achievements'.[37] She simply further draws our attention to the '*underside costs*'[38] of this 500-year process, a process that has in fact divided humanity, sometimes even in the name of it. These costs include the West's 'large-scale territorial expropriation and correlatedly unstoppable military conquests of the majority of the world's peoples, as well as their subsequent racialized reduction to "native" labor roles in a now globally incorporated world-systemic division of labor'.[39] She also includes in these costs the West's ongoing evangelisation, Christianisation and secularisation of the peoples it has conquered.[40] In another article written between the two ceremony essays, her 1989 article on Glissant, 'Beyond the Word of Man', Wynter stresses that Glissant's work can be read as an 'uprising' directed at the discourse of the 'Word of Man', meaning 'the tradition of discourse . . . Western Europe was to effect . . . in the secularization of human existence in the context of its own global expansion and to lay the basis of the plantation structure'.[41]

Indeed, the question of the secular becomes a focus of her second ceremony essay. The price paid for Western humanism – both Renaissance and liberal – she concludes, is the '*aporia* . . . *of the secular*', in which we have a 'humanly emancipatory process on the one hand' and a 'humanly subjugating processes on the other', with 'each nevertheless the lawlike condition of enacting of the other'.[42] With clear eyes, looking back on her earlier essay in 2015, Wynter says she left her own humanist heresy incomplete, because she did not offer 'a new secular', by which she means a new 'other' – an 'entirely new answer to the question of who-we-are over against our present globally hegemonic, (neo)Liberal . . . answer'.[43] Further, she says

the re-enactment of this heresy would have also required a corre-lated proposal with respect to a now *ecumenically human* order of knowledge – a *New Studia* – one able to come to grips with the ancil-lary question posed by the second part of the title of my 1984 essay . . . *after Humanism, what?*[44]

But she still thinks, as she asserted in 2003, that 'the struggle of our new millennium will be one . . . [around the] conception of the human'.[45] To speak to her question 'After Humanism, what?', she looks from the outside at the 'Western and west-ernized, middle and upper-class bourgeois *We*' and says that, from this outer view, one can see that there are steps we could take 'for the first time in our species' existence, now fully conscious agents in the autopoietic institution and reproduc-tion of a *new* kind of planetarily extended . . . community'.[46] These steps are on the way to becoming 'We-the-ecumeni-cally-Human', meaning the general or universal human as a species.[47] We become human differently through recognising a new 'order of consciousness', namely, a species-wide and planetary consciousness; our sense of ourselves shifts, and (I would argue) our obligations widen.[48]

If we are autopoietic, meaning we make ourselves, then how does that making happen? To speak to this question, Wynter looks to Judith Butler, extending their reading of the performance of gender to all genres of human life, including class, development, sexual orientation and race.[49] As Wynter acknowledged in a 2015 interview with McKittrick, 'Butler's illuminating redefinition of gender as a praxis rather than a noun . . . set off bells ringing everywhere!'[50] The method-ological or sociological task that follows is to see what Wynter calls 'the performative enactment of all our roles, of our role allocations as, in our contemporary Western/Westernized case, in terms of . . . race, class/underclass, and, across them all, sexual orientation'.[51] Hence Wynter's thesis that being human, in all its modes or roles, is praxis.[52]

In her reading of performance, Wynter's stresses that praxis is always ordered and oriented symbolically. Because – whatever we call ourselves – we are creatures who desire, desire can condition our symbolic orientation. To live under any dominant conception of the human means that for each of us, as Wynter says, 'she/he thereby reflexly and normally desires to realize her/himself in the lawlike terms of the discursively *positively marked* code of *symbolic life*' while avoiding what is negatively marked and considered deviant.[53] While she singles out 'academics/intellectuals' as functioning to replicate the Western world-system, her analysis applies to everyone.[54] This means that there will always be social costs to those who are marked, or who practise or live, on the 'negative' side of the lines of the ordering system – whether dressing 'poorly', eating with 'bad' manners, being born with a certain skin colour, or practising a faith tradition deemed 'primitive' or 'irrational' or 'cult-like'. And yet there are always also those who can stand outside of the lines and point them out for what they are, or those who simply see the lines/borders in the first place. In this regard Wynter names as examples the 'parallel conclusions' of Virginia Woolf and Carter G. Woodson regarding gender and race respectively in the early twentieth century.[55]

To recognise that up to this point in the history of humanism only a Western mode of being human has been 'overrepresented as if it were . . . humankind' is to relativise and de-naturalise how we live at present.[56] This relativisation rarely happens because most of us, including intellectuals, Wynter observes, tend to act like anthropologists who examine the rituals, morals and activities only *of other societies/faiths/cultures/ traditions without examining the stories we tell about ourselves*. Thus, we guard against the falling apart of our meaning- and role-making story that we are beings for economic growth and beings marked in hierarchical ways.[57] And thus, we have rendered our own agency opaque to ourselves.[58] All of us – Wynter insists all of us – remain encoded and incorporated in this system.[59]

* * *

The stakes of the over-representation of Western *Man* could not be higher. Wynter takes as her key example the 2007 Fourth Assessment Report of the Intergovernmental Panel on Climate Change (IPCC) as well as its 2014 Fifth Assessment Report. She criticises the reports for speaking about climate change in terms of generic 'human activities' without qualifying what mode of human is being performed. She is also worried about how the IPCC frames 'solutions' in economic terms.[60] She proposes instead that enacting the specific form of Western *Man* causes climate change, and thus she leaves room for what it means to be truly or generally or ecumenically human regarding the climate. She also warns against taking 'such an over-representation as an *empirical fact*', implying the need once again to recognise the social and cultural processes at play in determining how we are in the world.[61]

Her description leaves us with so many practical questions. What are we to do in the face of 'daily *sacrificing* of the interest of the referent "We" of our *species being*'?[62] Wynter says we need to overturn one answer to what it means to be human and to give another one.[63] She concludes with an insight from Vico: what we have made we can make again (differently).[64] About our agency, she writes that with the ceremony now found, with a *New Studia* of the world, 'we will now find that we humans no longer need the illusions of our hitherto story-telling, extra-human projection of that Agency'.[65] Here I wonder: Is this *New Studia* a sufficient response amidst many of our desires to join what she calls in a footnote in the second essay an 'ethno-class ensemble of behaviors' that people across the planet want to perform?[66] That is, is a new *studia* what is needed amidst IPCC reports about the rising waters and warming lands, reports that fail to change our desires away from that ethno-class behaviour – Starbucks, Marriott, Tesla, Calvin Klein and all?

Wynter keeps the faith in the importance of culture, or what she would come to call 'institution' and our capacity for 'auto-institution'.[67] She argues that '[e]mpire's most powerful apparatus is the education system. It initiates us into a culture and a knowledge system that instructs us to want to be of a specific ethnoclass of humanity'; indeed '[t]here is no order in the world that can exist or hold together, including an empire', she goes on, 'without a founding story', so 'the question for academia in the twenty-first century is, will you make space within it to be able to write a new foundation?'[68] If we grant this point and start to offer a response to this question that Wynter poses to the academy, then how would such a study work against what Wynter (reading Glissant) calls an imposed consumerism that is 'the reality of a colonization of the cultural Imaginary so successful at the level of the assimilation of the psyche'?[69] In other words, how could a new form of study help us check against our psychic need to be, identify as, and express ourselves through our consumption, particularly our aspirational ethno-class consumption? And again, how 'to write a new foundation', what Glissant called 'new founding works' for today? What would be a model or an example to follow?

* * *

As I read Wynter, I often find myself wishing she gave us more concrete examples of what she proposes, or that she spelled out more the practical implications of what she proposes. Is this new *studia* still to be found in the New Studies Departments she highlighted in the earlier essay? Or have these new studies become too theoretical, too abstracted away from ordinary life, too distanced from a real attention to material conditions and political economy, to speak productively to these questions, much less to draft new founding stories?[70] But if not there, then where? And what would be the curriculum of this new *studia*? If the Renaissance *studia humanitatis* – a term that the Italian humanists borrowed from Cicero in order to focus on rhetoric, poetry and philosophy, as well as Greek and Latin – was always understood as part of educating the elite, then how would Wynter's new *studia* attend to the underside of humanism that she wants to address? And what does this new performative enactment, this new mode of practising the human, look like, anyway? More specifically, what does it look like as we live our precarious lives, as we try to afford health care and make rent and teach histories and traditions being outlawed as I write this? The political theorist Neil Roberts comments that Wynter 'holds concerns that world civilization is stuck in the paradigm of various concepts of the *human* but has not come to grips with how to represent modes of producing the *human*'.[71] That is true – it's just that coming to grips with how to represent or produce the human still does not give us so much in terms of how to live out our new ceremonies, rituals and practices of study so needed today in the very real, non-abstract, non-glamorous circumstances in which we find ourselves. It is in search of these more concrete examples that I return to the very start of Wynter's 1984 essay, the two epigraphs that mention a specific kind of ceremony. Indeed, what was the original 'ceremony' Wynter was trying to find, anyway?

* * *

The first two epigraphs to her 1984 essay both use the word 'ceremony'; in both this term refers to interracial marriage. The first epigraph is from a John Peale Bishop poem about Othello, about Desdemona marrying Othello. The second comes from William Faulkner's *Absalom, Absalom* and is about Judith Sutpen marrying Charles Bon. I read these ceremonies as much more than just a metaphor or a figure in Wynter's essays. After all, when Wynter was writing the first essay, interracial marriage in the US had been legal across the country for fewer than twenty years. The US Supreme Court only ruled that anti-miscegenation laws were unconstitutional in *Loving v. Virginia* in 1967, in the wake of the same struggles that gave rise to the New Studies Departments that Wynter names. Further, it is so-called interracial marriages that arguably normalise human life across the subjugating lines that humanisms have both drawn and challenged. And it is from interracial marriages, or at least those relationships of varying kinds, that lead to so-called 'biracial' or 'mixed' children (I don't like these words), children who look back on our histories and more clearly see a plurality of ancestries. To look back at your history and see multiplicity is not insignificant for the question of the 'outer view' that Wynter is speaking to in these essays. As Stuart Hall has stressed in many places, it is this perspective, the perspective of more and more of us in a world becoming increasingly diasporic, that never feels fully at home in any 'pure' ethnicity or nation. It is the thinkers from this perspective, the double- or multiple-consciousness of thinking from diasporas, who, perhaps more than thinkers from any other position, have achieved the epistemological stance Wynter says we need, the 'outer view' to the lawlike systems that define how we as humans understand ourselves today.

Indeed, one of Wynter's examples of 'differing observer positions' from the 1984 essay is Edward Said's *Orientalism*.[72] And Said, although born to Palestinian parents and so not a product of the interracial ceremony Wynter starts from, lived in exile as part of the Palestinian diaspora, and thus lived from an 'outer view' regarding his own nation as well as regarding the West, feeling always 'out of place', as he put it in the title to his memoir.[73] There are other reasons it is perhaps not surprising that Wynter would turn there to Said; both share key influences in Vico and Foucault, and both share the project of trying to think through and unsettle the colonial problematic they were living through. Perhaps most importantly, both Wynter and Said are humanists. They understood, and indeed have taught many of us, the limitations of the category of the human, but they ultimately maintained a sense of species-being in their criticism.[74] And so I want to follow Wynter's lead in turning next to Edward Said's articulation of secular criticism.[75] When Wynter says that Renaissance humanism offered 'a new *secular*' as an answer to who we are as humans and that she will follow that answer but also emphasizes that we are living through 'the *underside costs* of the *aporia* of the *secular* West' – and that these costs are 'generated by' our performance and practise of the 'secular Western . . . *genre* of being . . . human', meaning, as she says elsewhere, that 'the subjects of the techno-industrial North are hegemonically oriented in their behaviors by the contemporary secular metaphysics of productivity and profitability' – is she ultimately *endorsing* or *departing from* the secularism of traditional humanism?[76] Reading Said on secularism will help us gain clarity on Wynter's position.

Secular Criticism

Said calls his Introduction to his 1983 book *The World, the Text, and the Critic* 'Secular Criticism'.[77] Before he defines his terms, he contextualises his intervention within the US academy, writing not in regard to New Studies as Wynter did, but making a similar point about specialisation and provincialism in regard to literature, criticism and the humanities more broadly. '[T]he whole edifice of humanistic knowledge resting on the classics of European letters', he says, 'represents only a fraction of the real human relationships and interactions now taking place in the world.'[78] 'New cultures, new societies, and emerging visions of social, political, and aesthetic order now lay claim to the humanist's attention', he goes on, 'with an insistence that cannot longer be denied.'[79]

When he does get around to talking about the secular, he says he is interested in how 'the political and social world becomes available for critical and secular scrutiny'.[80] He adds that secular criticism 'deals with local and worldly situations, and that it is constitutively opposed to the production of massive, heretic systems'.[81] This is a point he makes within a larger point about *form*, arguing that the essay – 'a comparatively short, investigative, radically skeptical form' – is the form of secular criticism.[82] He summarises his main point: '[C]riticism must think of itself as life-enhancing and constitutively opposed to every form of tyranny, domination, and abuse; its social goals are noncoercive knowledge produced in the interests of human freedom.'[83] For Said, then, secular criticism leverages the big concepts that some would rather critique or deconstruct, such as 'the human' and 'freedom'. What is 'secular' about it is its focus on this human level, its focus on engaging the world as opposed not just to metaphysics, but also opposed to methodologically staying within texts. This sense of secularity is brought into further relief in his conclusion to that book, 'Religious Criticism', in which he describes the religious tendency as 'an agent of closure, shutting off human investigation . . . and effort in deference to the authority of the more-than-human, the supernatural, the other-worldly'.[84] If a religious approach gives us 'group solidarity' and 'communal belonging', he is saying, it can also compel subservience and adherence.[85]

Said saw religiosity not just in writing about holy texts and theology, but also in 'those versions of such actively radical positions as Marxism, feminism, or psychoanalysis that stress the private and hermetic over the public and social'.[86] He explains this point: 'This new mood superficially resembles, but is very unlike the utopianism of Ernst Bloch' – 'resembles' for its turn to the religious with a view towards solving social problems; 'unlike' because instead of returning from the religious to 'everyday reality' as Bloch did, religious critics offer only 'theory liberated from the human'.[87] 'All of it', Said summarises, 'expresses an ultimate preference for the secure protection of systems of belief . . . and not for critical activity or consciousness.'[88] He goes as far as to say, in his concluding lines, that the critic has become a cleric, and the most important task of the day is returning criticism to 'a truly secular enterprise'.[89] This return is a corrective in that the secular focus returns to us 'a sense of history and human production'.[90] 'Said, in his own work', the literary critic Emily Apter comments, 'never lets the reader forget the human in the humanities.'[91] 'If at times . . . it seems as if Said minimizes humanist Orientalism in order to salvage humanism tout court', Apter continues, 'it is perhaps because he believed that there was simply too much at stake within the humanism tradition to justify simplistic denunciations.'[92]

* * *

Reading Wynter with Said, we see that their ultimate concern is that we are telling ourselves stories about who we are that place our agency outside of ourselves, that take away from ourselves our ability to tell different stories and to re-make the world. But how they go about making this point, if it shares a content, departs significantly in form. When Said writes in *The World, the Text, and the Critic* (one year before Wynter's first article on the ceremony) that 'having given up the world entirely for the aporias and unthinkable paradoxes of a text, contemporary criticism has retreated from its constituency, the citizens of modern society, who have been left to the hands of "free" market forces, multinational corporations, the manipulations of consumer appetites', it is as if he is summarising my difficulties with the form of both of Wynter's essays on the ceremony.[93] Perhaps Wynter's example of the IPCC does bring her analysis down to the world, you might respond. But besides calling for a new *studia* and performance of the human, more than fleshing out what that would look like in the world, she leaves us with the aporias she outlined. This is itself a major contribution: it allows us to see the fundamental contradictions in what Western humanism has meant so far, and perhaps more than anyone else, Wynter urges the need to perform or enact our roles differently, according to a different script, as part of reminding us that we can define and live out what it means to be human differently. These are the reasons I stay with Wynter. And yet, I am reminded of Said's point that one hurdle to understanding any 'historical and social configuration' is when an interpretive community evolves 'camouflaging jargon'.[94] Might Wynter's framing of our contemporary problems in terms of an aporia, might the fact that her work is only understandable to those who have followed her post-structuralist jargon, itself be a hurdle to achieving the 'outer view' that she suggests we take? It is noteworthy to me that her examples for taking the outer view – including Du Bois, Woolf, Woodson and Said – generally wrote in strikingly clear prose and (precisely because of their humanist commitments) often avoided jargon. It is also noteworthy that Wynter in 1984 turned to Said's 1978 *Orientalism* as an example of gaining this 'outer view', and not to his 1979 *The Question of Palestine* or 1983 *The World, the Text, and the Critic*. Both of those less famous texts call for (and enact) a more self-consciously situated, essayistic and largely jargon-free mode of writing. In my view, those books – more than *Orientalism* – allow us to understand our new genre of being human as one that descends from the level of the text, from the level of aporia, *down* to the grounded, with-others, indeed political level of self-determination and human rights, his keywords in *The Question of Palestine*. Where Said turns to the world, Wynter stays with the Word.[95] (That said, and equally importantly, Wynter turned to the question of Being because of her commitments to praxis, because of her reflections emerging out of revolutionary Guyana.) For these reasons, Said's criticism is more 'secular' than Wynter's.

Moreover, it was not just Said's criticism that was more secular than Wynter's in the sense I have been using the term, following Wynter and Said. His life was also secular in the colloquial sense. Even if by 'secular criticism' Said does not mean criticism of religious institutions, and even if some readers of Said have read his secularism primarily as a critique of nationalism or as a critique of metaphysics and transcendence,[96] Said certainly *would* and *did* criticise those institutions. Born and having spent summers in Jerusalem, he was always wary of the tensions created by competing claims to religious significance, and the violence that followed from those disagreements. In turn, when he described 'the idea of Palestine', he described it as 'a non-exclusivist, secular, democratic, tolerant, and generally progressive ideology, not about colonizing and dispossessing people but about liberating them'.[97]

But to disregard religion as a source of knowledge or liberating energy is to throw away much of human experience and tradition. In his book on Said and religion, the scholar of religious studies William Hart said that on this point Said demonstrated a 'lack of insight', because '[r]eligion is an important site of struggle. It is more important', Hart went on, 'than Western classical music for the elaboration of civil society and as a form of ideology critique.'[98] And in his striking critique in *Restating Orientalism*, the philosopher Wael Hallaq goes as far as to say that Said's liberalism and secularism, including his apprehension about religion, prevented a true critical engagement with human claims to domination and sovereignty.[99] For Hallaq it is ultimately *religion* that allows what Wynter called an 'outer view', meaning that the role of religion is to allow humans to re-evaluate our place in the world and who we are, including recognising that sovereignty is a concept that belongs only to God, never to a human as property owner, never to a nation state as a political unit.[100] What is needed, Hallaq goes on, is an inversion of 'the entire value structures of modernity, amounting to a revolution not only against how we think but, more importantly, against who we, as humans, ultimately are'.[101] He concludes:

Integral to this revolution is a major adjustment geared toward compelling us – initially and until it becomes ingrained in us as a second nature – to see the world as a unity. And this cannot be successfully undertaken without realizing the full potential of our capacities of love, sympathy, and solidarity, capacities that may reestablish the desideratum of harmony within life and the world.[102]

* * *

Here I want to pose a paradoxical question, one I take very seriously: If, as Wynter noted, one of the exports of the modern West has been secularisation – and if Wynter is searching for a new secular, which she defines carefully as fundamentally meaning 'otherness' as well as coming from the world and not the church, as the realm of fallen time and not the transcendent divine realm – then *pace* Said, might we find *this* new secular not in the clergy or the clerics, not in search of a transcendent or divine realm, but in the natural world around us that is very much in time, that grows and passes away, that changes and dies and begins again? And – here is the paradox – isn't it different forms of human religion that, in passing down natural law, have emphasised this point most consistently?

Natural Law and Humanism

This is a paradoxical question because to pose it – to hint at a natural law we can apprentice ourselves to – suggests that the new *studia* is a recollection of the old one that the original humanist heresy departed from: the sense, to repeat Wynter's summary, 'that God had ordered the world according to certain principles, and the role of fallen man was to decipher these principles and abide by them, but not seek to question or have knowledge of things celestial which, unaided, his corrupted human knowledge could not encompass'.[103] The difference is that returning to the order of the world through the humanist heresies, as well as through the debate between Said and Hallaq, we return to it not as fallen, without questions, and seeking the supernatural or celestial, as Wynter worries, but as agential, with our questions, and seeking to understand, as Hallaq puts it, whether 'the cosmos contains an underlying ethical order'.[104]

Taking our cue from Said, we might briefly examine how Ernst Bloch is different from the unworldly critics Said criticises, at least to bring into further relief the kind of (how to say it?) *cosmological* secular criticism that Said might allow, provided that it remains concrete, worldly and public. That is the challenge which I will take up to conclude this chapter. Because my topic is humanism, my focus in reading Bloch will be his 1961 *Natural Law and Human Dignity*. In his Preface to that book, he begins with the simple, ancient philosophical question 'What is justice?' and immediately looks to a tradition of natural law in offering an answer.[105] 'No matter what position one took with respect to this idea of natural law, whether critical or undecided', Bloch begins, 'what it referred to could never be a matter of indifference.'[106] 'Where everything has been alienated', he goes on, 'inalienable rights stand out in sharp relief.'[107] 'Yet because these rights had no real, enduring place for themselves, this provided little comfort for the obedient subject.'[108] So Bloch recognises, as Arendt put it in her critique of human rights in *Origins* a decade earlier, that 'the world found nothing sacred in the abstract nakedness of being human'.[109] But unlike Arendt, who looks to state-supported civil rights, Bloch keeps his faith in the natural rights tradition. Why?

Part of Bloch's faith comes from his observation that natural law remains a fount from which we can call into question positive law and the state.[110] But in addition to this critical or judgemental function, he stays with natural law for the constructive potential he sees in it. Importantly, Bloch's method starts from the premise that natural law is part of a radical tradition that threatens nationalism and fascism because it is a site of imagination. It can be understood as radical and emancipatory as well as *conservative* in a literal sense of conserving a liberatory idea and not simply as a tool to justify or ground oppressive forms of positive law. His use of natural law, a concept almost lost today on much of the Left, brings to mind Walter Benjamin's sixth thesis on the philosophy of history, namely, that one of the central dangers for thinking the present anew is that a radical tradition faces the danger of 'becoming a tool of the ruling classes', such that '*even the dead* will not be safe'.[111] This is a point resonant with an observation Leslie Marmon Silko makes in her novel *Ceremony*, noting that one way the nation state operates is to 'destroy the stories' and to make truly radical human concepts 'confused or forgotten'.[112]

In *Natural Law and Human Dignity*, Bloch's specific goal is to bring together a tradition of natural law with a tradition of social utopianism, two traditions, he observes, that while agreeing on the goal of 'a more humane society' overall 'marched separately'; they 'did not strike together'.[113] Separate marches because they have understood their goals as separate: for natural law, upholding dignity; for social utopias, achieving happiness. 'It is high time', Bloch says, 'that we finally came to see how the differences between the intentions of happiness, which belonged to previous social utopias, and of dignity, which belonged to previous theories of natural law, are functionally connected and surmounted.'[114]

Although in Western antiquity the light of utopias was, as Bloch puts it, 'faint', in Sophocles' *Antigone* we find the heart of natural law calling into question positive law, and thus framing the social problem as 'the conflict of two laws'.[115] He also cites the Roman jurist Ulpian, whose dates are around 170–228, in offering an expansive sense of natural law beyond human life: 'Natural law is that which nature has taught all living beings; for this law is not solely the possession of the human race, but is common to all living beings that live on the land, are born in the seas, indeed it belongs even to birds.'[116] '[B]irds', Bloch comments, 'were always highly symbolic as beings that were not bound by any barriers. This is an ancient revolutionary image: to be free as a bird in the sky.'[117] Bloch adds to this ancient sense of natural law the utopianism of Marx and Marxism, while underscoring that Marxists have rarely given natural law its due.[118] Better to understand these traditions as intertwined, Bloch says: their similarities 'consist in *passing beyond* givenness, in the belief that present existents must be pushed aside in order to liberate and open the way to a better status'.[119] What brings natural law and Marxism concretely together is socialism.[120]

'Socialism is the path', Bloch, resonating with Du Bois, states clearly in the final pages of *Natural Law and Human Dignity*.[121]

[T]he red faith was always more than a private matter; there is a basic right to community, to humanism, that is equally political and in the goal. This is what the demanding right was en route to: the *eunomia* of the upright carriage in community. Art is not alone in holding the dignity of humankind in its hand.[122]

This concluding emphasis, that demanding a better society is 'more than a private matter', answers Said's concern about criticism that remains withdrawn and private, and so Bloch's criticism, *even as it works through theological sources*, remains more secular than religious, in Said's terms. And Bloch responds to Said, if you'll allow the anachronism: Bloch's final line implies turning to law in addition to turning to art; it could be read as a critique of Said's primarily aesthetic focus in his work on music as well as on literature, as seen in *Cultural and Imperialism*. In other words, Bloch (like Du Bois) offers a critique of starting from the aesthetic, and he would worry (as would Said) about what today has been called the micro-political, which puts its faith in small individual actions, in ever-shifting self-expression, as foundational for building a new society.

In my view, we are living in a moment where the utopian focus on happiness has become so individuated as to almost have lost its communal dimension as it spirals into self-expression and the hedonism of new clothes, music festivals, drugs taken with no consideration of the labour and risk required to produce and transport them, and quick videos of ourselves to be shared immediately with others. This usually digital performance, including understanding our reception in terms of likes and comments, means that as we post and check our phones we often decrease our ability to attend to the world in extended contemplation, to pay attention over a sustained period of time. At the very least, my reading of Wynter, Said and Bloch in this chapter would ask that we connect our micro-political, everyday negotiations of self, identity and belonging to what some consider a passé twentieth-century political and collective vocabulary, the vocabulary that – no matter how much he wrote on art – Said maintained in *The Question of Palestine* and in *The Politics of Dispossession*, including a call for self-determination, decolonisation, debt forgiveness, human rights, repatriation and reparations. In other words, Bloch's grounding in natural law asks us to go beyond the sense of performance that Wynter draws from Butler; it asks not only for us to see our roles and assemblies as performative, but also and first for us to orient ourselves to a greater truth or order, and then to live according to that order in our actions or praxis. To name just one example, in the water wars of Cochabamba, Bolivia, the performative element was not the emphasis of the individual's declaration; rather, the stress was on the right to water as a communal right, against the nationalisation and privatisation that worked together.

With my reading of Bloch, you might be thinking, we are a long way from the question of a new *studia*, of a ceremony that performs a new kind of humanity, so let me try to make what I see as the connection as clearly and succinctly as possible. Bloch understood that for social movements to be more than isolated flash points – for social movements to inaugurate new social realities or utopias – they need both a negative or critical element (a critique of injury and degradation) and a positive or constructive element (a vision of happiness and flourishing). In turn, Bloch offers a radical sense of natural law, what he calls '[g]enuine natural law', a law not from above but a fount for 'an active justice of below'; he returns to the tradition of natural law to remind his twentieth-century readers that natural law was 'the first to reclaim the justice that can only be obtained by struggle'.[123] At the very least, this genuine natural law can offer the critique of the state or the market or any social order that leads to illness or poverty or degradation – any denial of human dignity. After all, as the theologian Vincent Lloyd has recently argued, natural law is also the tradition of Frederick Douglass, Anna Julia Cooper, W. E. B. Du Bois and Martin Luther King.[124] If theorists since before Said's *The World, the Text, and the Critic* and very much into our own time have tried to offer theory liberated *from* the human, Bloch is helpful because he shows that theory liberated *through* the human might do well to orient ourselves to what is *beyond* the human (not necessarily towards a God, but perhaps towards the landscape and seascape that surrounds and engulfs and moves beneath us, as Glissant might put it). In the line from *Natural Law and Human Dignity* that called most strongly to me and is perhaps most relevant to this chapter, Bloch writes, 'Ethical freedom, where it appears, is not formed in tranquility, but precisely as character in the river of the world.'[125]

* * *

To return to the question of ceremony and study, and to conclude, I now depart from Said's strict and loose sense of secularism, and I depart from Wynter's concern about looking to the 'extra-human'; instead, I will stay with Hallaq's return to the cosmos understood through Bloch's humanist return of natural law to the world. But Bloch's Marxism and focus on socialism means his archive in *Natural Law and Human Dignity* is one of jurists and philosophers; it does not draw much of its impulse from the mystics, theologians and prophets who, in the Abrahamic tradition with which Bloch is in dialogue, have given natural law much of its spiritual and indeed ethical and political charge. Of the figures I have staged a dialogue between in this chapter, only Hallaq, because of his turn to

religion as serving to orient humans in our humility and rela-
tivity, really offers a sense of ceremony that includes not just
the human world, but the presence of the earth, an earth that
is tied to an ordering knowledge that is beyond human com-
prehension, but that we can nevertheless tap into, apprentice ourselves to, learn from and tell stories about. This is an
everyday sense of ceremony resonant with Tiffany Lethabo
King's description of being human as 'to be ceremony'.[126] If in
reading Glissant's novels Wynter finds promise in a character
who learned to study 'not only that . . . which lies around him,
but . . . that inside him as he leaves behind the certainty of the
transcendental for the provisional', if in other words Wynter ultimately comes down on the side of human autonomy
over an understanding of the earth as transcendental, I would
underscore that a study of the transcendental can remain very
much uncertain, very much provisional, open and riven as we
try to learn from that which lies around us.[127] Glissant himself
remains abstract on this topic, offering not so much more than
his 'poetics of relation' and call to listen to the landscape, and
Wynter and Said are perhaps too influenced by Marxism, or
perhaps too focused on the problematic of secular humanism,
to grant the earth, the cosmos, or natural law this re-orienting
role (though this ethical element is arguably at play in *Hills
of Hebron*). A character in Silko's novel *Almanac of the Dead*
puts the strengths and limitations of the Marxian inheritance
this way:

[Marx and Engels] had been far ahead of their time; they had been
close, but they still hadn't got it quite right. They had not understood that the earth was mother to all beings, and they had not
understood anything about the spirit beings. But at least Engels and
Marx had understood the earth belongs to no one. No human, individuals or corporations, no cartel of nations, could own the earth; it
was the earth who possessed the humans and it was the earth that
disposed of them.[128]

(Here, like Fanon in *Wretched*, I am thinking of the need to 'stretch' Marxism, not only with respect to race, but with respect to religion.) So, my question becomes: Could we, in studying this cosmological, earthly law, find the grounds for a worldly utopian vision? And if we could, how could we make that vision public and legible and widely shared and informed by those we are in dialogue with, while emphasising our agency within that vision (thus bringing Wynter and Said together)? In calling for new 'founding works today', Glissant looks to the models of the Old Testament and the *Odyssey*, among others; in closing, I want to suggest that one base for 'a modern form of the sacred', what he calls 'a Poetics of Relation', might not be found in a book; we might first look, with others, to read the reality of the world that surrounds us.[129]

Returning to Ceremony

The struggle over the Line 3 pipeline both *was* and *was not*, as Bloch read *Antigone*, 'the conflict of two laws'. It *was not* because there was a conflict over *one* law, namely, US law, and specifically interpretations of an 1837 treaty between the US government and the Anishinaabe people. The treaty specifies Anishinaabe rights to hunt, fish and harvest wild rice. In the 1999 US Supreme Court case *Minnesota v. Mille Lacs Band of Chippewa Indians*, the Court affirmed the 1837 treaty rights. Some Anishinaabe argued that Line 3 would violate these treaty rights because the Minnesota Department of Natural Resources granted a permit to the pipeline company Enbridge on 4 June 2021 to draw water from wild rice beds, to use the water, and to return the now-contaminated water to other places. Some also argued that potential pipeline spills would poison the treaty-bound land and water. Our ceremony at the Mississippi headwaters, like so many Indigenous-led protests and prayers across Turtle Island in this century, called for the treaties to be honoured; for this reason, we were calling for the affirmation of positive law.

But there was also a second law at play in the struggle over Line 3. The second law at play at our river gathering was what we could call a natural law, whether it be the metaphysics of different Abrahamic faiths that were present at the gathering, or whether it be informed by an Anishinaabe understanding of creation, which includes a First Man who performed a naming ceremony and gave us language, as well as a co-creating Thunderbird who ties human capabilities to ancestors and reminds us that birds are connections to both our spiritual hearts and to the universe. If, in Glissant's terms of a 'right to opacity', this creation story and metaphysics remain largely opaque to me, in the same terms, we at the headwaters chose to defend not just the treaty rights, but also the cultural rights of the Anishinaabe – rights which are deeply tied to the wild rice and the river and the land, because culture and land are not separated according to this second law.

According to the first law, the positive law of the treaties, our ceremony didn't really make sense. Our reading of the 1837 treaty was not upheld in the practice of the state, and we were not at the river just to mark this failure or to mourn our loss. If we gathered only amidst discrete political struggles, only to achieve one policy victory at a time, then we would not have gathered at the river at all. For we had already lost this specific struggle. No, we were there as part of what Wynter called the 'long process' of humanity.[130] Our ceremony crossed the colour line, but we were not simply autonomous subjects. We were trying not just to study, but to receive the lessons of the water, and to do so publicly, no matter how small our gathering was. We were taking an 'outer view' on our still-modern order, not just from multiple consciousnesses, but also from the perspective of the river and the transitions it was teaching us.

My sense is that, if we are to defend human rights beyond separate struggles – between the performances of Occupy and Standing Rock and the protests at Cop City – then we might follow the rules of Standing Rock (no alcohol, no weapons, dress simply) not just at the event, but throughout our lives, because the water and the birds teach us that the world is a unity, and that everywhere is a prayer camp, but we have dis-covered or covered over that relational sacred. If this is a practice that acknowledges the 'extra-human', it is also one that situates the human into a cosmos much bigger than ourselves. We could think of this ultimately as undermining humanism. We could read this acknowledgement and receptivity as abandoning our agency, our ability to tell a new story. But for me, situating human life as relative to an earthly order much bigger than us is better understood as affirming precisely the conditions that make our agency possible 'in the river of the world'.

Notes

1. Glissant, *Traité du Tout-Monde*, p. 29. The French is: 'Que l'opacité . . . nous soit une fête, non une terreur.' I am perhaps a bit loose here with 'fête' as 'ceremony' and not 'celebration'. I am simply trying to resonate with Wynter's keyword.
2. Glissant, *Poetics of Relation*, p. 16.
3. See Charles Taylor, *A Secular Age* (Cambridge, MA: The Belknap Press of Harvard University Press, 2007). Similarly, Janine Jones argues that 'the *ism* of Humanism implies fixity and necessity' (Janine Jones, 'Modern African humans effecting Atlantic middle passes', *Cultural Studies* 37, no. 6 (2022): p. 995).
4. Joshua Myers, *Of Black Study* (London: Pluto Press, 2023), p. 54.
5. Xhercis Méndez and Yomaira C. Figueroa, 'Not Your Papa's Wynter: Women of Color Contributions toward Decolonial Futures', in *Beyond the Doctrine of Man: Decolonial Visions of the Human*, eds. Joseph Drexler-Dreis and Kristien Justaert (New York: Fordham University Press, 2020), p. 60.

6. See Zimitri Erasmus, 'Sylvia Wynter's Theory of the Human: Counter-, not Post-humanist', *Theory, Culture & Society* 37, no. 6 (2020): pp. 47–65.

7. Méndez and Figueroa, 'Not Your Papa's Wynter', p. 63.

8. Sylvia Wynter, 'The Ceremony Must Be Found: After Humanism', *boundary 2* vol. 12, no. 3–vol. 13, no. 1 (1984): pp. 19–70.

9. Ibid. p. 28.

10. Ibid. p. 27.

11. Ibid. p. 28.

12. Ibid. p. 43.

13. Ibid. pp. 37, 38.

14. Ibid. p. 50.

15. Elisabeth Paquette, 'Ceremonies of Liberation: On Wynter and Solidarity', *The CLR James Journal* 28, nos. 1–2 (2022): p. 65.

16. Ibid. p. 56.

17. Ibid.

18. Sylvia Wynter, '"No Humans Involved": An Open Letter to My Colleagues', *Forum N.H.I: Knowledge for the 21st Century* 1, no. 1 (1994): p. 42.

19. Ibid. p. 43.

20. Ibid. p. 45

21. Ibid. p. 49.

22. Ibid. p. 59.

23. Ibid. pp. 44, 47, 48.

24. Ibid. pp. 68, 69.

25. Ibid. p. 69.

26. Ibid. pp. 69–70.

27. Myers, *Of Black Study*, p. 97.

28. Ibid. p. 15.

29. Wynter, 'No Humans Involved', p. 52.

30. Ibid. p. 69.

31. McKittrick, *Demonic Grounds*, p. xxv.

32. Sylvia Wynter, 'The Ceremony Found: Towards the Autopoetic Turn/Overturn, its Autonomy of Human Agency and Extraterritoriality of (Self-)Cognition', in *Black Knowledges/Black Struggles: Essays in Critical Epistemology*, eds. Jason R. Ambroise and Sabine Broeck (Liverpool: Liverpool University Press, 2015), p. 185.

33. Ibid. p. 187.
34. Ibid.
35. Rafael Vizcaíno, 'Sylvia Wynter's New Science of the Word and the Autopoetics of the Flesh', *Comparative and Continental Philosophy* 14, no. 1 (2022): p. 74. For the relationship between war and settlement in the US, see Helen M. Kinsella, 'Settler Empire and the United States: Francis Lieber on the Laws of War', *American Political Science Review* 117, no. 2 (2023): pp. 629–42.
36. Wynter, 'The Ceremony Found', p. 188.
37. Ibid.
38. Ibid.
39. Ibid. pp. 188–9.
40. Ibid. p. 189.
41. Wynter, 'Beyond the Word of Man: Glissant and the New Discourse of the Antilles', p. 639.
42. Wynter, 'The Ceremony Found', p. 189.
43. Ibid. pp. 190, 191. For how she uses 'secular', see p. 190, n. 9.
44. Ibid. p. 192.
45. Wynter, 'Unsettling the Coloniality of Being/Power/Truth/Freedom', p. 260.
46. Wynter, 'The Ceremony Found', p. 194.
47. Ibid.
48. Sylvia Wynter, *We Must Learn to Sit Down Together and Talk about a Little Culture: Decolonising Essays, 1967–1984* (Leeds: Peepal Tree Press 2022), p. 9.
49. Wynter, 'The Ceremony Found', p. 195.
50. McKittrick, ed., *Sylvia Wynter*, p. 33.
51. Ibid.
52. Wynter, 'The Ceremony Found', p. 196.
53. Ibid. p. 199. See also ibid. p. 200.
54. Ibid. p. 186.
55. Ibid. p. 212.
56. Ibid. p. 216.
57. Ibid. p. 227.
58. Ibid. p. 224.
59. Ibid. p. 230.

60. Ibid. p. 231.

61. Ibid. p. 232.

62. Ibid. pp. 239–40.

63. Ibid. p. 235.

64. Ibid. p. 242.

65. Ibid.

66. Ibid. p. 237, n. 56.

67. On this shift, see Demetrius L. Eudell, 'To Change the Order of the World: Decolonising Culture, Decolonising the Self', in Wynter, *We Must Learn to Sit Down Together*, p. 39.

68. Quoted in Bayani Rodriguez, 'Introduction'.

69. Wynter, 'Beyond the Word of Man', p. 639.

70. Cf. Jonathan Fenderson, 'Black Studies Post-Janus', pp. 1–7.

71. Neil Roberts, 'Sylvia Wynter's Hedgehogs: The Challenge for Intellectuals to Create New "Forms of Life" in Pursuit of Freedom', in *After Man Towards the Human: Critical Essays on Sylvia Wynter*, ed. Anthony Bogues (Kingston, Jamaica: Ian Randle Publishers, 2006), pp. 159–60.

72. Wynter, 'The Ceremony Must Be Found', p. 47. See also ibid. p. 48.

73. Edward Said, *Out of Place* (New York: Vintage, 1999).

74. My reading is different from Paquette's, which argues that in the second ceremony essay, Wynter proposes 'a move away from a species-being conception of what it means to be human' and 'a turn towards genre' (Paquette, 'Ceremonies of Liberation', p. 67). My view is that Wynter emphasises genre while maintaining a sense of the species, arguing for instance that what the civic humanism of the Renaissance negated was 'our co-humanity as a species' (Wynter, 'The Ceremony Found', p. 187). She continues to speak positively later about a new emergence or becoming in 'our species' existence' (ibid. p. 194).

75. Wynter, 'The Ceremony Must Be Found', pp. 34, 42, 47.

76. For the first lines, see Wynter, 'The Ceremony Found', p. 222; for the 'elsewhere' line, see Wynter, 'Unsettling', p. 331, n. 4.

77. Edward Said, *The World, the Text, and the Critic* (Cambridge, MA: Harvard University Press, 1983), p. 1.

78. Ibid. p. 21.
79. Ibid.
80. Ibid. p. 24.
81. Ibid. p. 26.
82. Ibid.
83. Ibid. p. 29.
84. Ibid. p. 290.
85. Ibid.
86. Ibid. p. 292.
87. Ibid. p. 291.
88. Ibid. p. 292.
89. Ibid.
90. Ibid. p. 290.
91. Emily Apter, 'Saidian Humanism', *boundary 2* 31, no. 2 (2004): p. 53.
92. Ibid. p. 45.
93. Said, *The World, the Text, and the Critic*, p. 4.
94. Ibid. p. 26. When asked in 1991 what would it mean to rewrite Chomsky's 1967 essay 'Responsibility of Intellectuals' today, Said argued first, 'One would have to pretty much scuttle all the jaw-shattering jargonistic postmodernisms that now dot the landscape. They are worse than useless. They are neither capable of understanding and analyzing the power structure of this country nor are they capable of understanding the particular aesthetic merit of an individual work of art. Whether you call it deconstruction or postmodernism or poststructuralism or post-anything, they all represent a sort of spectacle of giving back tickets at the entrance and saying, we're really out of it. We want to check into a private resort and be left alone' (Said, *The Politics of Dispossession*, p. 316).
95. For Wynter's understanding of the 'Word' as a specific discursive tool that draws lines so as to order not the clergy/laity but the settler/Indigenous, settler/enslaved, sane/mad, rational/poor, see Wynter, 'Beyond the Word of Man', p. 641. I have struggled to find whether Wynter published comments explicitly on Palestine, and relatedly whether she explicitly theorised

Black and Palestinian dispossession and resistance together. She mentions in her *Small Axe* interview with David Scott that after World War II, her first husband, Hans Ragnar Isachsen, 'was training the El Al airline pilots in Israel, as well as flying for them'; thus, Wynter had some proximity to the nation-building project of Israel (Scott, 'The Re-Enchantment of Humanism: An Interview with Sylvia Wynter', p. 132). In a later interview with Katherine McKittrick, Wynter says that we are living in '[a] global order' in which 'the nuclear "haves" (United States/Israel) vie with Islamic Iran's ongoing attempt to join the nuclear club' and concludes that 'once again, we find ourselves in a nuclear-threatened world. The fundamental issue is therefore one having to do not only with all of the above costs but also with the species-threatening nature of these negative costs, including that of the relentlessly increasing fossil fuel-driven climate instability's ongoing catastrophe' (Wynter and McKittrick, 'Unparalleled Catastrophe for Our Species?', p. 43). Wynter's slash in aligning the US and Israel resonates with how I will conclude this book, and this critical move perhaps suggests some distance from her earlier connection with El Al.

96. See e.g. the work of Bruce Robbins and Stathis Gourgouris.
97. Said, *The Politics of Dispossession*, p. xix.
98. William Hart, *Edward Said and the Religious Effects of Culture* (Cambridge: Cambridge University Press, 2000), p. 37.
99. Wael Hallaq, *Restating Orientalism: A Critique of Modern Knowledge* (New York: Columbia University Press, 2018), p. 110. Thanks to Shadi Anello for discussion on this point.
100. See ibid. p. 256.
101. Ibid. p. 254.
102. Ibid.
103. Wynter, 'The Ceremony Must Be Found', p. 28.
104. Hallaq, *Restating Orientalism*, p. 156.
105. Ernst Bloch, *Natural Law and Human Dignity*, trans. Dennis J. Schmidt (Cambridge, MA: The MIT Press, 1996), p. xxvii.
106. Ibid.

107. Ibid.

108. Ibid.

109. Arendt, *Origins*, p. 299.

110. See Bloch, *Natural Law*, p. 243.

111. See Walter Benjamin, 'On the Concept of History' (1940), https://www.marxists.org/reference/archive/benjamin/1940/history.htm. I thank Max Tomba for guiding me to see that natural law is part of a radical tradition, for pointing me to Bloch, and for drawing out Benjamin's theses on history as a reminder that conserving the past can be radical, and that the true victory of the dominant classes comes when radicals forget our own history.

112. Leslie Marmon Silko, *Ceremony* (New York: Penguin, 2016), p. 2. Consider also how academic movements have forgotten their spiritual motivation. See e.g. Peter Gabel, 'Critical Legal Studies as a Spiritual Practice', *Pepperdine Law Review* 36, no. 5 (2009): pp. 515–34.

113. Bloch, *Natural Law*, p. xxix.

114. Ibid. p. xxx.

115. Ibid. p. 114. This is also the conflict in Roberto Rossellini's compelling 1945 film *Rome Open City*, when towards the end the Nazi officer tries to get the radical priest to give up information by threatening to subject the priest to the Nazi military law that applies to traitors, and the priest says, 'God will judge.' You might say that the atheist and communist Manfredi needed no appeal to a higher law not to talk even when tortured, and I take your point. Both died a martyr's death; and as the officer (Major Bergmann) stressed, even the atheist's death – had the public heard his real name and not the pseudonym that the Nazis used to hide their crime – would have been understood as martyrdom.

116. Quoted in Bloch, *Natural Law*, p. 22.

117. Ibid. p. 23.

118. See ibid. p. 186.

119. Ibid. p. 206.

120. See ibid. p. 208.

121. Ibid. p. 279.
122. Ibid. p. 280.
123. Ibid. p. xxx.
124. See Vincent Lloyd, *Black Natural Law* (Oxford: Oxford University Press, 2016).
125. Bloch, *Natural Law*, p. 157.
126. King, *The Black Shoals*, p. 204.
127. Wynter, 'Beyond the Word of Man', p. 646.
128. Leslie Marmon Silko, *The Almanac of the Dead* (New York: Simon & Schuster, 1991), p. 749.
129. Glissant, *Poetics of Relation*, p. 16.
130. Wynter, 'The Ceremony Must Be Found', p. 50.

4 Edward Said's Postcolonial Humanism

The first time I went to an academic archive, it was to the Beinecke Library at Yale, to study the manuscripts of Édouard Glissant. As a boy, Glissant would accompany his father to work at some of Martinique's sugarcane plantations.[1] Through his poetry and philosophy, Glissant would go on to become an important voice of the Caribbean, whose fate he always connected to the traditions and struggles of the whole world. I rather enjoyed my time at the Beinecke. The Vermont marble exterior looks like an emperor's arbitrary attempt to put honeycomb in building form, and once inside, the visitor realises that the marble is in fact translucent. The way it lets in only some light gives the interior an almost magical feel. Walking down the regal stairs to access the manuscripts, I felt very important. The man who welcomed me to the archive wore a Tag Heuer watch. When I got to my table, I recognised the man at the table next to me; he was a famous poet who had recently started teaching at Yale.

As far as I could tell, no cane cutters were in the room. I could afford to visit Glissant's archive only because the university where I went to graduate school, Emory, provided travel funding for its students – the prominent Atlanta families who owned Coca-Cola have given generously to Emory over the years, leading to a nimble endowment. One company's violation of water rights, generation of global emerging markets and donations for tax purposes become a graduate student's ticket to Yale for a research project about human rights. Such a de facto class-based and geographical segregation of material access can be captured in the phrase 'the coloniality of the archive'.[2]

I have been thinking about this performative contradiction. I have been thinking about it amidst louder and louder discussions of positionality in (and calls for decolonisation of) the US academy today. I have been thinking about it as a person of European descent who writes about Caribbean philosophy, teaches in a Black Studies Department (at the time of this writing), and is asked around once a month, upon sharing that I write about Glissant or that I teach in a Black Studies Department, if I am Black – a question I never got before, and so that (among other things) testifies to how few white people read Black philosophers seriously, carefully, or as part of a larger tradition today, such that if you do, it can justifiably be assumed that you are not white.[3] (Of course, there is a lot else going on in these questions, but that is for another essay.) And so I have begun to wonder: What obligations come with studying archives we were not born into, meaning whose authors have an ancestry different from our own?

* * *

At a conference in 2022, I made the above point about access and Glissant's archive, again, that Yale's holding Glissant's work without digitising it or making it more accessible – to Martinicans, to those in the Caribbean and to humanity – reflects a colonial pattern of resource acquisition, and upon making that point, I was asked to write an essay about the coloniality of the archive. But this point is rather small, and what to do about it seems rather straightforward: increase global access through digitisation and enact material repatriation when called to by the people in the places from which the materials were taken (or purchased). In any case, I have not spent enough time in archives to be anything close to an expert on how collection, preservation and distribution function.

Upon being asked to write about the archive, what I really wanted to do was to return to Edward Said's archive, whose collection I whimsically began to study a few years ago on a weekend trip to New York, a trip taken ostensibly to see art with my brother and his partner. So I drew up a proposal to study a question that had been on my mind for some time: How did postcolonial theory, which many say Edward Said inaugurated with his 1978 *Orientalism*, become so focused on texts, and garner such strong critiques from anti-colonial Marxists, when many of Said's own deepest influences – e.g. Antonio Gramsci, C. L. R. James, E. P. Thompson, Raymond Williams – were Marxists? In his 1992 *In Theory*, Aijaz Ahmad says that in *The World, the Text, and the Critic* Said 'singled out' Marxism when Said argued that '[t]he net effect of "doing" Marxist criticism' is 'to put oneself outside a great deal of things going on in the world', and Ahmad adds that while in Said we find 'an eloquence, a style', ultimately in Said's work 'the notable feature, underlying all the ambivalences, is the anti-Marxism and the construction of a whole critical apparatus for defining a postmodern kind of anti-colonialism'.[4] But despite Said's critique of representation through Michel Foucault and by extension critique of 'truth' through Nietzsche in *Orientalism*, didn't Said, already by his 1979 *The Question of Palestine*, return more strongly to a sense of truth, human rights and self-determination? If it is correct that Said was more comfortable with putting words others than 'Marxist' before 'criticism' – 'secular', 'oppositional' and finally 'democratic' – couldn't we also read those lines at the end of his introduction to *The World, the Text, and the Critic* as in fact *sharing a concern* with Ahmad that Marxism has become, as Said says, 'an academic, not a political, commitment'? If so, could

Said also be offering a corrective to a false Marxism very much 'in need of systematic decoding, demystifying, [and] rigorous clarification'?[5] If so, could we read Said's anti-colonial critique of Marxism in *Culture and Imperialism* as a similar corrective?[6] Even if Said remains a liberal in his vocabulary and solutions, doesn't the clear prose, call to universality and emphasis on human rights that runs straight through from his 1979 *The Question of Palestine* to his 2003 speech against war entitled 'Memory, Inequality, and Power: Palestine and the Universality of Human Rights' share much more with a line of Marxist criticism that always leveraged human rights claims – the Marxism of W. E. B. Du Bois, Claudia Jones and Stuart Hall – than it does with our contemporary, jargon-heavy postcolonial theory that emphasises particularity and generally avoids appealing to 'the human' or to 'human rights'?[7] But of course, once I got to Said's archive, it was much less these theoretical questions and much more personal questions that tugged at my interest.

* * *

I first went to study Said's papers at Columbia University in March of 2022. I examined a few boxes, just getting started, and then left the library to meet a colleague at Columbus Circle. After my colleague, a political theorist, kindly bought me an americano, and as we walked around Central Park, he reflected on the richness and the mixture – the richness *because of* the mixture – of his university education in Puerto Rico, where he was taught by Republicans who had fled fascist Spain. He might read Plato in the morning and Glissant in the afternoon, he said, and that form of creolised reading was normal for him. I told him about my time at Said's archive, and he asked me what I thought about Timothy Brennan's 2021 biography of Said, *Places of Mind*. I demurred, then said it helped me to put Said's work in context – not much of an answer! He expressed some reservations as well, even if we couldn't exactly name them.

I have come to think that no one will fully endorse a biography of Said. His work is too personal to us. '[T]here are many aspects of the memoir I shall not touch upon', Nadia Gindi writes in her review of Said's memoir, *Out of Place*.[8] She goes on with a wonderful honesty perhaps more of us should take up: 'This essay is solely concerned with my personal reaction to Edward's early memories.'[9] Let's face it: We who read Said's work have our own individual readings of, and reasons for returning to, his corpus. We disagree so strongly not only about how best to understand his writings, but also about how best to understand his life.

As Sadik Jalal al-'Azm asked from Beirut in 1980, does Said's framing of a linear progression of Orientalism result in *hindering* his own stated goals, because to describe the West as continuously mis-representing others in fact makes more difficult 'the task of combating and transcending [Orientalism's] essentialistic categories, in the name of this common humanity'?[10] As Wael Hallaq asked from New York in 2018, does Said's confident secularism prevent a robust engagement with the role of religion in anti-colonial efforts, and thus at best return to a Western secular liberalism?[11] And as I would ask from St Louis in 2022, are Said's Rolex watches and Burberry suits a disavowal of any true anti-colonial politics, or does my pause at seeing a Palestinian speaking so eloquently at the best universities and in the best clothes itself reflect a colonial stereotype that expects to see the 'barbaric' or 'undeveloped' Other?

Representations

It was my professor of Islam in college who introduced me to Said. I read selections of *Orientalism* and *Covering Islam* then, and I listened to his 1993 BBC Reith Lectures 'Representations of the Intellectual' more than once, later learning that the lectures had been turned into a book by the same name. Perhaps no text has influenced my sense of intellectual life more – or been such a consistent talking point. When I did a post-doc in Toronto, I would meet the political theorist Neil Roberts in a park ostensibly to discuss Caribbean philosophy, but more than once we ended up talking about Said's *Representations*. My tennis partner in Toronto was a critical theorist, and he and I mostly just talked tennis – he was teaching me the game – but when we didn't, it was usually to talk about humanism and what, at the end of his life, Said called 'democratic criticism'.[12] When I interviewed for the job I had when I started writing this book, a job in an African American Studies Department, the search committee and I ended up speaking about Said; and when I was later familiarising myself with the research of our Department, I smiled when I saw that Chris Tinson used Said to think through the history of the radical Black magazine *The Liberator*.[13] Why does Said speak to so many of us?

For me it was first and foremost his voice, how clearly he wrote in defence of Islam and of Palestine, of traditions not his own as much as his own (though he would caution us not to see traditions in terms of ownership). This defence was part of a larger mode of intellectual life he outlines in *Representations*: oppositional, certainly, but never so far from the public to be unheard or irrelevant.[14] In his first lecture in *Representations*, he notes that intellectual life is marked by a combination of private and public life. It is about how private life, how our experiences and history, enter the social world. It is about how our commitments can inform how people think about war and peace, domination and liberation. Intellectual life, he says, is public by definition, because by publishing and speaking we enter a broader conversation, but not to make our audiences feel good: 'The whole point is to be embarrassing, contrary, even unpleasant.'[15]

To this contrarian style Said adds how each of us are situated. Each 'situation', he says, using Jean-Paul Sartre's term, has its own 'problems, triumphs, and peculiarities'.[16] And each of us speaks to a particular public. Said argues, however, that no matter one's situation, the intellectual makes a claim to universality. Quite simply, in his view intellectuals operate to advance 'universal principles', namely, 'that all human beings are entitled to expect decent standards of behavior concerning freedom and justice from worldly powers or nations, and that deliberate or inadvertent violations of those standards need to be testified against courageously'.[17] 'Courageously', because speaking truth to power always involves exposing oneself to the force of the powerful. Therefore, the intellectual's vocation involves 'both commitment and risk, boldness and vulnerability'.[18] Such a combination is in part what Jeanne Morefield has in mind when, beautifully reading Said alongside the poet Mahmoud Darwish, she describes what Said offers as 'a disposition toward critique' instead of a systematic theory.[19] Indeed, Said never resolved the tensions he underscored and embodied. Rather, as Morefield goes on to say in the final page of her elegant 2022 book *Unsettling the World*, 'He simply painted richer, more complicated portraits of the whole world while simultaneously looking loss in the face and demanding a better world.'[20]

If Said insisted that one's private life informs one's public stances, he did not say that this happens easily or seamlessly. Perhaps in focusing on Said's eloquent and confident public tone we can overlook the internal struggles that weighed on him, the human-all-too-human side of him that is harder to see in his publications in the best academic journals and easier to see in his letters and personal journals – easier to see in his own handwriting. In an 8 January 1978 entry in a personal journal now collected in his archive, a journal that is nearly empty save these lines, Said reflected that 'magazines, lectures, platforms . . . even books, are all about what *needs to be said, about fitting an occasion*, about saying the *stateable* thing', but that 'there is the more important reason at work in this journal, that so much of what one knows and feels has no place in the various public places of one's writing'. He would write in a 16 October 1978 entry, now in black and not blue ink, 'There is a great confusion about me.'[21]

Style

As compelling as I have always found Said's language, there were parts of his (public) style that I found, and still find, largely inaccessible – that I found hard to read myself into. The photos of him that circulate online show someone in perfectly tailored clothes, and often speaking in London or teaching in New York. Having grown up in a rural place, for much of my life I wouldn't have known where to find those kinds of blazers and scarfs, much less how to wear them. And intellectual events circulating from New York to Paris can imply to those of us not from those cities, or not from any city, that we simply aren't to be part of the conversation.

At the same time, no matter where I have been when reading Said, I have felt that his contradictions – or what *I* read as his contradictions – are part of a vast and complex project, one ultimately more welcoming than it may have initially felt. Because no matter what pen Said chose to write with, the words that his surely expensive ink formed carry with them a humanism that still inspires people, particularly students and exiled people, in Ramallah as much as London, New Delhi as much as New York, rural Minnesota as much as rural Tindouf.

Indeed, as he closes his famous 1982 essay 'Traveling Theory', one of the tasks of criticism is to 'preserve some modest . . . belief in noncoercive human community'.[22] When I write this line now, I still feel the promise of this task: for as long as some people maintain such a belief, in spite of the forces we face, then we know there remains, however hidden in social life, a rejection of the 'realist' claim that, by nature or fate, there will always be violence, war, colonisation and domination. Said always saw state violence for what it was. In a little notebook entry on a page titled 'War', he wrote 'the *meanness* of it all. No sense of life lost.'

I still wonder in what circumstances the skills Said says in *Representations* the intellectual must cultivate – knowing how to use language well and knowing how to intervene in language – are necessary but not sufficient, needed but not enough by themselves to bring about the required social changes our species so urgently needs today. I wonder what other skills would supplement those textual skills. Is the problem of an oil pipeline that violates treaties with Indigenous nations, or of a checkpoint that allows only Israeli citizens and certain permit-holders to pass, a problem that the right language can solve? I wonder if what Said's position of the intellectual as never being a consensus-builder, as maintaining a critical posture to the very end, if what this position gains in terms of never being co-opted, it loses in the chance of building alternative communities with others. Is it too critical at the expense of communal construction? And does not this focus on language by and large miss the more significant point that is less about conceptual connections and more about physical dependencies and entanglements, wrought through centuries of invasion and extraction?

* * *

In addition to his voice and vision (both deeply complicated), Said offers a method of reading in times when coloniality contaminates all concepts. In a paragraph he first wrote out by hand, with black ink, on a long white page, he says of human rights:

To be 'for' human rights means, in effect, to be willing to venture inter-pretations of those rights in the same place and with the same language employed by the dominant power, to dispute its hierarchy and methods, to elucidate what it has hidden, to pronounce what it has silenced or rendered unpronounceable. These intellectual procedures require, above all, an acute sense not of how things are separated but of how they are connected, mixed, involved, embroiled, linked.[23]

In such a passage we see the result, regarding human rights, of Said's signature method: starting small in the spirit of Giambattista Vico, reading closely like Erich Auerbach, tracking discourse like Aimé Césaire, writing courageously in the wake of C. L. R. James, and steadfastly holding on to the language of rights, as many Jerusalemites still do.[24] For me, the idea of maintaining a position 'for' something flawed, but nevertheless worth fighting for, so thoroughly captures the practice of reading and writing I have tried to cultivate since first reading Said, that I selected the above quotation as the epigraph to my book on Glissant and human rights, a selection that resulted in a journey through the intellectual places Said frequented. Indeed, upon my inquiring about the permissions, Harvard University Press pointed me to Said's copyright holder, the Wylie Agency, a WASP establishment that has not just Said but also Henry Kissinger as its client.[25] We could say of Said what Sylvia Wynter said of C. L. R. James: that he 'lived all the contradictions'.[26]

Perhaps, beyond their shared condition of exile, this is why Said sought out a meeting with James. Said's notes show that he met James in Brixton on Saturday, 27 June 1987. Said described James as 'warm and funny', and they spoke about – among other things – Paul Robeson's performance in the theatrical version of *The Black Jacobins*. In a typewritten follow-up letter dated 13 August 1987, James wrote to 'My dear Edward' at his Hamilton Hall address at Columbia, noting that he 'just listened to the Bach which you sent me'. He said in his pen-ultimate paragraph, 'I am glad that you remembered I would be interested in it. If at any other time you feel I would be interested in something, please send it to me. If there is any expense I will meet it', and in his ultimate paragraph, 'Again thank you for sending me such a wonderful body of music' before signing off simply, in blue ink, 'C. L. R.'

Positionality

If Said provides an example of voice, vision and method, what does he say about positionality? In 'Yeats and Decolonization', he argues that the elite Protestant poet W. B. Yeats, despite being 'almost completely assimilated to the canon', also offers 'another fascinating aspect', namely, 'that of the indisputably great *national* poet who articulates the experiences, the aspirations, and the vision of a people suffering under the dominion of an offshore power'.[27] His next lines are perhaps the most important for this chapter:

From this perspective Yeats is a poet who belongs to a tradition not usually considered his, that of the colonial world ruled by European imperialism now – that is, during the late nineteenth and early twentieth centuries – bringing to a climactic insurrectionary stage, the massive upheaval of anti-imperialist resistance in the colonies, and of metropolitan anti-imperialist opposition that has been called the age of decolonization. If this is not a customary way of interpreting Yeats for those who know a great deal more about him as an Irish European modernist poet of immense stature than I do, then I can only say that he appears to me, as I am sure to many others in the Third World, to belong naturally to the other cultural domain.[28]

In other words, Said reads the question of postcolonial position-ality less as about who Yeats was – as if who we are were essentially a question of ethnicity[29] – and more about the political positions he took. He would reiterate this point, again about perspective and position, in *Representations*:

Exile is a model for the intellectual who is tempted, and even beset and overwhelmed, by the rewards of accommodation, yea-saying, set- tling in. Even if one is not an actual immigrant or expatriate, it is still possible to think as one, to imagine and investigate in spite of barriers, and always to move away from the centralizing authorities towards the margins, where you see things that are usually lost on minds that have never traveled beyond the conventional and the comfortable.[30]

'Identity, for him, be that national, cultural, or other', the sociologist Gurminder Bhambra summarises, 'was best under- stood as a starting point for a more interesting journey. It is not all that human life is about.'[31]

For those who want Said to represent the particular and not the universal, to only perform pleas in Arabic as a victim and not to be actively intervening in discourse in *Le Monde*, what was Said doing reading Yeats, anyway? Or founding the West-Eastern Divan Orchestra with the Argentine-Israeli con- ductor and pianist Daniel Barenboim? Or teaching a seminar on T. S. Eliot? Or maintaining so many correspondences, later collected in his archive, with letters written to him in Ara- bic, French, Spanish and English, among other languages? Or defending Joseph Conrad to the very end? Or returning again and again to English literature? In a comment placed on the bottom of the first page of a student's paper saved in his archive, Said (or was it one of his graduate students – the handwriting is different) wrote in a parenthetical about the Rudyard Kipling novel '(maybe there are competing ideolo- gies in *Kim*)'. Perhaps that is the true lesson of Said's archive, that in these modern/colonial times when more and more of us feel out of place, we also all have within us competing ide- ologies. That no category, label or identification can contain that tension or be more accurate than that 'maybe'.

To put my cards on the table, I sympathise more with the norms of Standing Rock – dress simply, this is a prayer camp – than with the idea that the model for postcolonial theory is found wearing Burberry, writing with a Montblanc pen, in Fournier notebooks, from Brown's Hotel in London.[32] And yet, for me, it was. And yet, as Esmat Elhalaby summarised so perfectly in his review of *Places of Mind*, 'It was precisely these kinds of efforts to juxtapose culture or refinement from the symbols and practices of political action that Said perennially opposed.'[33] And yet, as Al-Azm highlights in his summary concept 'Ontological Orientalism' – now not criticising but praising Said – to focus only on a few of Said's habits assumes an essential difference between his quotidian life and the kind of politics I want to affirm, and thus misses the point that such a politics needs to be based on a more complicated understanding of human culture. These objections are right. Granting them, I'll add that I'd prefer a colleague who has the courage to write about Palestine – or Ferguson, or Fairy Creek, or #RhodesMustFall, or that our university sits on Osage land and was built by enslaved people, and that we owe something to their descendants for that land and labour – over one who doesn't, no matter their threads.[34]

I admit: I like the idea of a world where one of the most compelling scholars of a Polish-British novelist who wrote about the Belgian Congo is an Anglican Palestinian Christian who was raised in Egypt and lived in New York City, and whose ashes are now buried in a Quaker cemetery in the mountains just outside of Beirut. That is a world where theory travels not just to be domesticated, but to be read in new contexts and in different ways – to be revised and revisited. That is a colonial world. It is our world. It is a world where the established professor of social theory still today guides students trying to think through questions of race, class, gender and dispossession to the work of Émile Durkheim more than to that of Ida B. Wells. Here I recite my lessons from Said: If we have responsibilities in a world this complicated, this injured, this 'connected, mixed, involved, embroiled, linked', then they are humanist responsibilities. An idea cannot be owned. A tradition is always already plural. The worth of a theory is not based on where it comes from, but on whether it inspires, whether it gives breath. But – humanist responsibilities, yes, and all of this – we should start, perhaps, with our responsibilities to those we have dehumanised. We should start, perhaps, from Gaza, from African diasporas, from Indigenous nations our universities have dispossessed – from those who 'suffocate more', as Darwish laments in 'To Our Land'.[35]

Coda

In 1950 the United Nations Relief and Works Agency for Palestine Refugees in the Near East (UNRWA) leased land from Jordan to establish the Aida Refugee Camp in Bethlehem, a response to the need to shelter Palestinians displaced from the 1948 *nakba*. In 2000, eleven young people from Aida founded the Lajee Center, a cultural gathering place for the camp's inhabitants. In Arabic, 'lajee' means 'refugee'. On the day in May 2023 that I visited Aida and Lajee with other academics from the US, people there were having a gathering to remember 1948. Many wore shirts with 194 in one colour and the 8 in another, the 194 thus highlighted to reference United Nations General Assembly Resolution 194, which resolved that

refugees wishing to return to their homes and live at peace with their neighbours should be permitted to do so at the earliest practicable date, and that compensation should be paid for the property of those choosing not to return and for loss of or damage to property which, under principles of international law or equity, should be made good by the Governments or authorities responsible.

For many Palestinians, this Resolution is understood as part of the basis for their 'right of return'. For all, it has yet to be granted.

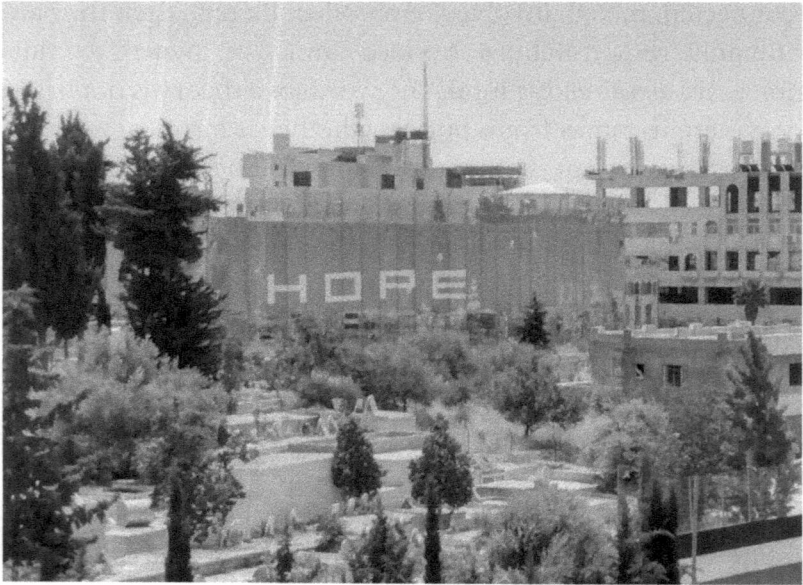

Figure 4.1 Apartheid/Separation Wall, viewed from the roof of the Lajee Center. Photo by author.

We were told that, because of the gathering that refused to forget the *nakba*, it was likely that the Israeli Occupying Forces would raid the camp at some time during the day. The occupying forces raid the camp with tremendous frequency – not a hard task because they built a sniper tower and a base only a few hundred metres from the camp, the base's blue gate above Aida always ready to open, allowing soldiers to march in formation down the hill and into the camp. According to a January 2018 report from the Human Rights Center at the University of California, Berkeley, School of Law, 100 per cent of residents at Aida camp were exposed to tear gas in the previous year.[36] In practice, the IOF uses Aida as a ground to test new equipment and techniques; without rights or effective international support, the camp's inhabitants have no recourse.[37] Worse yet, insofar as we participate in our university-provided retirement plans that invest in the military and technology companies that profit from this violence, both our theory and our practice remains colonial.[38] As middle-class US citizens, we are not just implicated in Israel's occupation; with our taxes and investments, we throw our money at it. Mirroring how it was Said's *Orientalism* and not *The Question of Palestine* that would gain so much currency in the US academy, we US academics are often more worried about being 'orientalist' in how we talk about others than we are with whether our money works to displace, maim and kill others.[39]

We toured the camp rather slowly, I thought. I have trouble breathing, and I was eager to return quickly to the Lajee building. Even if the cultural centre, like the homes of those in the camp, has also been shelled with tear gas innumerable times before, it still felt safer than walking through the camp's narrow streets, away from Aida's single entrance/exit. On the tour we saw where camp residents had burned an IOF watchtower. We saw murals to Leila Khaled, as well as a variety of other graffiti. Our guide said the separation/annexation wall should be kept unpainted, lest we make something horrifying beautiful. I carried with me the Castelli notebook I had purchased a few days before at the Educational Bookshop on Salah Eddin Street in East Jerusalem, and I carried merely (unfortunately) a ballpoint pen, but I was too jittery to take notes. Instead, I kept glancing back at the blue gate.

We made it back to Lajee and were served a delicious meal of green beans over rice. A colleague with ancestry visibly different from my own offered me a cup of Coca-Cola, which I accepted. She filled my cup, poured some for herself, and spilled some on the table. I was glad I was not pouring, for I would've spilled too, my hands still unsteady from fear of being teargassed, my whole body panicked from placing myself, for less than an hour, in a reality that for many forms a whole life. If my colleague and I were thinking of anything in that moment, as the fizzy drink pooled on the table, it was not where our ancestors came from or which stories are ours to tell. It was not the contradictions of that day or what we felt we had to prove. It was simply the pleasantness and the normalcy of a crisp drink on a hot day, a day that for us would continue with a tour of Bethlehem, our Mercedes van taking us out of the camp thirty minutes before the IOF started to fire tear gas into it.

This too is Said's archive, this space of dispossession and rightlessness, this space where, as he said about post-Oslo Palestine, 'sufferings had been reduced to the status of terrorism and violence, to be renounced retrospectively or passed over in silence'.[40] 'There never seems to be enough time', Said reflected in 1986, 'and one always has the impression that one's enemy – in this case the Israelis – is trying to take the archive away.'[41] But perhaps this space could also be a future-oriented archive, where rights claims and creative histories would expose, challenge and divest from the companies and governments that connect tear gas production in Pennsylvania to denials of humanity in Bethlehem. As Said himself noted in opening *The Question of Palestine*, what academics can offer is simply, but not insignificantly, 'a series of experienced realities, grounded in a sense of human rights and the contradictions of social experience, couched as much as possible in the language of everyday reality'.[42] Such an offering is especially meaningful in a climate of fear and silence, he went on:

How many ex-politicians or actively engaged intellectuals still say privately that they are horrified by Israeli military policy and political arrogance, or that they believe the occupation, creeping annexation, and settlement of the territories is inexcusable, and yet say little or nothing in public, where their words might have some effect?[43]

If, as Said insisted, 'the question of Palestine is a concrete historical one that can be comprehended in human terms',[44] then should not our response to it also be given in those ordinary human terms? Why *choose* to see Aida in the first place, if only to return to our comfortable lives? I would wager most of us had made this choice from carrying our own problematic or virtuous or, in any case, deeply human burdens – to 'help' the downtrodden, to bear witness, to link struggles and hopes across artificial boundaries, to denounce violence, or to redeem ourselves. But intellectual links do little in the face of state force, and they do nothing if they remain our own personal musings on a godforsaken world, a thought experiment we spin around internally without taking the outward-facing risks that might well cost us our careers in an increasingly politicised, nationalised and repressive state of discourse across the world. Edward Said taught us that academic power is a sham unless it is leveraged to speak truth to power – unless it builds power, across positionalities we didn't choose, towards international communities that remain ours to make. What we are left with might be less questions about Palestine and more questions about ourselves, including an examination not just of who we are or of what we are willing to build, but also, because many of us are ourselves settlers, of what we are willing to let go.

Notes

1. See David Macey, *Frantz Fanon: A Biography* (New York: Verso, 2000), p. 42.
2. Cf. Maldonado-Torres, 'The Coloniality of Being'. Writing about Michel Foucault, whom Said both brought into fashion and from whom he (later) departed, Lynne Huffer describes the archive as 'both concrete place and abstract operating system, as both visible and invisible' (Lynne Huffer, *Foucault's Strange Eros* (New York: Columbia University Press, 2020), p. 7). In this chapter, I follow Huffer's dual understanding of the archive. I thank Lauren Guilmette for directing me to these lines in Huffer.

3. Cf. Lewis Gordon, *Disciplinary Decadence: Living Thought in Trying Times* (London: Routledge, 2006).

4. Ahmad, *In Theory*, pp. 219, 222.

5. See Said, *The World, the Text, and the Critic*, pp. 28, 29. A previous version of this chapter was published as 'Edward Said's Archive: Toward Postcolonial Theory' in *Philosophy & Global Affairs*.

6. There he writes: 'Much of Western Marxism, in its aesthetic and cultural departments, is similarly blinded to the matter of imperialism. Frankfurt School critical theory, despite its seminal insights into the relationship between domination, modern society, and the opportunities for redemption through art as critique, is stunningly silent on racist theory, anti-imperialist resistance, and oppositional practice in the empire . . . Much the same thing can be said of most Anglo-Saxon cultural theory, with the important exception of feminism, and a small handful of work by young critics influenced by Raymond Williams and Stuart Hall' (Edward W. Said, *Culture and Imperialism* (New York: Vintage, 1993), p. 278).

7. Said described Palestine in the following way: 'It is the idea of a human community.' See 'Edward Said on The Idea of Palestine – 1982', https://kpfa.org/area941/episode/edward-said-on-the-idea-of-palestine/. There he also describes Palestine as 'a wedge opening up a whole can of worms'. Thanks to Ashleigh Elser for suggesting this interview.

8. Nadia Gindi, 'On the Margins of a Memoir: A Personal Reading of Said's Out of Place', *Alif: Journal of Comparative Poetics* 20 (2000): p. 284.

9. Ibid.

10. See Sadik Jalal al-'Azm, 'Orientalism and orientalism in reverse', https://libcom.org/article/orientalism-and-orientalism-reverse-sadik-jalal-al-azm.

11. See Hallaq, *Restating Orientalism*, pp. 239, 110. Further, in his study of Said's relationship to religion, William Hart observes Said's 'lack of insight' regarding the socially transformative role religion can play: 'Religion is an important site of struggle. It is more important, I would say, than Western classical music for

the elaboration of civil society and as a form of ideology critique' (Hart, *Edward Said*, p. 37).

12. Said, *Humanism*, p. 11. In his final book, Said outlines both the need and the requirements for 'a different kind of humanism', a humanism avoidant of Eurocentrism, resistant to *idées reçues*, and that discloses the present (ibid.; see also pp. 22, 43, 61 and 73). Cf. Nikolas Kompridis's enlightening review of Akeel Bilgrami's *Secularism, Identity, and Enchantment*, a review in dialogue with Said: https://ndpr.nd.edu/reviews/secularism-identity-and-enchantment/.

13. Lucius Outlaw, who is building an archive of Africana philosophy at Haverford College, provides a thoughtful answer in his chapter in an edited volume: While 'a discipline is an inherently social enterprise in which some degree of consensus is necessary, shared rules are required' and '[t]he rules – the norms – for obtaining such agreement are not provided by melanin', it is also the case that Black Studies 'offer[s] a critical *mediation* of competing normative agendas relative to the goals and objectives of the particular people in question. Such a contribution requires the fulfillment of one of the definitive commitments of contemporary Black Studies to be in touch with and service to the communities that are the object of study; but, refined through the criticist frame, it also redefines the limits of this same commitment. The sincerity and intensity of our commitment must not degenerate into authoritarian dogmatism' (Lucius Outlaw, 'Africology: Normative Theory', in *The African American Studies Reader*, ed. Nathaniel Norment, Jr (Durham, NC: Carolina Academic Press, 2007), pp. 557, 559).

14. What could it mean for a tradition to be 'ours'? Is a tradition singular? Would it be more accurate (with Said) to talk about the many beginnings, as opposed to *an* origin, of a tradition? Could a tradition be thought of in forward-looking terms, as in how it travels, as opposed to from where it originates? If so, what erasures would occur, and how would those be ethically problematic?

15. Edward Said, *Representations of the Intellectual: The 1993 Reith Lectures* (New York: Vintage, 1996), p. 12.

16. Ibid. p. 26. To the many who know Said better than I: Would it be fair to say his critique of nationalism, his emphasis on what someone has done more than who they are, is in the spirit of Sartre's claim that transcendence is more important than facticity?

17. Said, *Representations*, pp. 11–12.

18. Ibid. p. 13.

19. Jeanne Morefield, *Unsettling the World: Edward Said and Political Theory* (Lanham, MD: Rowman and Littlefield, 2022), p. 112.

20. Ibid. p. 206.

21. Said was always writing in notebooks, appointment books and journals, as well as commenting on those notes in the margins of those texts. He was asking questions about himself, about Palestinian politics, about the classes he was teaching, about the US media landscape, and so on. His notes are so mixed that they confound the archivist's categories. For instance, his above note about what he couldn't say in public is housed in a folder labelled 'research notebook', yet the 'notebook' says nothing about his research (understood in a traditional sense) and is probably better understood as a journal or diary.

22. Said, 'Traveling Theory', p. 247. There is, of course, also the way that some ideas gain *more* of a political edge, become *more* popular, as they travel not from an insurrectionary context to an academic one, but from nation state to empire. This is what Said documented when he noted that the idea of Zionism 'has become effective' in the West (Said, *The Question of Palestine*, p. 56). Hence the need for a historical examination of ideas. 'The task of criticism, or, to put it another way, the role of the critical consciousness in such cases is to be able to make distinctions, to produce differences where at present there are none. To write critically about Zionism in Palestine has therefore never meant, and does not mean now, being anti-Semitic; conversely, the struggle for Palestinian rights and self-determination does not mean support for the Saudi royal family, nor for the antiquated and oppressive state structures of most of the Arab nations' (ibid. p. 59).

23. See Edward Said, 'Nationalism, Human Rights, and Interpretation', in *Reflections on Exile and Other Essays* (Cambridge, MA: Harvard University Press, 2000), p. 430. All of my references to Said's physical archive come from the Edward Said Papers, Rare Book & Manuscript Collection, Columbia University in the City of New York. Not all of what I cite is dated.

24. Perhaps the reader wonders here about how much influence Said gleaned from women philosophers. The gendered, non-relational language of one of his 1956 exams at Princeton, housed in his archive at Columbia, is informative: 'I pledge my honor as a gentleman that during this examination I have neither given nor received assistance.'

25. Said himself observed: 'Henry Kissinger and the two presidents he served gave Israel more arms in a shorter period of time than ever in its history. U.S. policy [under Kissinger] was deliberately to ignore the Palestinians, to try to whittle down Arab nationalist sentiment in the region, to force political movement into bilateral, step-by-step processes' (Said, *The Question of Palestine*, p. 225).

26. See Sylvia Wynter, 'Beyond the Categories of the Master Conception: The Counterdoctrine of the Jamesian Poiesis', in *C. L. R. James's Caribbean*, eds. Paget Henry and Paul Buhle (Durham, NC: Duke University Press, 1992), p. 70. As Gerard Aching reminded me while I was composing this chapter, Said comes from the generation of postcolonial theorists that attempted to 'master the masters'. We could ask: What is the most fruitful method for a next generation of theorists? And: How do we read this previous method in dialogue with Audre Lorde's famous line about the master's tools?

27. See Edward W. Said, 'Yeats and Decolonization', in Eagleton et al., *Nationalism, Colonialism, and Literature* (Minneapolis: University of Minnesota Press, 1990), p. 69.

28. See ibid. pp. 69–70. Said adds in an interview: 'We've had a tendency, you see, to think of experiences in national terms. We say there's the Polish experience . . . there's the Haitian experience . . . It seems to me that that's pretty much over, where one

could give a certain amount of fidelity and attention to basic national identities. What's interesting is the way that national identities have historically, in fact – and the present moment facilitates that – interacted and depended upon each other. I mean the relationship between Brazil and North America is very, very dramatic now in the situation of the rain forests . . . What you begin to realize is the universality, therefore, not of stabilities, which have been the prevailing norm in cultural studies, but of migrations' (Edward W. Said, 'Criticism, Culture, and Performance', in *Power, Politics, and Culture: Interviews with Edward Said*, ed. Gauri Viswanathan (New York: Vintage, 2001), pp. 114–15).

29. This is one of Said's frustrations with Michael Walzer, namely, the appeal to the ad hominem, the hugely reductive emphasis on the ethnic: 'I am a "Palestinian Christian," he tells us, deducing my world view from that ethno-religious fact; what would he say if I drew conclusions from his family background? Is this the kind of political analysis we are to expect from a professor at the Institute for Advanced Study?' (Hart, *Edward Said*, p. 197). This is different from, for instance, the playful way the author Nadine Gordimer would write to Said: 'This atheist white African Jew spent Christmas in the company of the Christian (lapsed?) Arab Palestinian Edward Said. And excellent company he was, too' (letter from 28 December 2000).

30. Said, *Representations*, p. 63. He would add in *Cultural and Imperialism*: 'If one believes with Gramsci that an intellectual vocation is socially possible as well as desirable, then it is an inadmissible contradiction at the same time to build analyses of historical experience around exclusions, exclusions that stipulate, for instance, that only women can understand feminine experience, only Jews can understand Jewish suffering, only formerly colonial subjects can understand colonial experience' (Said, *Culture and Imperialism*, p. 31).

31. Gurminder Bhambra, 'Beginnings: Edward W. Said and Questions of Nationalism', *Interventions: International Journal of Postcolonial Study* 8, no. 1 (2006): p. 1. He would say himself 'that

"identity" does not necessarily imply ontologically given and eternally determined stability, or uniqueness, or irreducible character, or privileged status as something total and complete in and of itself' (Said, *Culture and Imperialism*, p. 315).

32. Hart explains these high-culture attachments by saying that 'Said is a Marxist-oriented thinker with Arnoldian sympathies' (Hart, *Edward Said*, p. 97). It is noteworthy that Said's model, as a celebrity academic, contrasts sharply with, say, the call of Duncan Kennedy (especially in his splendid 'Legal Education and the Reproduction of Hierarchy') and Critical Legal Studies to create a university where pay is equal and professors spend time sweeping the floors. Can you even sweep in Burberry, or does the jacket automatically disintegrate upon realising that you are about to do working-class labour?

33. See Esmat Elhalaby, 'The World of Edward Said', 13 May 2021, *Boston Review*, https://www.bostonreview.net/articles/the-world-of-edward-said/.

34. Cf. Valerie Lambert's unofficial Land and Labor Acknowledgment on her University of North Carolina page: https://anthropology.unc.edu/person/valerie-lambert/. Cf. 'Manan Ahmed, Gurminder K. Bhambra and Valerie Lambert: Post-Colonial Knowledge', https://www.youtube.com/watch?v=A8_94VY3XQ4&ab_channel=COMITResearch. Hamid Dabashi notes that one of the biggest barriers to carrying out Said's idea of the humanist intellectual is the professionalism that dominates both students and faculty alike on most US campuses (see Hamid Dabashi, *On Edward Said: Remembrance of Things Past* (Chicago: Haymarket Books, 2020), pp. 97–101).

35. Mahmoud Darwish, 'To Our Land', *Poetry* (2005): p. 198. Also, although an idea cannot be owned, it can be guarded – or locked up at Yale.

36. See the report 'No Safe Space', https://humanrights.berkeley.edu/programs-projects/past-projects/no-safe-space.

37. See Antony Loewenstein, *The Palestine Laboratory: How Israel Exports the Technology of Occupation Around the World* (New York: Verso, 2023).

38. See Noam Perry, 'Is your 401(k) funding state violence and human rights violations?' American Friends Service Committee, https://afsc.org/news/your-401k-funding-state-violence-and-human-rights-violations.

39. In a line that was very influential for how I have come to see postcolonial theory in the US academy, Ann Stoler writes, 'One could argue that (post)colonial studies made no conceptual place for the very forms of colonial governance that motivated Said's work. Reading *The Question of Palestine* alongside *Orientalism* might have provoked a different set of questions that are more present in vastly reconfigured colonial studies now: about the relations among imperial formations; about the network of power relations that joined British colonialism, European racism, U.S. investments in the Middle East, and the persistent encroachment of Israeli settlements on working Palestinian land and lives' (Stoler, *Duress*, p. 55). For how Israel debilitates Palestinians, and for an important distinction between disabling and debilitating state practices, see Jasbir Puar, *The Right to Maim*.

40. See Edward W. Said, 'The Morning After', *London Review of Books* 13, no. 20 (1993).

41. Said, *The Politics of Dispossession*, p. 119.

42. Said, *The Question of Palestine*, p. xli.

43. Ibid. p. xxii.

44. Ibid. p. 230.

5 Hannah Arendt's Ordinary Humanism

I went to Nablus in May 2023. This was the time when the militant group the Lions' Den had gained support in the city for its armed attacks against Israeli checkpoints, soldiers and settlements. As a consequence, the Israeli Occupying Forces had increased their surveillance and raids not just of Lions' Den hideouts, but of the city of Nablus as a whole. Foreigners by and large had stopped going to the city. It was deemed too dangerous.

I was there with a group of academics from the United States. I have breathing problems that can be triggered by many factors, including airborne pollutants such as the exhaust from a car, the mould of an old building, or the fragrance of cologne (or of a plant). So when the other academics toured one of Nablus's famous soap factories, I stood and waited outside. I looked around and took in all the black water tanks on the roofs of the buildings. Ubiquitous across the West Bank, the tanks collect rainwater for the weeks at a time when the Israeli forces shut off Palestinian access to water. Israel controls over 80 per cent of the water in the West Bank, sending it to settlements, where it is used for pools and car washes while the majority of Palestinians struggle to access sufficient clean water.[1] As I stood outside the factory, a group of Nablusi youths approached me, perhaps wondering if I – like many of the pale-skinned people who remained in the city? – was ultimately there to infiltrate Palestinian organisations on behalf of Israel. I don't speak Arabic, so I only smiled and waved, wondering myself when my group would finish its tour.

After the soap factory we walked through the densely populated Old City, starting at the Manara Clock Tower, which had been adorned by posters honouring Lions' Den martyrs – the stern gazes of dead young men, armed with automatic rifles, watching us as we passed under the clock. Our local guide taught us about the Roman history of Nablus as well as how it has been ruled by multiple empires in its history, which includes a history of coexistence, at different times, between Jews, Muslims and Christians. Before we ended our tour with *knafeh*, a sweet cheese pastry Nablus has made famous, but after seeing the house where a prominent barber had been killed (or 'martyred') for his involvement with the Lions' Den, we walked down another narrow street in the Old City to visit a historic spice shop.

Avoiding strong smells once again, I stood outside the shop and waited. The director of the academic programme joined me outside so she could smoke one of her American Spirits. I desperately wanted to join her in the ordinary pleasure of smoking. The sun beat down on us in the alley, which smelled of exhaust from the scooters many Palestinians use to get around the narrow roads of the Old City. Several young Nablusi boys, their hair cut high and tight in the military fashion of the martyrs, walked by. Then an old sedan turned into the alley.

The narrowness of the alley meant that the director and I had to press up against the stone wall to allow the sedan to pass. We saw that an older man was driving. He approached us slowly, and we remained pressed against the wall.

Smoke from the director's cigarette mixed with the car's exhaust and the alley's gravel dust. The man stopped his car next to us. He rolled down the window. He looked at me.

He said something in Arabic. I didn't understand. He reached across the passenger seat, picked up a small, square cardboard box, and extended it out the window. I stared at the box intently. He looked into my eyes and opened the box. It was filled with *raha*, a Nablusi sweet made from sugar, starch and sometimes rose or orange water. The director and I each took one and told him *shukran*, thanks. He smiled and drove on.

I have revisited that moment many times since that hot afternoon, not least to grapple with the fact that, perhaps because I grew up in post-9/11 America, when the man approached us in the alley, and especially when he stopped his car next to me, I was afraid. Essentially, I had feared a man who gave me a snack. I was afraid of someone who was going about his day, and who, upon seeing two people who certainly looked more Israeli than Nablusi, and so might've been involved in the death of his beloved barber, had decided the proper approach was to offer us something sweet.

And because he likely has limited clean water at home, the food he shared with us was not just a simple dessert, but a delicacy cobbled together in the face of great constraints.

What that man's generosity demonstrates, I feel, hints at what it looks like to live beyond the modern categories into which we are born, and in which most of us remain (including me, above all in that moment) – in our thinking and our actions, in our self-understanding and our relations – for the rest of our lives. The man demonstrated an ordinary ethics lived out in the face of tremendous loss and ongoing deprivation. And in that way, his gift might also be understood as an invitation for its recipients to live differently, beyond our own categories and fears with respect to self and Other, friend and enemy, stranger and kin. He offered an example of how, in Glissant's words, '[w]ithin this universe of domination and oppression, of silent or professed dehumanization, forms of humanity stubbornly persisted'.[2]

Caught in Categories

Because that *raha* might be understood as symbolising a refusal of categorical thinking, because it was offered across the usual and easy distinctions – between citizen and foreigner, native and infiltrator, perhaps even Israeli and Palestinian – when I reflect on that day, I also return to the philosopher Hannah Arendt, whose writing maintained a thoroughgoing critical examination of modern responses to modern problems, yet who personally struggled to realise the promise of her thought. Indeed, it was Arendt who, in the 'Imperialism' section of *The Origins of Totalitarianism* – a section Edward Said almost always included in his syllabi related to empire or postcolonial theory – wrote:

Hitler's solution of the Jewish problem, first to reduce the German Jews to a nonrecognized minority in Germany, then to drive them as stateless people across the borders, and finally to gather them back from everywhere in order to ship them to extermination camps, was an eloquent demonstration to the rest of the world how really to 'liquidate' all problems concerning minorities and stateless. After the war it turned out that the Jewish question, which was considered the only insoluble one, was indeed solved – namely, by means of a colonized and then conquered territory – but this solved neither the problem of the minorities nor the stateless. On the contrary, like virtually all other events of our century, the solution of the Jewish question merely produced a new category of refugees, the Arabs, thereby increasing the number of the stateless and rightless by another 700,000 to 800,000 people. And what happened in Palestine within the smallest territory and in terms of hundreds of thousands was then repeated in India on a large scale involving many millions of people. Since the Peace Treaties of 1919 and 1920 the refugees and the stateless have attached themselves like a curse to all the newly established states on earth which were created in the image of the nation-state.[3]

To respond to the modern 'problem' of minorities through the modern 'solution' of the nation state, Arendt teaches, only perpetuates the problem. She reiterated this claim later, in *Eichmann in Jerusalem*, arguing there that the minority problem remained 'insoluble' as long as we are living 'within the political framework of the nation-state'.[4] Importantly, in this line she does not say that the question of living together in right relations is impossible *for human beings*. Her claim is more specific; it is about the political form in which we have organised ourselves, inherited, and not successfully moved beyond. The form of the nation state creates the problem of the minority. 'The strength of Arendt's analysis', Jacqueline Rose comments, 'is that she recognises that there is something deadly in the law.'[5] Such criticism of the nation state does not necessarily equate to pessimism, nor does it entail eschewing law *tout court*. A different political order, perhaps one in which the human being is indeed found and treated as sacred, remains a possibility. To get there, Arendt proposed in her 'Prologue' to *The Human Condition*, our first task 'is nothing more than to think what we are doing'.[6]

* * *

It is worth noting that I was cautioned against concluding a book largely focused on a Black Atlantic archive of ethics with a philosopher whose ideas were deeply tainted and limited by racism and colonialism. Arendt's racial politics leaves theorists who nevertheless want to think with her asking ourselves what the political theorist Patricia Owens has called a 'vexed question' regarding Arendt's utility.[7] For instance, in Arendt's article 'Reflections on Little Rock' – written for *Commentary* in 1957 but not published until 1959 in *Dissent* – she argued that integrating schools was 'to burden children, black and white, with the workings of a problem which adults for generations have confessed themselves unable to solve', as well as that '[t]o force parents to send their children to an integrated school against their will means to deprive them of rights which clearly belong to them in all free societies'.[8] Even if Arendt would concede in a letter to the writer Ralph Ellison that 'I now see that I simply didn't understand the complexities in the situation', nevertheless, as the philosopher Kathryn T. Belle notes, 'Arendt's concession does not prevent a repetition of her error in judgment in "Crisis in Education" and *On Violence*'.[9] 'The problem with violence' as Arendt sees it, Belle observes, 'is not the original or constitutive violence of America's founding fathers and Europe's imperialists, but rather the anticolonial violence and resistance of the colonized in Africa.'[10] As the political theorist Joy James has noted about how the Greek *polis* influenced Arendt, 'Arendt ignores the fact that enslavement and economic exploitation and forced relegation to the "powerless" private realm enabled an Athenian elite (of propertied males) to practice democracy.'[11] Further, as the historian Dirk Moses has noted about how Roman politics influenced Arendt, 'Arendt embraced an ideology of civilization modeled on the Roman republic and justified through its progressive incorporation of diverse people into a federated international order.'[12] Moses continues: 'Rome's mythic foundation in colonial conquest and settlement and its spread of civilization by violent expansion was, she thought, an acceptable, indeed necessary, theodicy that could be distinguished from modern imperialism.'[13] Here Moses perceptively underscores that even Arendt's critique of Zionism 'was ultimately undermined by its civilizational normativity'.[14] The historian Samuel Moyn summarises: '[G]iven Arendt's neo-Roman politics, empire was one form of exemplary grandeur implicit in her call for collective action.'[15] And in terms of more recent events, the architect Eyal Weizman has noted that in the case of Bosnia, thinking with Arendt and 'raising the flag of human rights meant military intervention'.[16]

So, Arendt – who was so perspicacious regarding many of the logics of modernity – also missed key aspects of its *racial* logics. As Owens asserts, 'Racism was also not a minor issue in Arendt's work, or something marginal to her substantive political theory. It affected core themes associated with what is most celebrated in her historical and theoretical work.'[17] The poet and theorist Fred Moten has added that there is 'an antiblackness that infuses and animates Arendt's work', which, Moten shows, is not just against Black Studies but also against black study itself.[18] All in all, Arendt's racism is another way of understanding that Arendt offered what the political theorist Seyla Benhabib has described as her 'reluctant modernism' – but still a modernism, one deeply tied to colonialism (its norms, its questions, its problematisations).[19] 'This information', Said reflected about a different but related context, Arendt's support of Israel in 1967 and 1973, 'is remarkable for someone otherwise so compassionate and reflective on the subject of what Zionism did to Palestinians.'[20]

It may therefore seem that, given all of these critiques (which I grant), to conclude this book with Arendt's correspondence is not just a curious, but a misguided choice. And to place Arendt's correspondence in apposition with a story from Palestine is, perhaps, *especially* misguided, given Arendt's Zionism, even if she did go on to criticise Zionists in *Eichmann* (for which she was attacked). In other words, Arendt – despite being a refugee and camp survivor herself – by and large missed the greater anti-colonial point about the need to stand in solidarity with the dispossessed in order to oppose how the nation state cheapens human life – a point that Palestinians have so strongly asked the world to account for today.

And yet, I stay with Arendt to think about the ethical questions the philosophers in this book have raised not only because she asks us to think about these questions as parts of a larger constellation but also because understanding her strengths and limitations sheds light on different forms of political theory today. Yes, she misunderstood Indigenous liberation movements due to her presuppositions that maintained a positive role for expanding Western empires. I agree with Benhabib when she argues that 'Arendt's own judgments were sometimes quite wrong, especially concerning what W. E. B. Du Bois called the "color line"'; but I also agree with Benhabib that 'Arendt's legacy is not a doctrine or a philosophical system. It is a bracing induction into thinking about the political and facing up to its promise as well as its failures.'[21] Indeed, Robert Gooding-Williams has productively read Arendt as a corrective to Du Bois in regard to the question of defining politics, because Arendt helps us move away from a sense of politics as leadership and being ruled and more towards understanding politics as actions we take together.[22] This method of reading, of facing up to promises and failures together in taking a longer and more holistic perspective of a topic or book or question or figure, remains underdeveloped in many strands of critical theory and social movements today, and it is one that both Said and Gilroy have modelled in their respective critical readings of Arendt; it is a method I am attempting to follow here.

Contradictions

Each philosopher with whom this book engages has offered an ethical theory rife with contradictions, and I would like my conclusion to be in that spirit. Indeed, returning to Arendt symbolises something else. Our political movements still need to make space for our own contradictions that all of us, feeling increasingly 'out of place', are still working through. Thinking with these tensions might proceed through a method that exemplifies what Jacqueline Rose said about Stuart Hall: that throughout his essays 'Hall is trying to let as much air and movement into our political and psychic lives as is humanly possible.'[23] After all, it was Hall who stressed, at the end of the last century, the need for us 'to wake up, to grow up, to come into the world of contradiction', which he also called 'the world of politics'.[24] While concluding with Arendt is noticeably a departure from the anti-imperial thinkers I have commented on thus far, in doing so I also recognise that to think in modern/colonial times *is* to proceed through unresolved tensions, complexities and contradictions. And – to speak to my readers who have participated in this century's social movements – we need more air in our political lives. We need to find a way to sustain one another in the struggle, as opposed to treating each other in a way that leads to *increasing* our alienation, now not just with the world around us, but with the movements, with each other, and with ourselves.

To return to Paul Gilroy, it is noteworthy that Gilroy cites Arendt several times in *Against Race*, and he has elsewhere said that *Against Race* is modelled on Arendt's 1951 *Origins of Totalitarianism*.[25] As is his custom, Gilroy not only builds on but also departs from this influence. While it remains implicit in *Against Race*, elsewhere Gilroy makes explicit that the 'vulnerable figure' of Arendt's basic human in *Origins* 'might', Gilroy says, 'be described much more accurately as a *racialized* human: a particular, infra-human creation rather than a specimen of the catastrophically empty humanity that she wishes to repudiate. Her error corresponds to a refusal to engage racism directly and critically.'[26] Nevertheless – or precisely because of these generative complications – Gilroy stays with Arendt.

But even if we move through, beyond, or perhaps simply past Arendt's racial oversights to think with her, isn't her concept of thinking itself anti-ethical? As Rei Terada has observed in reading Arendt to consider US delusions around the Iraq

War, 'There are more politicians whose imperial fantasies could be corrected by realism than there are ones who could be corrected by ethics: most imperial fantasies happily invoke ethics without encountering anything in the ethical field that can't be domesticated by a little interpretation.'[27] 'That is', Terada goes on, '"Don't harm another human being" is not necessarily helpful because there can be disagreement about what a human being is; indeed the very creation of the maxim also creates a motive to make sure that some people are not counted as human.'[28] Thus, as Terada concludes – *contra* the argument of much of this book – 'Arendt bets on reality rather than ethics, thinking as registration rather than thinking as process, only because the "inherent contingency" of facts, being less predictable and more palpably consequential, is more likely than ethical abstraction to take fantasy aback.'[29]

I still wonder if reading reality and practising an ethics could go together. I still wonder if one limitation of Arendt's approach lies in thinking ethics as what Terada calls 'ethical abstraction'. Is it not *this abstraction* that takes us out of ethical life as it is lived, and thus into the textual and terminological realms we pose ethical problems through, the categories we need to find a way to live beyond or transition away from? As the novelist and philosopher Frieda Ekotto has written about critiques of race that stay at the level of content without addressing the limits of *the form* of their criticism, 'such critiques do not take into account that race was invented as a category at the same time that categorial reason was invented as an all-important theoretical tool . . . One should also extend [the critique of racial categories] to the entire process of categorial reason.'[30]

Suggesting a distinction between ethics and ethical abstraction still requires addressing the sociological corrective, stressed over and over by feminists and others in the twentieth century, namely, that we do not begin our encounters from a pre-conceptual, unmediated 'pure' space, a space somehow without categories that mediate our theory and practice. According to this view, it is not the case that the man who offered me *raha* was not thinking categorically, for all human life is always already mediated by categories. And I certainly do not want to suggest that there is a pre-political sphere. Instead, what I wish to highlight is the material role of refusal, hesitation, reinterpretation and action. My suggestion, more specifically and existentially, is that there remains a moment of choice in how we act, something like a moment between ethics and categorial ethical abstraction. Put differently, there is a moment in which either we can try to solve a problem by reverting to the level of abstractions or we can offer an answer through our actions.[31] In this moment, we can (imperfectly) testify to another dimension of social relations, the dimension we are trying to build.

Giving an Account

All the philosophers who inform this book engaged the ancient philosophical idea of examining our lives – coming from Socrates' famous line that 'the unexamined life is not worth living'. All had encountered Plato and Plato's *Apology*, and it would have not been lost on Glissant that when Césaire articulated a 'systematic defense' of colonised civilisations in *Discourse*, his words in the original French were 'je fais l'apologie systématique des sociétés détruites par l'impérialisme'.[32] I want to say that Du Bois, Glissant, Wynter and Said also offer an ethics related to a less famous, later moment of the *Apology*, in which Socrates notes that he is being persecuted only because he asked his fellow citizens to give an account of their lives. 'You have killed me in the belief that you would avoid giving an account of your life', Socrates says, 'but I maintain that quite the opposite will happen to you. There will be more people to test you, whom I now held back, but you did not notice. They will be more difficult to deal with as they will be younger.'[33]

As Judith Butler writes about ethical encounters, '[W]hen the "I" seeks to give an account of itself, an account that must include the conditions of its own emergence, it must, as a matter of necessity, become a social theorist.'[34] Butler goes on: 'If the "I" is not at one with moral norms, this means only that the subject must deliberate upon these norms, and that part of deliberation will entail a critical understanding of their social genesis and meaning. In this sense, ethical deliberation is bound up with the operation of critique.'[35] Is this 'ethical deliberation' another form of what Terada called 'ethical abstraction'? I do not think it necessarily has to be. Yes, one way of reading Butler here is to stress that any person, or any 'I' who gives an account, becomes a social *theorist*, and so turns to an abstracted sociology or cultural theory in order to examine norms in 'their social genesis and meaning'. But as it was for Socrates in the *agora*, it could also be the case that this deliberation proceeds not only or even mostly through a *studia* in the library, but also through ongoing worldly *action*, Arendt's translation of Aristotle's *praxis*.

And perhaps this *praxis* would make room – in its form or style – for all the fallibility that characterises human life. Perhaps it would be informed by some of Arendt's most pressing observations in her writings on literature: as she says of Stefan Zweig's response to the Nazi influence on German 'better classes' in the early 1930s, 'he failed to perceive that the dignified restraint, which society had no longer considered a criterion of true *Bildung*, was under such circumstances tantamount to plain cowardice'; as she says learning from Franz Kafka, 'A true human life cannot be led by people who feel themselves detached from the basic and simple laws of humanity nor by those who elect to live in a vacuum, even if they be led to do so by persecution'; and as she says of W. H. Auden, 'The main thing was to have no illusions and to accept no thoughts – no theoretical systems – that would blind you to reality.'[36]

Arendt draws these conclusions – against respectable restraint in unethical times, against living without wide social contacts, against the ways we avoid reality, and so conclusions deeply relevant for living out political lives – from her literary analysis. Indeed, she offered them as public engagements with novels and poetry. Her points also read to me as possible ethical precepts: that restraint from public engagement can be a form of cowardice (as it so often is regarding the question of Palestine); that even under persecution one part of maintaining humanity is to continue not just to think, but to live relationally and through our attachments (to a world billionaires would rather destroy and then have us leave behind in space travel); and that systematic thought, including ethical systems or abstractions, can take us away from reality and thereby away from complicated human life as it is lived (on the ground and in ordinary ways). It is because of these lessons, offered through engagement with not philosophy per se but with literature, and learned from years of correspondence with friends and with writers – with many of whom she disagreed – that I suggest we receive Arendt's offering not just regarding *the content* of what she said, such as her misguided argument about Little Rock, but about *the form* of her humanist practice: her essays and book reviews and letters, her persistent and sometimes (like all of ours) problematic thinking, and her courage all the while to make her thoughts public. If we read Arendt with a view towards form and practice, then we begin to read her contributions perhaps more like how Gilroy read *Origins*, namely, as a model to follow.

But it is not, as it was for Gilroy, to *Origins* or *The Human Condition* that I wish to turn in order to conclude this book, nor is it to her striking reviews of literature. It is, rather, to her correspondence with her teacher and friend, Karl Jaspers. I do this for the rather simple reason that in the wake of Israel's collective punishment of Palestinians in October 2023, I found myself (surprised myself) returning not just to an old college practice I had of reading Yehuda Amichai and Mahmoud Darwish together, not just to call after call with friends, but I also found myself returning to Arendt's letters for their sense of thinking and friendship in what she called – in perhaps a troubling description – 'dark times'.[37]

If there is a form that outlines another dimension of humanity, lived out in the most ordinary way, might it be less the philosophical treatise with its sharp arguments, or the novel with its varying characters we can read ourselves into, or even the essay that tests a new form of thinking and being, and more the letter written intimately between friends? While a turn in ethics to such a private practice is, arguably, at best symptomatic of the limits of our agency in our neoliberal times, or at worst a fundamentally anti-political gesture, it is also the case that such practices are necessary to inform (in theory) and sustain (in empathy and understanding) our complicated political movements over time.

An Ethics of Correspondence

What is more reflective of an ordinary humanism than our fallibility, our blind spots, our failures and our personal (and political) mistakes? Might the task of our time be to find a communal, species-wide footing given these limitations and violations? Might letting more air and movement into our political lives involve starting from our own in-process tensions (including regarding the philosophers whose work we have come to love)? What I want to suggest – when today partisan sides trade blows over who is awake and who is not, who is cancelled and who gets to stay, who is called out and who is celebrated – is that part of living 'another humanity' is thinking with one another amidst these disagreements, missteps, and errors, as Arendt did in writing to Ellison. Not that we abandon critique. Not that there is always a place for forgiveness, much less redemption, even if Arendt observed in *The Human Condition* that '[t]respassing is an everyday occurrence which is in the very nature of action's constant establishment of new relationships within a web of relations, and it needs forgiving'.[38] Some action and structures are, I believe, unforgivable. But at the same time, much of ordinary life requires forgiving – Arendt stresses this 'need' only after giving an example of 'an everyday occurrence'.

At the end of this book, I turn to correspondence because, after all, it is in how we communicate with one another over time – and it must be over time – that these dimensions of awakening, trespassing and (perhaps) forgiving play out. Thinking is not just, as Arendt stressed in a lecture, like the wind and therefore unsettling.[39] It is also – as Arendt thought with Heidegger, as Du Bois thought with Bismarck, as Glissant thought with Hegel, as Wynter thought with Adorno, and as Said thought with Conrad – complicated, protean, 'contradictory', contrapuntal, unpredictable and en route. If these philosophers have taught us anything, it is that we do not always share a politics with those we think with, and we certainly don't necessarily share with them any identity, whether it be in terms of race, sexual orientation, nationality, theory of change, or otherwise. Though it is not what Arendt meant by her simile, this is another way that thinking is like the wind: thinking moves in gusts and lulls, storms and stillness, across all fabricated borders.

In my view, it would take a rather rigid position to see little of value for ethical life in the Arendt-Jaspers correspondence. For here is a conversation between teacher and student, German and Jew, man and woman; here is a conversation between countries, over time, and thus one that proceeds through an implicit acceptance of disagreement, an acceptance marked by censure, debate, joy, frustration, hurry, pause, patience and consistency. If the world finds nothing sacred in being human, it is so often left to friends, particularly those born into different positions, to find something sacred in each other. And such 'sustaining friendship', as Ramzi Fawaz puts it in concluding *Queer Forms* with a return to Arendt, is worth holding onto as we continually piece ourselves together in order to continue our movements in the face of increasing criminalisation and repression.[40]

* * *

I will not recapitulate the correspondence here, at the close of this book. Rather, I want to focus on a few letters that, for me, carry implications for Glissant's longed-for new practice of humanity. Might our letters be one way of practising the accountability that Socrates said we try so hard to avoid?

In his 2 December 1945 letter to Arendt, Jaspers writes, 'I sense in your words not only your personal loyalty but also the spirit of a natural humanity that is infinitely comforting.' 'Tears came to my eyes while I was reading your letter', he goes on, 'because I felt how rare that spirit is . . . There are others, many of them. But one doesn't meet them. The very few suffice to give one hope. They keep alive in us the awareness of a truth that is not tangible, a bright room that opens to us.'[41] Jaspers's is a sentiment all of us who are trying to live out another dimension of humanity have felt, the loneliness that is not generative solitude as part of solidarity, but that is the feeling that we don't meet enough of the kind of people who are also pursuing another path, and so too often we return to what is more widely considered normal and good; without a relational path ahead, we assimilate into the norms and desires of our still-colonial present.[42]

Jaspers goes on to note, in his own way, that he misses Arendt, saying how pleasant it would be if she joined him again in the rooms of his apartment: 'You could sit in the chair at my desk again the way you used to as a doctoral candidate.' And then, in the manner of an inviting teacher, he asks Arendt about a new opportunity to contribute some writing:

Would you like to write an essay for us? You can see that your length has to be limited, to about 12 pages of print. What you write is up to you. Perhaps you could write something on what truly unites us across all the barriers between us – and by us I mean Americans and Europeans, including Germans?

'Please forgive this prose', Jaspers concludes his short letter. 'Everything is jumbled together in one's head in this world, which is just starting on its way back, or perhaps is on its way back, to some kind of order in which it is possible to live for tasks worthy of human beings.'[43]

Even though Jaspers is writing here at the conclusion of World War II, fewer than seven months after the Nazi surrender, there is something of a universal quality to his letter, not just for professors and their students, I would wager, but also for all of us who read and write as our way of making sense of how the world unfolds around us.

I will tell you here, reader, that I started drafting this conclusion in early October 2023, when Hamas violently resisted Israel's occupation by killing some 1,200 Israelis (mostly civilians), and then when the Israeli Occupying Forces responded with aggressive (and illegal) collective punishment of Palestinian civilians. When I would then email friends, colleagues and students to see how they were doing, I often included in my emails my poor scan of this page of correspondence, asking my friends to also forgive my prose, for I too felt that everything was 'jumbled together' just as strongly as I desired for a world 'starting on its way'. We 'do our best every day, and every hour', Esra Akcan wrote back to me, capturing the texture of that painful moment, 'even with the knowledge that it will not be good enough'.

* * *

Arendt's 29 January 1946 response is as moving as Jaspers's invitation to write about 'what truly unites us across all the barriers between us'. She begins by recalling 'our last talks together in Berlin, in 1933' and adds that 'I didn't write after that because I was afraid of endangering you'.[44] She goes on, 'How could I explain to you on the telephone or even in the context of a letter the infinitely complex red-tape existence of stateless persons?' It had been so long since they were intimately part of each other's lives (save the intimacy of memory) that she can only note, 'I have a vague recollection that your birthday falls sometime in February, so let me begin by wishing you all the best and telling you how grateful I am that you were born.'

But the correspondence nevertheless hints at a possible world – 'What you wrote does indeed create that "bright room" in which things once again fall into their proper place.' And she takes some time to comment on Jaspers's invitation to return to his chair.

I think about your study, which has always been that 'bright room' for me – with the chair at the desk and the armchair across from it where you tied your legs in marvelous knots and untied them again. I can well imagine how your own apartment strikes you as ghostly, but I'm very glad it's still there, and I hope someday to sit once again on that aforementioned chair.[45]

She goes on to explain that she has gotten married, but that 'I continue to use my old name' and that she does so for a particular reason: 'I wanted my name to identify me as a Jew.' She then adds a few more details to assure her old teacher that she has not assimilated into US society: 'I'm still a stateless person . . . I haven't become respectable in any way. I'm more than ever of the opinion that a decent human existence is possible today only on the fringes of society, where one then runs the risk of starving or being stoned to death.' 'In these circumstances', she continues, 'a sense of humor is a great help.'[46] She goes as far as to say: 'Every intellectual here is a member of the opposition simply because he is an intellectual. The reasons for that are the all-pervasive social conformity, the necessity to rebel against the god of success, etc.'

After praising the US for how ordinary people feel a responsibility for public life, citing the 'genuine storm of protest' to the internment of Japanese Americans as her example, she goes on to note 'a flip side' to her adopted country, namely, 'that nobody worries about what cannot be changed'. This nonchalance towards death, she says, is 'only another expression of this country's fundamental anti-intellectualism, which, for certain special reasons, is at its worst in the universities'.[47]

'I know you will not misunderstand me when I say that it is not an easy thing for me to contribute to a German journal', she says later, now explicitly in response to Jaspers's offer. Her next lines merit more extended consideration:

At the same time, I am unhappy about the desperate resolve of the Jews to leave Europe (you are probably aware of the mood in all the refugee camps both in and outside Germany; and that mood cannot be ignored). I am also more anxious than I care to say about the frightening possibility of other catastrophes, particularly in Palestine, given the behavior of other governments and our own suicidal tendencies in politics. Yet one thing seems clear to me: If the Jews are to be able to stay in Europe, then they cannot stay as Germans or Frenchman, etc., as if nothing had happened. It seems to me that none of us can return (and writing is surely a form of return) merely because people again seem prepared to recognize Jews as Germans or something else. We can return only if we are welcome as Jews.[48]

Here she connects her own refusal to assimilate 'respectably' with a broader political demand, namely, that European nation states recognise Jews as Jews, that they recognise a minority in their particularly and not just in broader national (assimilated and erased) terms. In regard to this book, we could read her line as an implicit challenge to any humanism that would not account for how minorities have been denied through categories they might want to hold on to as part of their resistance. It is also noteworthy that by working out this political demand in a personal letter to an old teacher who is becoming a dear friend, a friend she might say she loved, perhaps Arendt is dissolving the private/public distinction she would later work so hard to maintain. (But what is the 'catastrophe' she worried about in Palestine, in part concerned about 'other governments'? What did she see and what did she miss in these lines, and how did she arrive at these particular ways of seeing and posing problems?)

What stands out here beyond the political demand suggested in this letter is Arendt's comment on writing itself. Glissant once said of using parentheses, '[I]t is my way of breathing.'[49] Arendt too here breathes in parentheses, saying '(and writing is surely a form of return)'. She has in mind here the geographical return of Jews to Europe, which is her immediate context, as well as writing an essay for publication. But I also want to suggest that writing is a form of return to ourselves, and not just a return to a form of ourselves we have previously been, because writing is also a technology of the self through which we become different kinds of people. For a return to ourselves, in the epistolary form, comes only through our accountability to another. In this way, Arendt's assertions of her lack of respectability, her insistence on keeping her Jewish name, and her reading of intellectual opposition take on heightened significance because they are not just her journal entries; they are positions she is testing in the world through her friendship with Jaspers. And in a spirit of encouraging friendship and future accountability, Jaspers immediately affirms Arendt's essaying of the world, opening his 12 March 1946 response from Heidelberg with enthusiastic gratitude: 'Dear Hannah Arendt! What a pleasure your letter of January 29 was! I've read it over and over again and reassured myself beyond all doubt of the solidarity we share.'[50]

* * *

The second letter I want to discuss in closing this book is Arendt's 13 May 1953 letter, which again brings up the role of the intellectual and the question of the university. By this point she has become deeply worried about the state of US society. 'You probably know a lot from the papers', she begins. 'Can you see from them how far the disintegration has gone and with what breathtaking speed it has occurred? And up to now hardly any resistance.' Writing about the ways the fear tactics and biographical investigations of Senator Joseph McCarthy have permeated the country (a senator to whom many Republicans are returning as we approach the 2024 elections), Arendt comments that this is a way of 'introducing police methods into normal social life'. What follows is self-censorship and an informal system of intellectuals informing on one another for their previous ties to Communism, anti-fascism, or support for Republicans in the Spanish Civil War. 'As you can see', she continues, 'I feel that we're looking at developments that are all too familiar.'

'To give you a more complete picture', she goes on, 'I would have to tell you about the role major foundations play in the universities.' Commenting on the Ford Foundation and the Rockefeller Foundation, she writes, 'The whole business operates in a vacuum and produces no results.' What is really happening is that some of 'the intellectual proletariat' are for once 'able to acquire positions of power or make positions of power out of ones that never had any power before.' The political climate has deteriorated so much that Arendt has started to question her loyalty to the US. 'I feel it is no longer possible, as it was only a few years ago, to stand up for America without any reservations.'

At the end of the letter, she writes about what she is reading, writing and thinking about, telling Jaspers that she has been studying Marx ('a terrible pain in the neck') and writing an essay on understanding. She concludes on a personal note: 'For the distant future we're planning to go to Europe in 1955', she says of her plans with her husband, but only 'if things stay the way they are now and we can afford it . . . Just thinking of it is like a dream!'

As I read this correspondence while Israel drops more bombs on Gaza in six days than the US dropped in one year of its trigger-happy operations in Afghanistan, it strikes me that there is an analogy between the McCarthy era and our present time in regard to writing about Palestine. In our time, as Arendt said about hers, 'Just about anything is possible here at the moment, among other reasons because neither free speech nor a free press are de facto prohibited. It is not the case either that one cannot publish.' Indeed, we can write about Palestine, but many of us – in the wake of what happened to Steven Salaita (whom very few took the risk of publicly defending), and with our jobs on the line if we cannot secure, in perfect neoliberal fashion, external funding from a granting agency – choose not to. 'Save that for after tenure', people tell you. In effect meaning: 'Never write about it at all.'

And many of us, too, like Arendt, remain relatively poor, working under our earning potential in the field of education, but nevertheless dreaming of travelling through Italy as much as Hannah and Heinrich did. If we lose our jobs, of course, we will not be able to travel. So we self-censor, effectively saying that our summer in Rome is more important than the lives of Palestinians. We get the grant. We stay quiet. To repeat Said's reflection from *The Question of Palestine*: 'How many ex-politicians or actively engaged intellectuals still say privately that they are horrified by Israeli military policy and political arrogance, or that they believe the occupation, creeping annexation, and settlement of the territories is inexcusable, and yet say little or nothing in public, where their words might have some effect?'[51]

* * *

I have participated in parts of the Boycott, Divest, Sanctions (BDS) movement with a view towards using non-violent means to uphold international law, in which Arendt places her faith as she concludes *Eichmann in Jerusalem*. Although international law remains, as Noura Erakat has stressed with respect to the case of Palestine, 'like all other structural asymmetries . . . brutally unfair and inescapable', the law also contains within it 'the capacity to dominate as well as to resist'.[52] In other words, Erakat reads law as I have read 'the human' in this book – as 'a tool' whose ultimate utility and performance relies on a wider movement.[53] Returning to the specific question of BDS, I have always wondered – but until this conclusion to this book have kept only as private reflections to my friends in our letters and in our bright rooms – how we could participate in BDS while supporting US universities 'without any reservations'.

For indeed it is that other kind of reservation in the US that continues to give me pause. If in the form of federal Indian reservations (to use the official term) our federal government holds title to land in trust, and if we continue to violate the treaties that our government made with these Indigenous nations – such as violating the Fort Laramie Treaties to build the Dakota Access Pipeline or violating an 1837 treaty granting Chippewa Bands hunting and fishing rights to 'renovate' the Line 3 pipeline – then are we not also a settler colonial country violating peoples' right to self-determination? And if so, should not our boycott, divestment and sanctions also apply to US universities? We can consider, for instance, that the Morrill Act – which granted federal land to states and led to the construction of schools such as Cornell University and the University of California (and Texas A&M, from which I finish revisions of this book now) – was also simultaneously an act of tremendous Indigenous dispossession. 'We can't talk about Israel because we can't talk about Wounded Knee', the Anishinaabe activist Winona LaDuke wrote a decade before this most recent intensification of the hundred-years' war on Palestine. She added, 'We can't talk about Israel because we are Israel.'[54] After all, many pro-Israel marches occurring in the US since October 2023 have included not just Israel flags, but also US flags, proving that the right wing of US politics understands LaDuke's point about connected struggles over settler colonialism better than many actors on the left. Here we would do well to follow Zalloua's ethical suggestion; we could replace 'the US' for 'Israel' and 'Indigenous' for 'Palestinian' when he writes, 'Those who are not willing to talk critically about Israel's egregious policies of dispossession should also keep quiet about the form that Palestinian resistance takes.'[55]

Here I have to ask myself: Why is it that I have adamantly and intentionally avoided any possible collaboration with, for instance, the University of Haifa, which houses the Department for Geo-Strategy (to 'solve' Israel's 'demographic problem') and instead have worked with academics at An-Najah National University in Nablus, but I have always accepted lecture invitations from US land-grant universities (and now work at one)? What would it look like, in other words, to make the decolonial practices we have learned from our Palestinian colleagues more truly universal, 'made to the measure of the world', as Césaire put it? What is the practical counterpart to the 'inter/nationalism' Salaita calls for in generatively reading Palestinian and Indigenous struggles together?[56] What would it look like to keep top of mind Said's reminder – *part of* his focus on the novel and on art – that humanism is ultimately about land? Said writes:

Everything about human history is rooted in the earth, which has meant that we must think about habitation, but it has also meant that people have planned to *have* more territory and therefore must do something about its indigenous residents. At some very basic level, imperialism means thinking about, settling on, controlling land.[57]

And what would it mean to work towards Indigenous sovereignty while remembering the 'double politics' at play here, the strategic necessity to cite sovereignty in treaty-based and legal struggles on the one hand, and the acknowledgement of our human need to move beyond thinking of political relations and land in terms of sovereignty on the other? Here we would do well to add to the conversation Arendt's argument that sovereignty 'is always spurious if claimed by an isolated single entity, be it the individual entity of the person or the collective entity of a nation', Hallaq's insistence that sovereignty ultimately 'commands the right over life and death' in its always rights-denying operations, and McKnight's observation that social orders today tend to operate 'in the subordination of persons to a sovereignty that exists for itself first, an idea that can be used to cover the absence of other ideas in the polity that define the human collective at large'.[58] We are left to make something of these tensions together.

* * *

Without a doctrine, without a system, perhaps without humanism in its traditional form, we are left with what Glissant called a poetics. We are left with what we make and re-make with others. We are left to our own internal struggles and our disagreements with each other. We are left to think not just 'from the standpoint of others', the capacity Arendt noted Eichmann lacked, but to think *with* others in our letters and conversations, on walks and at meals, and in the depths of our disagreements.[59] For living out another dimension of humanity need not come from some singular life-changing event: a mystical experience, a documentary that awakens us, *the* book that woke us out of our slumber. It might more often be part of what Wynter called the 'long process' of humanity.[60] 'To remain human at this juncture is to remain in agony', Hammad observes. 'Let us remain there: it is the more honest place from which to speak.'[61]

But do we listen; and what testimony could we give to show that we have listened? Living out another dimension of humanity might be seen in whether we receive what someone shares with us, whether in turn we make a very ordinary decision to purchase our goods from a different store, to decline an invitation to a university, or to call our representatives and demand a ceasefire; whether we stop our days to march outside of the weapons company our university retirement plan nevertheless keeps investing in – the decision, all in all, to live our lives 'on the fringes of society'. And if these decisions are truly to be part of a process, then each one could be understood as a new beginning to politics, a daily effort to own up to the promises and failures of the institutions we have inherited and that we can re-make. Our ordinary humanism, in other words, might be understood as a series of efforts and exchanges to give an account of our lives to others – not in a speech, not even directly, but in how we conduct our very lives.

Notes

1. See Bethan McKernan, 'A precious resource: how Israel uses water to control the West Bank', *The Guardian*, 17 May 2023, https://www.theguardian.com/world/2023/may/17/how-israel-uses-water-to-control-west-bank-palestine.
2. Glissant, *Poetics*, p. 65.
3. Arendt, *Origins*, p. 290.
4. Hannah Arendt, *Eichmann in Jerusalem: A Report on the Banality of Evil* (New York: Penguin, 2006), p. 182.
5. Jacqueline Rose, 'The Body of Evil: Arendt, Coetzee, and 9/11', in *The Jacqueline Rose Reader*, eds. Justin Clemens and Ben Naparstek (Durham, NC: Duke University Press, 2011), p. 177.
6. Hannah Arendt, *The Human Condition* (Chicago: University of Chicago Press, 1998), p. 5.
7. See Patricia Owens, 'Racism in the Theory Canon: Hannah Arendt and "the one Great Crime in which America Was Never Involved"', *Millennium: Journal of International Studies* 45, no. 3 (2017): p. 403.
8. Hannah Arendt, 'Reflections on Little Rock', *Dissent* (1958): pp. 48, 55.
9. Kathryn Gines, *Hannah Arendt and the Negro Question* (Indianapolis: Indiana University Press, 2014), p. 6.
10. Ibid. p. 3.
11. Joy James, 'All Power to the People! Hannah Arendt's Theory of Communicative Power in a Racialized Democracy', in *Race and Racism in Continental Philosophy*, ed. Robert Bernasconi (Bloomington: Indiana University Press, 2003), pp. 249–50.
12. A. Dirk Moses, '*Das römische Gespräch* in a New Key: Hannah Arendt, Genocide, and the Defense of Republican Civilization', *The Journal of Modern History* 85, no. 4 (2013): p. 876.

13. Ibid.

14. Ibid. 893.

15. Samuel Moyn, *Liberalism against Itself: Cold War Intellectuals and the Making of Our Time* (New Haven, CT: Yale University Press, 2023), p. 130.

16. Eyal Weizman, *The Least of All Possible Evils: Humanitarian Violence from Arendt to Gaza* (New York: Verso, 2011), p. 53.

17. See Owens, 'Racism in the Theory Canon', p. 405.

18. Fred Moten, *The Universal Machine* (Durham, NC: Duke University Press, 2018), p. 66. For the line on black study, see p. 67. Moten goes on: 'This is, then, not to say that any invocation of Arendt in the critique of the features and contours of the current conjuncture is thereby rendered illegitimate and irrelevant if it doesn't acknowledge and come to terms with Arendt's placement within the dominant intellectual apparatus of this conjuncture, where antiabolitionism meets the end of ideology' (ibid. p. 93).

19. See Seyla Benhabib, *The Reluctant Modernism of Hannah Arendt* (Lanham, MD: Rowman & Littlefield, 2003).

20. Said, *The Politics of Dispossession*, p. 95. Despite this critique, Said remained enthusiastic about Arendt's work. For example, in his archive I found an 8 May 1980 letter to Leon Botstein, the President of Bard College, in which Said thanked Leon for the invitation to participate in a conference on Arendt and expressed his delight in accepting.

21. Seyla Benhabib, 'Thinking Without Banisters', *The New York Review of Books*, 24 February 2022, https://www.nybooks.com/articles/2022/02/24/thinking-without-banisters-hannah-arendt/. Cf. Marilyn Nissim-Sabat and Neil Roberts, eds, *Creolizing Hannah Arendt* (Lanham, MD: Roman & Littlefield, 2024).

22. Robert Gooding-Williams, *In the Shadow of Du Bois: Afro-Modern Political Thought in America* (Cambridge, MA: Harvard University Press, 2011), pp. 1–18.

23. Jacqueline Rose, 'The Analyst', *The New York Review of* Books, 21 September, 2023, https://www.nybooks.com/articles/2023/09/21/the-analyst-stuart-hall-jacqueline-rose/. Consider also this paragraph from the novelist Philip Roth on human experience as getting people wrong: 'You fight your superficiality, your shallowness,

so as to try to come at people without expectations, without an overload of bias or hope or arrogance, as untanklike as you can be, sans cannon and machine gun and steel plating half a foot thick; you come at them unmenacingly on your own ten toes instead of tearing up the turn with your caterpillar treads, take them on with an open mind, as equals, man to man, as we used to say, and yet you never fail to get them wrong. You might as well have the *brain* of a tank. You get them wrong before you meet them, while you're anticipating meeting them, you get them wrong while you're with them; and then you go home to tell somebody else about meeting and you get them all wrong again. Since the same generally goes for them with you, the whole thing is really a dazzling illusion empty of all perception, an astonishing farce of misperception. And yet what are we to do about this terribly significant business of *other people*, which gets bled of the significance we think it has and takes on instead of a significance that is ludicrous, so ill-equipped are we to envision one another's interior workings and invisible aims? Is everyone to go off and lock the door and sit secluded like the lonely writers do, in a soundproof cell, summoning people out of words and then proposing that these word people are closer to the real thing than the real people that we mangle with our ignorance every day? The fact remains that getting people right is not what living is all about anyway. It's getting them wrong that is living, getting them wrong and wrong and wrong and then, on careful reconsideration, getting them wrong again' (Philip Roth, *American Pastoral* (London: Vintage, 1998), p. 35).

24. Hall, 'Old and New Identities', p. 80.

25. See Max Farrar, 'Paul Gilroy in Conversation', *darkmatter: in the ruins of imperial culture* (2007), http://www.darkmatter101.org/site/2007/05/07/paul-gilroy-in-conversation/.

26. Paul Gilroy, 'Multiculture and the Negative Dialectics of Conviviality', in *Retrieving the Human: Reading Paul Gilroy*, eds. Rebecka Rutledge Fisher and Jay Garcia (Albany: State University of New York Press, 2014), p. 105.

27. Rei Terada, 'Thinking for Oneself: Realism and Defiance in Arendt', *ELH* 71, no. 4 (2004): p. 858.

28. Ibid. pp. 858–9.

29. Ibid. p. 860.
30. Frieda Ekotto, *Race and Sex across the French Atlantic: The Color of Black in Literary, Philosophical and Theater Discourse* (Lanham, MD: Lexington Books, 2010), p. 38.
31. The paradigmatic example for me is when Levinas is asked whether the Palestinian is the Other of the Israeli, and he responds via the abstract categories of kin, neighbour and 'people who are wrong'. That is a move to abstraction that prevents an ordinary human answer and thus precludes a more fundamental and concrete sense of responsibility.
32. See Césaire, *Discours*, p. 25.
33. See *Apology* 39c–d.
34. Judith Butler, *Giving an Account of Oneself* (New York: Fordham University Press, 2005), p. 8.
35. Ibid.
36. Hannah Arendt, *Reflections on Literature and Culture*, ed. Susannah Young-ah Gottlieb (Stanford, CA: Stanford University Press, 2007), pp. 59, 88–9, 298.
37. See Hannah Arendt, 'On Humanity in Dark Times: Thoughts about Lessing', in *Men in Dark Times* (New York: Mariner, 1970).
38. Arendt, *The Human Condition*, p. 239.
39. Hannah Arendt, 'Thinking and Moral Considerations: A Lecture', *Social Research* 38, no. 3 (1971): p. 434.
40. Fawaz, *Queer Forms*, p. 346.
41. Hannah Arendt and Karl Jaspers, *Correspondence: 1926–1969* (New York: Houghton Mifflin Harcourt, 1992), p. 25. Henceforth *Correspondence*.
42. For the dialectic between solitude and solidarity, see Pablo Neruda's Nobel Lecture, 'Towards the Splendid City'.
43. Arendt, *Correspondence*, p. 26.
44. Ibid. p. 28.
45. Ibid. p. 29.
46. Ibid.
47. Ibid. p. 30.
48. Ibid. p. 31.
49. Édouard Glissant, *Poetic Intention*, trans. Nathalie Stephens and Anne Malena (Callicoon, NY: Nightboat Books, 2020), p. 43.

50. Arendt, *Correspondence*, p. 33.
51. Said, *The Question of Palestine*, p. xxii.
52. Noura Erakat, *Justice for Some: Law and the Question of Palestine* (Stanford, CA: Stanford University Press, 2019), pp. 11, xli.
53. Ibid. p. 4.
54. See Adam Horowitz, 'Winona LaDuke: "We can't talk about Israel because we are Israel"', *Mondoweiss*, 21 November 2012, https://mondoweiss.net/2012/11/winona-laduke-we-cant-talk-about-israel-because-we-are-israel/. For a discussion of how the US government aided and abetted settlement in what is now Hill Country in Texas, including a framing of white settlement as rendering 'the Hill country finally freed from the fear of the Comanche moon' under which Indigenous people resisted and thus rendering 'the Indians gone', see e.g. the first chapter in what is considered the standard-setting biography in regard to US political life: Robert E. Caro, *The Years of Lyndon Johnson: The Path to Power* (New York: Vintage, 1990), p. 21.
55. Zalloua, *Solidarity*, p. 22.
56. See Steven Salaita, *Inter/nationalism: Decolonizing Native America and Palestine* (Minneapolis: University of Minnesota Press, 2016).
57. Said, *Culture and Imperialism*, p. 7.
58. Hallaq, *Restating Orientalism*, p. 124; Arendt, *The Human Condition*, p. 245; McKnight, *Race and the Politics of Exception*, p. 115. Relatedly, Anne Orford thinks with Jacques Derrida to call for a renewed dialogue between law and the humanities. See Anne Orford, 'A jurisprudence of the limit', in *International Law and Its Others*, ed. Anne Orford (Cambridge: Cambridge University Press, 2009), pp. 29–31.
59. Arendt, *Eichmann in Jerusalem*, p. 39.
60. Wynter, 'The Ceremony Must Be Found', p. 50.
61. Hammad, *Recognizing the Stranger*, p. 60.

Bibliography

Adorno, Theodor. *Minima Moralia: Reflections from Damaged Life*. Translated by Edmund F. N. Jephcott. New York: Verso, 1974.

——. *Negative Dialectics*. Translated by E. B. Ashton. New York: Continuum, 2007.

Ahmad, Aijaz. *In Theory: Classes, Nations, Literatures*. New York: Verso, 1992.

Ajari, Norman. *Dignity or Death: Ethics and Politics of Race*. Translated by Matthew B. Smith. Cambridge: Polity, 2023.

Alagraa, Bedour. 'The Underlife of the Dialectic: Sylvia Wynter on Autopoeisis and Epistemic Rupture'. *Political Theory* 51, no. 1 (2023): pp. 279–86.

Alahmed, Nadia. 'From Black Zionism to Black Nasserism: W. E. B. Du Bois and the Foundations of Black Anti-Zionist Discourse'. *Critical Sociology* 49, no. 6 (2023): pp. 1053–64.

Apter, Emily. 'Saidian Humanism'. *boundary 2* 31, no. 2 (2004): pp. 35–53.

Arendt, Hannah. *Eichmann in Jerusalem: A Report on the Banality of Evil*. New York: Penguin, 2006.

——. *The Human Condition*. Chicago: University of Chicago Press, 1998.

——. *Men in Dark Times*. New York: Mariner, 1970.

——. *The Origins of Totalitarianism*. Boston: Mariner, 2001.

——. *Reflections on Literature and Culture*. Edited by Susannah Young-ah Gottlieb. Stanford, CA: Stanford University Press, 2007.

——. 'Reflections on Little Rock'. *Dissent* (1958): pp. 45–56.

——. 'Thinking and Moral Considerations: A Lecture'. *Social Research* 38, no. 3 (1971): pp. 417–46.

Arendt, Hannah and Karl Jaspers. *Correspondence: 1926–1969*. New York: Houghton Mifflin Harcourt, 1992.

Azoulay, Ariella. *Potential History: Unlearning Imperialism*. New York: Verso, 2019.

Bayoumi, Moustafa, 'They are "civilized" and "look like us": the racist coverage of Ukraine'. *The Guardian*, 2 March 2022.

Benhabib, Seyla. *The Reluctant Modernism of Hannah Arendt*. Lanham, MD: Rowman & Littlefield, 2003.

——. 'Thinking Without Banisters'. *The New York Review of Books*, 24 February 2022.

Benjamin, Walter. 'The Concept of Criticism in German Romanticism'. In *Walter Benjamin: Selected Writings Volume 1 1913–1926*. Edited by Marcus Bullock and Michael W. Jennings. Cambridge, MA: The Belknap Press of Harvard University, 1996.

Bennington, Geoffrey. *Scatter 2: Politics in Deconstruction*. New York: Fordham University Press, 2021.

Berg, Manfred. 'Black Civil Rights and Liberal Anticommunism: The NAACP in the Early Cold War'. *The Journal of American History* 94, no. 1 (2007): pp. 75–96.

Bhambra, Gurminder. 'Beginnings: Edward W. Said and Questions of Nationalism'. *Interventions: International Journal of Postcolonial Study* 8, no. 1 (2006): pp. 1–8.

——. 'Theory for a global age: From nativism to neoliberalism and beyond'. *Current Sociology Monograph* 68, no. 2 (2020): pp. 137–48.

Biko, Steve. *I Write What I Like*. Chicago: University of Chicago Press, 2002.

Bilgrami, Akeel. *Secularism, Identity, and Enchantment*. Cambridge, MA: Harvard University Press, 2014.

Bloch, Ernst. *Natural Law and Human Dignity*. Translated by Dennis J. Schmidt. Cambridge, MA: The MIT Press, 1996.

Britton, Celia M. *Edouard Glissant and Postcolonial Theory: Strategies of Language and Resistance*. Charlottesville: University of Virginia Press, 1999.

——. 'Globalization and Political Action in the Work of Edouard Glissant'. *Small Axe* 13, no. 3 (2009): pp. 1–11.

Burden-Stelly, Charisse. 'In Battle for Peace during "Scoundrel Time": W. E. B. Du Bois and United States Repression of Radical

Black Peace Activism'. *Du Bois Review: Social Science Research on Race* 16, no. 2 (2019): pp. 555–74.

Burden-Stelly, Charisse and Gerald Horne. *W. E. B. Du Bois: A Life in American History*. Santa Barbara: ABC-CLIO, 2019.

Butler, Judith. *Giving an Account of Oneself*. New York: Fordham University Press, 2005.

Caro, Robert E. *The Years of Lyndon Johnson: The Path to Power*. New York: Vintage, 1990.

Césaire, Aimé. *Discourse on Colonialism*. Translated by Joan Pinkham. New York: Monthly Review Press, 2001.

——. *Discours sur le colonialisme*. Paris: Éditions Présence Africaine, 1955.

——. 'Letter to Maurice Thorez'. Translated by Chike Jeffers. *Social Text 103* 28, no. 2 (2010): pp. 145–52.

Chevannes, Derefe. 'Black Lives Matter Toward Afromodernity: Political Speech, Barbarism, and the Euromodern World'. *Political Research Quarterly* 77, no. 1 (2024): pp. 213–25.

——. 'The Haitian Revolution and Afromodernity: Political Speech, Euromodernity & Black Universalism'. *Theory & Event* 26, no. 2 (2023): pp. 318–44.

Cole, Teju and Fazal Sheikh. *Human Archipelago*. Göttingen: Steidl, 2021.

Crabtree, John and Francisco Durand. *Peru: Elite Power and Political Capture*. Chicago: Zed Books, 2017.

Çubukçu, Ayça. 'Many Speak for Palestine'. *Boston Review*, 1 May 2024.

——. 'Thinking Against Humanity'. *London Review of International Law* 5, no. 2 (2017): pp. 251–67.

Dabashi, Hamid. *On Edward Said: Remembrance of Things Past*. Chicago: Haymarket Books, 2020.

Darwish, Mahmoud. 'To Our Land'. *Poetry* (2005): p. 198.

Davis, Benjamin P. *Choose Your Bearing: Édouard Glissant, Human Rights, and Decolonial Ethics*. Edinburgh: Edinburgh University Press, 2023.

——. 'Human Rights and Caribbean Philosophy: Implications for Teaching'. *Journal of Human Rights Practice* 12, no. 4 (2021): pp. 136–44.

——. 'On Conceptual Sufficiency: Humanity in Du Bois's *Black Reconstruction* and *John Brown*'. *Philosophy & Global Affairs* 3, no. 1 (2023): pp. 120–48.

——. 'The Politics of Édouard Glissant's Right to Opacity'. *The CLR James Journal: The Journal of the Caribbean Philosophical Association* 25, no. 1 (2019): pp. 59–70.

——. 'The Right to Have Rights in the Americas: Arendt, Monture, and the Problem of the State'. *Arendt Studies* 6 (2022): pp. 43–57.

Deleuze, Gilles and Félix Guattari. *Kafka: Toward a Minor Literature.* Translated by Dana Polan. Minneapolis: University of Minnesota Press, 1986.

——. *What Is Philosophy?* Translated by Hugh Tomlinson and Graham Burchell. New York: Columbia University Press, 1994.

Derrida, Jacques. *Rogues: Two Essays on Reason.* Translated by Pascale-Anne Brault and Michael Naas. Stanford, CA: Stanford University Press, 2005.

Dewey, John. *Experience and Nature.* Carbondale: Southern Illinois University Press, 2008.

Drabinski, John. *Levinas and the Postcolonial: Race, Nation, Other.* Edinburgh: Edinburgh University Press, 2011.

Du Bois, W. E. B. *An appeal to the world.* W. E. B. Du Bois Papers (MS 312). Special Collections and University Archives, University of Massachusetts Amherst Libraries.

——. *Black Reconstruction in America: 1860–1880.* New York: The Free Press, 1992.

——. *Color and Democracy.* New York: Oxford University Press, 2007.

——. *The Correspondence of W. E. B. Du Bois: Volume III: Selections, 1944–1963.* Edited by Herbert Aptheker. Amherst: University of Massachusetts Press, 1978.

——. 'The ethics of the problem of Palestine, ca. 1948'. W. E. B. Du Bois Papers (MS 312). Special Collections and University Archives, University of Massachusetts Amherst Libraries.

——. 'Fifth Pan-African Congress final resolution, ca. October 1945'. W. E. B. Du Bois Papers (MS 312). Special Collections and University Archives, University of Massachusetts Amherst Libraries.

——. 'Human Rights for All Minorities, April 29, 1947'. W. E. B. Du Bois Papers (MS 312). Special Collections and University Archives, University of Massachusetts Amherst Libraries.

——. *In Battle for Peace: The Story of My 83rd Birthday.* New York: Oxford University Press, 2007.

——. *John Brown: A Biography*. New York: Routledge, 2015.

——. 'My Evolving Program for Negro Freedom'. *Clinical Sociology Review* 8, no. 1 (1990): pp. 27–57.

——. *The Souls of Black Folk*. Boston: Bedford/St. Martin's, 1997.

——. *The World and Africa*. New York: Oxford University Press, 2007.

Eagleton, Terry, Frederic Jameson and Edward W. Said. *Nationalism, Colonialism, and Literature*. Minneapolis: University of Minnesota Press, 1990.

Ekotto, Frieda. *Race and Sex across the French Atlantic: The Color of Black in Literary, Philosophical, and Theater Discourse*. Lanham, MD: Lexington Books, 2011.

Elhalaby, Esmat. 'The World of Edward Said'. *Boston Review*, 13 May 2021.

Erakat, Noura. *Justice for Some: Law and the Question of Palestine*. Stanford, CA: Stanford University Press, 2019.

Erasmus, Zimitri. *Race Otherwise: Forging a New Humanism for South Africa*. Johannesburg: Wits University Press, 2017.

——. 'Sylvia Wynter's Theory of the Human: Counter-, not Post-humanist'. *Theory, Culture & Society* 37, no. 6 (2020): pp. 47–65.

Fanon, Frantz. *Les damnés de la terre*. Paris: La Découverte, 2002.

——. *The Wretched of the Earth*. Translated by Constance Farrington. New York: Grove Press, 1963.

Farar, Max. 'Paul Gilroy in Conversation'. *darkmatter: in the ruins of imperial culture* (2007).

Fawaz, Ramzi. *Queer Forms*. New York: New York University Press, 2022.

Fenderson, Jonathan. 'Black Studies Post-Janus'. *The Black Scholar* 48, no. 4 (2018): pp. 1–7.

Ferreira da Silva, Denise. 'Before *Man*: Sylvia Wynter's Rewriting of the Modern Episteme'. In *Sylvia Wynter: On Being Human as Praxis*. Edited by Katherine McKittrick. Durham, NC: Duke University Press, 2015.

Fields, Karen E. and Barbara J. Fields. *Racecraft: The Soul of Inequality in American Life*. New York: Verso, 2014.

Foran, Clare. 'Hillary Clinton's Intersectional Politics'. *The Atlantic*, 9 March 2016.

Gabel, Peter. 'Critical Legal Studies as a Spiritual Practice'. *Pepperdine Law Review* 36, no. 5 (2009): pp. 515–34.

Getachew, Adom. *Worldmaking after Empire: The Rise and Fall of Self-determination*. Princeton, NJ: Princeton University Press, 2019.

Gilroy, Paul. *Against Race: Imagining Political Culture beyond the Color Line*. Cambridge, MA: The Belknap Press of Harvard University Press, 2000.

——. *The Black Atlantic: Modernity and Double Consciousness*. Cambridge, MA: Harvard University Press, 1993.

——. 'A Dialogue on the Human'. In *Retrieving the Human, Reading Paul Gilroy*. Edited by Rebecka Rutledge Fisher and Jay Garcia. Albany: State University of New York Press, 2014.

——. 'Multiculture and the Negative Dialectics of Conviviality'. In *Retrieving the Human: Reading Paul Gilroy*. Edited by Rebecka Rutledge Fisher and Jay Garcia. Albany: State University of New York Press, 2014.

——. 'Never Again: refusing race and salvaging the human'. The 2019 Holberg Lecture.

——. *Postcolonial Melancholia*. New York: Columbia University Press, 2004.

——. 'Race Is the Prism'. In *Selected Writings on Race and Difference*. Edited by Paul Gilroy and Ruth Wilson Gilmore. Durham, NC: Duke University Press, 2021.

Gindi, Nadia. 'On the Margins of a Memoir: A Personal Reading of Said's Out of Place'. *Alif: Journal of Comparative Poetics* 20 (2000): pp. 284–98.

Gines, Kathryn. *Hannah Arendt and the Negro Question*. Indianapolis: Indiana University Press, 2014.

Glendon, Mary Ann. *A World Made New: Eleanor Roosevelt and the Universal Declaration of Human Rights*. New York: Random House, 2001.

Glissant, Édouard. *Caribbean Discourse*. Translated by J. Michael Dash. Charlottesville: University of Virginia Press, 1991.

——. *Le discours antillais*. Paris: Gallimard, 1997.

——. *L'imaginaire des langues*. Paris: Gallimard, 2010.

——. *Mahogany*. Translated by Betsy Wing. Lincoln: University of Nebraska Press, 2020.

——. *Philosophie de la Relation*. Paris: Gallimard, 2009.

——. *Poetic Intention*. Translated by Nathalie Stephens and Anne Malena. Callicoon, NY: Nightboat Books, 2020.

——. *Poetics of Relation*. Translated by Betsy Wing. Ann Arbor: University of Michigan Press, 1997.

——. *Poétique de la Relation*. Paris: Gallimard, 1990.

——. *Tout-monde*. Paris: Gallimard, 1993.

——. *Traité du Tout-Monde*. Paris: Gallimard, 1997.

——. *Treatise on the Whole-World*. Translated by Celia Britton. Liverpool: Liverpool University Press, 2020.

Gooding-Williams, Robert. *In the Shadow of Du Bois: Afro-Modern Political Thought in America*. Cambridge, MA: Harvard University Press, 2011.

Gordon, Jane. *Statelessness and Contemporary Enslavement*. New York: Routledge, 2020.

Gordon, Lewis. *Disciplinary Decadence: Living Thought in Trying Times*. London: Routledge, 2006.

——. *Existentia Africana: Understanding Africana Existential Thought*. New York: Routledge, 2000.

——. *Fear of Black Consciousness*. New York: Farrar, Straus and Giroux, 2022.

——. *Freedom, Justice, and Decolonization*. New York: Routledge, 2021.

——. *What Fanon Said: An Introduction to His Life and Thought*. New York: Fordham University Press, 2015.

Gumbs, Alexis Pauline, China Martens and Mai'a Williams, eds. *Revolutionary Mothering: Love on the Front Lines*. Oakland, CA: PM Press, 2016.

Hadot, Pierre. *Philosophy as a Way of Life: Spiritual Exercises from Socrates to Foucault*. Translated by Michael Chase. Malden: Blackwell, 1995.

Hall, Stuart. 'Culture, Resistance, and Struggle'. In *Cultural Studies 1983*. Edited by Jennifer Daryl Slack and Lawrence Grossberg. Durham, NC: Duke University Press, 2016.

——. 'Cultural Studies and Its Theoretical Legacies'. In *Essential Essays, Volume 1: Foundations of Cultural Studies*. Edited by David Morley. Durham, NC: Duke University Press, 2019.

——. 'Cultural Studies: Two Paradigms'. In *Essential Essays, Volume 1: Foundations of Cultural Studies*. Edited by David Morley. Durham, NC: Duke University Press, 2019.

——. 'The Empire Strikes Back'. In *Selected Political Writings*. Edited by Sally Davison, David Featherstone, Michael Rustin and Bill Schwartz. Durham, NC: Duke University Press, 2017.

——. 'The Great Moving Right Show'. In *Selected Political Writings*. Edited by Sally Davison, David Featherstone, Michael Rustin and Bill Schwartz. Durham, NC: Duke University Press, 2017.

——. 'Ideology and Ideological Struggle'. In *Cultural Studies 1983*. Edited by Jennifer Daryl Slack and Lawrence Grossberg. Durham, NC: Duke University Press, 2016.

——. 'Old and New Identities, Old and New Ethnicities'. In *Essential Essays, Volume 2: Identity and Diaspora*. Edited by David Morley. Durham, NC: Duke University Press, 2019.

——. 'Political Commitment'. In *Selected Political Writings*. Edited by Sally Davison, David Featherstone, Michael Rustin and Bill Schwartz. Durham: Duke University Press, 2017.

——. 'The Problem of Ideology – Marxism without Guarantees'. *Journal of Communication Inquiry* 10, no. 2 (1986): pp. 28–44.

——. 'Race, Articulation and Societies Structured in Dominance'. In *Essential Essays, Volume 1: Foundations of Cultural Studies*. Edited by David Morley. Durham, NC: Duke University Press, 2019.

——. 'Race, the Floating Signifier: What More Is There to Say about "Race"?' In *Selected Writings on Race and Difference*. Edited by Paul Gilroy and Ruth Wilson Gilmore. Durham, NC: Duke University Press, 2021.

——. 'Teaching Race'. In *Selected Writings on Race and Difference*. Edited by Paul Gilroy and Ruth Wilson Gilmore. Durham, NC: Duke University Press, 2021.

——. 'Through the Prism of an Intellectual Life'. In *Essential Essays, Volume 2: Identity and Diaspora*. Edited by David Morley. Durham, NC: Duke University Press, 2019.

——. 'The West and the Rest: Discourse and Power'. In *Essential Essays, Volume 2: Identity and Diaspora*. Edited by David Morley. Durham, NC: Duke University Press, 2019.

Hallaq, Wael. *Restating Orientalism: A Critique of Modern Knowledge*. New York: Columbia University Press, 2018.

Hallward, Peter. *Absolutely Postcolonial: Writing between the singular and the specific*. Manchester: Manchester University Press, 2002.

Hammad, Isabella. *Recognizing the Stranger: On Palestine and Narrative.* New York: Black Cat, 2024.

Harcourt, Bernard. *Cooperation: A Political, Economic, and Social Theory.* New York: Columbia University Press, 2023.

Harjo, Joy. 'Break My Heart'. In *An American Sunrise: Poems.* New York: W. W. Norton & Co., 2019.

Harris, Christopher Paul. *To Build a Black Future: The Radical Politics of Joy, Pain, and Care.* Princeton, NJ: Princeton University Press, 2023.

Hart, William. *Edward Said and the Religious Effects of Culture.* Cambridge: Cambridge University Press, 2000.

Henry, Paget. *Caliban's Reason: Introducing Afro-Caribbean Philosophy.* New York: Routledge, 2000.

hooks, bell. *Feminist Theory: From Margin to Center.* New York: Routledge, 2015.

Horne, Gerald. *Black and Red: W. E. B. Du Bois and the Afro-American Response to the Cold War, 1944–1963.* Albany: State University of New York Press, 1985.

——. 'Introduction'. In *Color and Democracy.* New York: Oxford University Press, 2007.

Horowitz, Adam. 'Winona LaDuke: "We can't talk about Israel because we are Israel"'. *Mondoweiss*, 21 November 2012.

Huffer Lynne. *Foucault's Strange Eros.* New York: Columbia University Press, 2020.

Issar, Siddhant. 'Listening to Black Lives Matter: Racial Capitalism and the Critique of Neoliberalism'. *Contemporary Political Theory* 20, no. 1 (2021): pp. 48–71.

Itzigsohn, José and Karida Brown. *The Sociology of W. E. B. Du Bois: Racialized Modernity and the Global Color Line.* New York: New York University Press, 2020.

Jackson, Shona N. *Beyond Constraint: Middle/Passages of Blackness and Indigeneity in the Radical Tradition.* Durham, NC: Duke University Press, 2024.

Jackson, Zakiyyah Iman. *Becoming Human: Matter and Meaning in an Antiblack World.* New York: New York University Press, 2020.

Jalal al-'Azm, Sadik. 'Orientalism and orientalism in reverse'.

James, C. L. R. 'The Olympia Statues, Picasso's *Guernica* and the Frescoes of Michelangelo in the Capella Paolina'. In *The Future in the Present*. Westport, CT: Lawrence Hill and Company, 1977.

James, Joy. 'All Power to the People! Hannah Arendt's Theory of Communicative Power in a Racialized Democracy'. In *Race and Racism in Continental Philosophy*. Edited by Robert Bernasconi. Bloomington: Indiana University Press, 2003.

——. *Contextualizing Angela Davis*. London: Bloomsbury, 2024.

——. 'Incarceration (Un)Interrupted: Reclaiming Bodies, Lands, and Communities'. Talk given at Macalester College, St Paul, Minnesota, 10 October 2019.

——. *Resisting State Violence: Radicalism, Gender, and Race in U.S. Culture*. Minneapolis: University of Minnesota Press, 1996.

Jones, Janine. 'Modern African humans effecting Atlantic middle passes'. *Cultural Studies* 37, no. 6 (2022): pp. 993–1008.

Kamugisha, Aaron. *Beyond Coloniality: Citizenship and Freedom in the Caribbean Intellectual Tradition*. Indianapolis: Indiana University Press, 2019.

Katz, Cindi and Neil Smith. 'An interview with Edward Said'. *Environmental and Planning D: Society and Space* 21 (2003): pp. 635–51.

Keating, AnaLouise. 'Risking the Personal: An Introduction'. In Gloria Anzaldúa, *Interviews/Entrevistas*. New York: Routledge, 2000.

Khalidi, Rashid. *The Hundred Years' War on Palestine: A History of Settler Colonialism and Resistance, 1917–2017*. New York: Picador, 2020.

Khatibi, Abdelkebir. *Plural Maghreb*. Translated by P. Burcu Yalim. London: Bloomsbury, 2019.

King, Tiffany L. *The Black Shoals: Offshore Formations of Black and Native Studies*. Durham, NC: Duke University Press, 2019.

Kinsella, Helen M. 'Settler Empire and the United States: Francis Lieber on the Laws of War'. *American Political Science Review* 117, no. 2 (2023): pp. 629–42.

Kirkland, Sean D. *Heidegger and the Destruction of Aristotle: On How to Read the Tradition*. Evanston, IL: Northwestern University Press, 2023.

Kompridis, Nikolas. *Critique and Disclosure: Critical Theory between Past and Future*. Cambridge, MA: The MIT Press, 2006.

Lara, María Pía. *Beyond the Public Sphere: Film and the Feminist Imaginary*. Evanston, IL: Northwestern University Press, 2021.

Lederach, John Paul. *The Moral Imagination: The Art and Soul of Building Peace*. New York: Oxford University Press, 2005.

Lefebvre, Alexandre. *Human Rights and the Care of the Self*. Durham, NC: Duke University Press, 2018.

Leupin, Alexandre. *Édouard Glissant, Philosophe*. Paris: Hermann, 2016.

Lewis, David Levering. 'Introduction'. In *Black Reconstruction in America: 1860–1880*. New York: The Free Press, 1992.

——. *W.E.B. Du Bois: A Biography*. New York: Henry Holt and Company, 2009.

Lloyd, Vincent. *Black Natural Law*. Oxford: Oxford University Press, 2016.

Loewenstein, Antony. *The Palestine Laboratory: How Israel Exports the Technology of Occupation Around the World*. New York: Verso, 2023.

Loichot, Valérie. 'Between Breadfruit and Masala: Food Politics in Glissant's Martinique'. *Callaloo* 30, no. 1 (2007): pp. 124–37.

——. *Water Graves: The Art of the Unritual in the Greater Caribbean*. Charlottesville: University of Virginia Press, 2020.

Lustgarten, Abrahm. 'Oceans of Debt'. *The New York Times Magazine*, 31 July 2022.

Macey, David. *Frantz Fanon: A Biography*. New York: Verso, 2000.

McKernan, Bethan. 'A precious resource: how Israel uses water to control the West Bank'. *The Guardian*, 17 May 2023.

Mackinnon, Emma. 'Declaration as Disavowal: The Politics of Race and Empire in the Universal Declaration of Human Rights'. *Political Theory* 47, no. 1 (2019): pp. 57–81.

McKittrick, Katherine. *Demonic Grounds: Black Women and the Cartographies of Struggle*. Minneapolis: University of Minnesota Press, 2006.

McKnight, Utz. *The Everyday Practice of Race in America: Ambiguous Privilege*. New York: Routledge, 2010.

——. *Race and the Politics of the Exception: Equality, Sovereignty, and American Democracy*. New York: Routledge, 2013.

Maldonado-Torres, Nelson. 'On the Coloniality of Being'. *Cultural Studies* 21, no. 2 (2007): pp. 240–70.

——. 'Lewis Gordon: Philosopher of the Human'. *The CLR James Journal: The Journal of the Caribbean Philosophical Association* 14, no. 1 (2008): pp. 103–37.

Mbembe, Achille. *Necropolitics*. Translated by Steven Corcoran. Durham, NC: Duke University Press, 2019.

Meeks, Brian. *After the Postcolonial Caribbean: Memory, Imagination, Hope*. London: Pluto Press, 2023.

Melas, Natalie. *All the Difference in the World: Postcoloniality and the ends of Comparison*. Stanford, CA: Stanford University Press, 2007.

Méndez, Xhercis and Yomaira C. Figueroa. 'Not Your Papa's Wynter: Women of Color Contributions toward Decolonial Futures'. In *Beyond the Doctrine of Man: Decolonial Visions of the Human*. Edited by Joseph Drexler-Dreis and Kristien Justaert. New York: Fordham University Press, 2020.

Mignolo, Walter D. *The Darker Side of Western Modernity: Global Futures, Decolonial Options*. Durham, NC: Duke University Press, 2011.

——. 'The Enduring Enchantment: Or the Epistemic Privilege of Modernity and Where to Go from Here'. *The South Atlantic Quarterly* 101, no. 4 (2002): p. 934.

——. 'Who Speaks for the "Human" in Human Rights?' *Hispanic Issues On Line* (2009): pp. 7–24.

Mihai, Mihaela. *Political Memory and the Aesthetics of Care: The Art of Complicity and Resistance*. Stanford, CA: Stanford University Press, 2022.

Mikulak, Marcia. 'The Symbolic Power of Color: Constructions of Race, Skin-color, and Identity in Brazil'. *Humanity & Society* 35, nos. 1–2 (2011): pp. 62–99.

Monture-Angus, Patricia. 'Thinking about Aboriginal Justice: Myths and Revolution'. In *Continuing Poundmaker and Riel's Quest: Presentations Made at a Conference on Aboriginal Peoples and Justice*. Edited by Richard Gosse. Purich: Saskatoon, 1994.

Morefield, Jeanne. *Unsettling the World: Edward Said and Political Theory*. Lanham, MD: Rowman and Littlefield, 2022.

Moreiras, Alberto. *The Exhaustion of Difference*. Durham, NC: Duke University Press, 2001.

——. *Uncanny Rest: For Antiphilosophy*. Translated by Camila Moreiras. Durham, NC: Duke University Press, 2022.

Moreiras, Alberto and Geoffrey Bennington. 'On Scatter, the Trace Structure, and the Opening of Politics'. *Diacritics* 45, no. 2 (2017): pp. 34–51.

Morris, Aldon. *The Scholar Denied: W. E. B. Du Bois and the Birth of Modern Sociology*. Berkeley: University of California Press, 2017.

Moses, A. Dirk. '*Das römische Gespräch* in a New Key: Hannah Arendt, Genocide, and the Defense of Republican Civilization'. *The Journal of Modern History* 85, no. 4 (2013): pp. 867–913.

Moten, Fred. 'to consent not to be a single being'. *Poetry Foundation*, 15 February 2010.

——. *The Universal Machine*. Durham, NC: Duke University Press, 2018.

Moyn, Samuel. *Liberalism against Itself: Cold War Intellectuals and the Making of Our Time*. New Haven, CT: Yale University Press, 2023.

Murphy, Ann V. 'Corporeal Vulnerability and the New Humanism'. *Hypatia: A Journal of Feminist Philosophy* 26, no. 3 (2011): pp. 575–90.

Myers, Ella. 'Beyond the Psychological Wage: Du Bois on White Dominion'. *Political Theory* 47, no. 1 (2019): pp. 6–31.

Myers, Joshua. *Of Black Study*. London: Pluto Press, 2023.

Nissim-Sabat, Marliyn and Neil Roberts, eds, *Creolizing Hannah Arendt*. Lanham, MD: Roman & Littlefield, 2024.

Nehamas, Alexander. *The Art of Living: Socratic Reflections from Plato to Foucault*. Berkeley: University of California Press, 2000.

Neruda, Pablo. 'Towards the Splendid City'. Nobel Lecture.

Nesbitt, Nick. *Voicing Memory: History and Subjectivity in French Caribbean Literature*. Charlottesville: University of Virginia Press, 2003.

Nkrumah, Kwame. *Neo-colonialism: The Last Stage of Imperialism*. London: Thomas Nelson & Sons, 1965.

Noël, Samantha A. *Tropical Aesthetics of Black Modernism*. Durham, NC: Duke University Press, 2021.

Nyong'o, Tavia. 'Black Humanitarianism'. In *Retrieving the Human: Reading Paul Gilroy*. Edited by Rebecka Rutledge Fisher and Jay Garcia. Albany: State University of New York Press, 2014.

Odysseos, Louiza. 'Prolegomena to Any Future Decolonial Ethics: Coloniality, Poetics and "Being Human as Praxis"'. *Millennium: Journal of International Studies* 45, no. 3 (2017): pp. 447–72.

Orford, Anne. 'A jurisprudence of the limit'. In *International Law and Its Others*, ed. Anne Orford (Cambridge: Cambridge University Press, 2009), pp. 29–31.

Outlaw, Lucius. 'Africology: Normative Theory'. In *The African American Studies Reader*. Edited by Nathaniel Norment Jr. Durham, NC: Carolina Academic Press, 2007.

Owens, Patricia. 'Racism in the Theory Canon: Hannah Arendt and "the one Great Crime in which America Was Never Involved"'. *Millennium: Journal of International Studies* 45, no. 3 (2017): pp. 403–24.

Pagden, Anthony. *The Fall of Natural Man: The American Indian and the Origins of Comparative Ethnology*. Cambridge: Cambridge University Press, 1986.

Paquette, Elisabeth. 'Ceremonies of Liberation: On Wynter and Solidarity'. *The CLR James Journal* 28, nos. 1–2 (2022): pp. 61–83.

Parris, LaRose T. *Being Apart: Theoretical and Existential Resistance in Africana Literature*. Charlottesville: University of Virginia Press, 2015.

Perry, Noam. 'Is your 401(k) funding state violence and human rights violations?' American Friends Service Committee.

Plessner, Helmuth. *Political Anthroplogy*. Translated by Nils F. Schott. Evanston, IL: Northwestern University Press, 2018.

Puar, Jasbir. *The Right to Maim: Debility: Capacity, Disability*. Durham, NC: Duke University Press, 2017.

Quijano, Aníbal. 'Colonialidad y modernidad/racionalidad'. *Perú Indígena* 13, no. 29 (1992): pp. 11–20.

Ramírez, Miguel Gualdrón. 'Resistance and Expanse in *Nuestra América*: José Martí, with Édouard Glissant and Gloria Anzaldúa'. *Diacritics* 46, no. 2 (2018): pp. 12–29.

Rampersad, Arnold. *The Art and Imagination of W. E. B. Du Bois*. Cambridge, MA: Harvard University Press, 1976.

Reed, Adolph. *The South: Jim Crow and Its Afterlives*. New York: Verso, 2022.

——. *W. E. B. Du Bois and American Political Thought: Fabianism and the Color Line*. New York: Oxford University Press, 1997.

Revilla, No'u.'The Land is the Center'. Poetry Off the Shelf Podcast.

Roberts, Neil. 'Sylvia Wynter's Hedgehogs: The Challenge for Intellectuals to Create New "Forms of Life" in Pursuit of Freedom'.

In *After Man Towards the Human: Critical Essays on Sylvia Wynter*. Edited by Anthony Bogues. Kingston, Jamaica: Ian Randle Publishers, 2006.

Robinson, Cedric. *Black Marxism: The Making of the Black Radical Tradition*. Chapel Hill: University of North Carolina Press, 1983.

Rodriguez, Anthony Bayani. 'Introduction: On Sylvia Wynter and the Urgency of a New Humanist Revolution in the Twenty-First Century'. *American Quarterly* 70, no. 4 (2018): pp. 831–6.

Rose, Jacqueline. 'The Analyst'. *The New York Review of Books*, 21 September 2023.

——. 'The Body of Evil: Arendt, Coetzee, and 9/11'. In *The Jacqueline Rose Reader*. Edited by Justin Clemens and Ben Naparstek. Durham, NC: Duke University Press, 2011.

Roth, Philip. *American Pastoral*. London: Vintage, 1998.

Rothstein, Richard. *The Color of Law: A Forgotten History of How Our Government Segregated America*. New York: Liveright, 2017.

Ruwe, Dalitso. 'Can Black males be subjects of human rights violations?' *The International Journal of Human Rights* (2024): pp. 1–25.

Said, Edward W. *Beginnings: Intention & Method*. New York: Columbia University Press, 1985.

——. 'Criticism, Culture, and Performance'. In *Power, Politics, and Culture: Interviews with Edward Said*. Edited by Gauri Viswanathan. New York: Vintage, 2001.

——. *Culture and Imperialism*. New York: Vintage, 1993.

——. 'Edward Said on The Idea of Palestine – 1982'. KPFA Radio.

——. *Humanism and Democratic Criticism*. New York: Columbia University Press, 2004.

——. 'Memory, Inequality, and Power: Palestine and the Universality of Human Rights'. *The Electronic Intifada*, 25 September 2013.

——. 'The Morning After'. *London Review of Books* 13, no. 20 (21 October 1993).

——. *Out of Place*. New York: Vintage, 1999.

——. *The Politics of Dispossession: The Struggle for Palestinian Self-Determination, 1969–1994*. New York: Vintage, 1995.

——. *The Question of Palestine*. New York: Vintage, 1992.

——. 'Introduction'. In *Reflections on Exile*. Cambridge, MA: Harvard University Press, 2000.

——. *Reflections on Exile and Other Essays*. Cambridge: Harvard University Press, 2000.

——. *Representations of the Intellectual: The 1993 Reith Lectures*. New York: Vintage, 1996.

——. 'Traveling Theory'. In *The Selected Works of Edward Said: 1966–2006*. Edited by Moustafa Bayoumi and Andrew Rubin. New York: Vintage, 2019.

——. *The World, the Text, and the Critic*. Cambridge, MA: Harvard University Press, 1983.

——. 'Yeats and Decolonization'. In Eagleton et al. *Nationalism, Colonialism, and Literature*. Minneapolis: University of Minnesota Press, 1990.

Salaita, Steven. *Inter/nationalism: Decolonizing Native America and Palestine*. Minneapolis: University of Minnesota Press, 2016.

——. 'My Life as a Cautionary Tale: Probing the Limits of Academic Freedom'. *The Chronicle of Higher Education*, 28 August 2019.

Schürmann, Reiner. *Broken Hegemonies*. Translated by Reginald Lilly. Bloomington: Indiana University Press, 2003.

Scott, David. 'The Re-enchantment of Humanism: An Interview with Sylvia Wynter'. *Small Axe* 8 (2000): pp. 119–207.

——. *Refashioning Futures: Criticism after Postcoloniality*. Princeton, NJ: Princeton University Press, 1999.

——. 'Universalism & Reparation'. ERC Minor Universality.

Seale, Lebogang. *One Hundred Years of Dispossession: My Family's Quest to Reclaim Our Land*. Johannesburg: Jacana, 2024.

Sharpe, Christina. 'Black Life, Annotated'. *The New Inquiry*, 8 August 2014.

——. 'Black Studies: In the Wake'. *The Black Scholar* 44, no. 2 (2014): pp. 59–69.

Silko, Leslie Marmon. *The Almanac of the Dead*. New York: Simon & Schuster, 1991.

——. *Ceremony*. New York: Penguin, 2016.

Simeon-Jones, Kersuze. *The Intellectual Roots of Contemporary Black Thought: Nascent Political Philosophies*. New York: Routledge, 2021.

Smith, Ted A. *Weird John Brown: Divine Violence and the Limits of Ethics.* Stanford, CA: Stanford University Press, 2014.

Stoler, Ann Laura. *Duress: Imperial Durabilities in Our Times.* Durham, NC: Duke University Press, 2016.

Táíwò, Olúfẹ́mi O. *Elite Capture: How the Powerful Took Over Identity Politics (And Everything Else).* Chicago: Haymarket, 2022.

TallBear, Kim. 'Making Love and Relations Beyond Settler Sex and Family'. In *Making Kin Not Population.* Edited by Adele E. Clarke and Donna Haraway. Chicago: Prickly Paradigm Press, 2018.

Taylor, Charles. *A Secular Age.* Cambridge, MA: The Belknap Press of Harvard University Press, 2007.

Terada, Rei. *Looking Away: Phenomenality and Dissatisfaction: Kant to Adorno.* Cambridge, MA: Harvard University Press, 2009.

——. *Metaracial: Hegel, Antiblackness, and Political Identity.* Chicago: University of Chicago Press, 2023.

——. 'Thinking for Oneself: Realism and Defiance in Arendt'. *ELH* 71, no. 4 (2004): pp. 839–65.

Thomas, Deborah. *Political Life in the Wake of the Plantation: Sovereignty, Witnessing, Repair.* Durham, NC: Duke University Press, 2019.

Tippett, Krista. 'The Art of Peace', *On Being*, 2012.

——. 'The Ingredients of Social Change', *On Being*, 2018.

Tomba, Massimiliano. *Insurgent Universality: An Alternative Legacy of Modernity.* Oxford: Oxford University Press, 2019.

Trouillot, Michel-Rolph. *Global Transformations: Anthropology and the Modern World.* New York: Palgrave MacMillan, 2003.

Valdez, Inés. 'Cosmopolitanism without National Consciousness Is Not Radical: Creolizing Gordon's Fanon through Du Bois'. *Philosophy and Global Affairs* 1, no. 2 (2021): pp. 283–96.

Vallega, Alejandro. *Latin American Philosophy from Identity to Radical Exteriority.* Indianapolis: Indiana University Press, 2014.

Vizcaíno, Rafael. 'Sylvia Wynter's New Science of the Word and the Autopoetics of the Flesh'. *Comparative and Continental Philosophy* 14, no. 1 (2022): pp. 72–88.

Wainaina, Binyavanga. *How to Write about Africa.* London: Penguin, 2024.

Walcott, Rinaldo. *The Long Emancipation: Moving toward Black Freedom.* Durham, NC: Duke University Press, 2021.

Warren, Calvin. *Ontological Terror: Blackness, Nihilism, and Emancipation*. Durham, NC: Duke University Press, 2018.

Weheliye, Alexander. *Habeas Viscus: Racializing Assemblages, Biopolitics, and Black Feminist Theories of the Human*. Durham, NC: Duke University Press, 2014.

Weil, Simone. 'Reflections on the Right Use of School Studies with a View to the Love of God'. In *Waiting for God*. New York: G. P. Putnam's Sons, 1959.

Weir, Allison. *Decolonizing Freedom*. Oxford: Oxford University Press, 2024.

Weizman, Eyal. *The Least of All Possible Evils: Humanitarian Violence from Arendt to Gaza*. New York: Verso, 2011.

Wilder, Gary. *Concrete Utopianism: The Politics of Temporality and Solidarity*. New York: Fordham University Press, 2022.

——. *Freedom Time: Negritude, Decolonization, and the Future of the World*. Durham, NC: Duke University Press, 2015.

Wilderson, Frank B. *Afropessimism*. New York: Liveright, 2020.

——. *Red, White & Black: Cinema and the Structure of U.S. Antagonisms*. Durham, NC: Duke University Press, 2010.

Williams, Eric. *Capitalism and Slavery*. New York: Penguin, 2022.

Williams, Patricia J. *The Alchemy of Race and Rights*. Cambridge, MA: Harvard University Press, 1992.

Williams, Randall. *The Divided World: Human Rights and Its Violence*. Minneapolis: University of Minnesota Press, 2010.

Wirzba, Norman. *This Sacred Life: Humanity's Place in a Wounded World*. Cambridge: Cambridge University Press, 2021.

Wynter, Sylvia. 'Beyond the Categories of the Master Conception: The Counterdoctrine of the Jamesian Poiesis'. In *C. L. R. James's Caribbean*. Edited by Paget Henry and Paul Buhle. Durham, NC: Duke University Press, 1992.

——. 'Beyond the Word of Man: Glissant and the New Discourse of the Antilles'. *World Literature Today* 63, no. 4 (1989): pp. 637–48.

——. 'The Ceremony Found: Towards the Autopoetic Turn/Overturn, its Autonomy of Human Agency and Extraterritoriality of (Self-) Cognition'. In *Black Knowledges/Black Struggles: Essays in Critical Epistemology*. Edited by Jason R. Ambroise and Sabine Broeck. Liverpool: Liverpool University Press, 2015.

——. 'The Ceremony Must Be Found: After Humanism'. *boundary 2* 12, no. 3 / 13, no. 1 (1984): pp. 19–70.

——. '"No Humans Involved": An Open Letter to My Colleagues'. *Forum N.H.I: Knowledge for the 21st Century* 1, no. 1 (1994): pp. 42–71.

——. *Sylvia Wynter: On Being Human as Praxis*. Edited by Katherine McKittrick. Durham, NC: Duke University Press, 2015.

——. 'Unsettling the Coloniality of Being/Power/Truth/Freedom: Toward the Human, After Man, its Overrepresentation – An Argument'. *The New Centennial Review* 3, no. 3 (2003): pp. 257–337.

——. *We Must Learn to Sit Down Together and Talk about a Little Culture: Decolonising Essays, 1967–1984*. Leeds: Peepal Tree Press, 2022.

Wynter, Sylvia and Katherine McKittrick. 'Unparalleled Catastrophe for Our Species?: Or, to Give Humanness a Different Future: Conversations'. In *Sylvia Wynter: On Being Human as Praxis*. Edited by Katherine McKittrick. Durham, NC: Duke University Press, 2015.

Yancy, George. 'Reaching beyond "Black faces in high places": An Interview with Joy James'. *Truthout*, 1 February 2021.

Yussof, Kathryn. *A Billion Black Anthropocenes or None*. Minneapolis: University of Minnesota Press, 2018.

Zalloua, Zahi. *Solidarity and the Palestinian Cause: Indigeneity, Blackness, and the Promise of Universality*. London: Bloomsbury, 2023.

Zwartjes, Arianne. *These Dark Skies: Reckoning with Identity, Violence, and Power from Abroad*. Iowa City: University of Iowa Press, 2022.

Index

EU representative:
Easy Access System Europe
Mustamäe tee 50, 10621 Tallinn, Estonia
Gpsr.requests@easproject.com